Talking Race in Young Adulthood

At a time in which race lies at the heart of so much public debate, *Talking Race in Young Adulthood* comes at an important moment.

Drawing on ethnographic research with young adults in Manchester, Harries engages with ideas of the post-racial to explore how young adults make sense of their identities, relationships and new forms of racism, consequently revealing how and in what ways race remains a salient dimension of social experience. Indeed, this book presents news ways of thinking about how we live with difference, as Harries analyses the relationship between racism, generational identities and the spatial configurations of a city.

Offering a distinct contribution to the sociology of race, this book will appeal to undergraduate and postgraduate students interested in fields such as Race and Ethnicity, Urban Sociology, Human Geography, Youth Studies, Cultural Studies and Social Anthropology.

Bethan Harries is a Research Fellow in the Department of Sociology at the University of Manchester, UK

Routledge Research in Race and Ethnicity

For a full list of titles in this series, please visit www.routledge.com/sociology/series/RRRE

19 **Mapping the New African Diaspora in China**
Race and the Cultural Politics of Belonging
Shanshan Lan

20 **Doing Violence, Making Race**
Mattias Smangs

21 **Critical Reflections on Migration, 'Race' and Multiculturalism**
Australia in a Global Context
Edited by Martina Boese, Vince Marotta

22 **Mixed Race in Asia**
Past, Present and Future
Zarine L. Rocha and Farida Fozdar

23 **Lived Experiences of Multiculture**
The New Social and Spatial Relations of Diversity
Sarah Neal, Katy Bennett, Allan Cochrane and Giles Mohan

24 **The Body, Authenticity and Racism**
Lindsey Garratt

25 **Australia's New Migrants**
International Students' Affective Encounters with the Border
Maria Elena Indelicato

26 **Talking Race in Young Adulthood**
Race and Everyday Life in Contemporary Britain
Bethan Harries

Talking Race in Young Adulthood
Race and Everyday Life in Contemporary Britain

Bethan Harries

LONDON AND NEW YORK

First published 2018
by Routledge
2 Park Square, Milton Park, Abingdon, Oxon OX14 4RN

and by Routledge
711 Third Avenue, New York, NY 10017

Routledge is an imprint of the Taylor & Francis Group, an informa business

© 2018 Bethan Harries

The right of Bethan Harries to be identified as author of this work has been
asserted by her in accordance with sections 77 and 78 of the Copyright,
Designs and Patents Act 1988.

All rights reserved. No part of this book may be reprinted or reproduced or
utilised in any form or by any electronic, mechanical, or other means, now
known or hereafter invented, including photocopying and recording, or in
any information storage or retrieval system, without permission in writing
from the publishers.

Trademark notice: Product or corporate names may be trademarks or
registered trademarks, and are used only for identification and explanation
without intent to infringe.

British Library Cataloguing-in-Publication Data
A catalogue record for this book is available from the British Library

Library of Congress Cataloging-in-Publication Data
A catalog record for this book has been requested

ISBN: 978-1-138-12085-3 (hbk)
ISBN: 978-1-315-65148-4 (ebk)

Typeset in Times New Roman
by Apex CoVantage, LLC

Hope is the thing with feathers.

—Emily Dickinson

Contents

Acknowledgements		ix
1	**Introduction**	1
	The research 6	
	The book 10	
2	**The conflicted city**	15
	The multi-layered city 16	
	The city 17	
	The 'other' side of the city 23	
	Beyond the city 30	
	Conclusion 33	
3	**The imaginings of a 'post-racial' generation**	39
	A 'post-racial' generation? 41	
	The myth of sameness and the fantasy of non-racism 43	
	Other times and 'othered' places 47	
	Mixing ≠ multiculture 50	
	Conclusion 57	
4	**Anticipating race: race and the recognition of difference in encounters with diversity**	63
	Expectations of difference 65	
	No difference here 68	
	Contrasted spaces: encountering the white working class 71	
	Comfortable conceptions of difference 74	
	Proximities to difference 78	
	Learned encounters: the "unspoken code" 80	
	Conclusion 84	

viii   *Contents*

**5   Going against the grain: resistance to identifications
   and the claim for multiple subjectivities**   89

Starting from the point of misrecognition 91
White working class identities 94
Being 'different' and undermining identities of difference 98
De-categorising identities 102
Reworking the label: claiming a multi-faceted identity 107
"I am not who I am supposed to be" 110
Conclusion 116

6   When is racism?   121

The problem of racism 121
Talking racism 127
Racism and the weight of categorisation 127
Social mixing – an inadequate counter to racism 130
Naming racism, naming racists 134
Conclusion 139

7   Conclusion   143

Final comments 149

Index   153

Acknowledgements

I have been lucky to receive support and advice from lots of people in the process of writing this book. I would particularly like to thank Bridget Byrne who has been an incredible, patient and generous source of support throughout my PhD and beyond, including during this book. Thanks also to my colleagues at the Universities of Manchester, Glasgow and UC Berkeley for their supportive comments during the research and more latterly on presentations of drafts. And thank you to all those I've conferenced with along the way.

I must express sincere thanks to dear friends who have read chapters and offered thoughtful, helpful and kind comments, but have also been there to stimulate and challenge ideas – especially Abril Saldaña, Sivamohan Valluvan, Naaz Rashid, Malcolm James, James Rhodes and Andrew Taylor. Special thanks to Martí López Andreu who has always been there to listen and has encouraged me to the end.

Most importantly, I am hugely grateful to the young people who allowed me in to their lives and gave up their time to speak to me, often at great length. Thanks also to my bandmates in Gorton who were always patient with me and to the cafés that let me sit for hours on end and often generously gave me free cups of tea.

Finally, I would like to thank the Economic and Social Research Council who funded the research for my PhD on which this book is based.

1 Introduction

Whilst I was preparing the research for this book I was also teaching an undergraduate course called, 'Racism and ethnicity in the UK'. In one seminar I asked the students to think about how we might answer the question: 'What is racism?' Their responses almost universally drew on historical references to situate racism firmly in the past. I then asked them specifically about racism in the present and many students appeared confused. One woman said that she remembered one incident in the police, but that was "years ago" – she was referring to the police handling of the murder of Stephen Lawrence. Others claimed that there is no racism "really", but only occasional examples of some people "being mean" to other people. The majority of students on this course were white. A couple of things are worth noting about these responses. In the first place, racism had been almost eradicated or suppressed from the students' consciousness and second, when they did acknowledge people "being mean", the relationship to structures and instruments of power was entirely absent. This anecdote is symptomatic of conditions in the UK (and elsewhere) that silence race and relegate it to the past.

Given the events and political shifts of the last year across Europe and the US we might assume that such a response in the classroom would now be different. However, whilst the pace of political change appears rapid and ferocious, we must be cautious before we suppose that the extent to which racism is recognised as a structural feature of society has moved at a similar pace. Whilst broadly speaking there is a prevailing notion that we have moved beyond race, there has always been room for exceptions within a dominant discourse. The likes of Donald Trump, le Front National, UKIP and the EDL would now fall into this camp, but prior to them it has long been possible to lay the responsibility of racism at the feet of other far right groups and to the margins of society, where, for example, the occasional racist name-calling incident on the football field is imagined as disrupting a status quo. Indeed, the presidency of Trump is treated not so much as an exception, but as an anomaly in the US and the west more broadly. Hence, he is readily recognised as racist whilst other governments (including in the UK), rarely face such accusations despite similar approaches to immigration and border control. Without diverging to discuss the kind of racism that this new wave of nationalism represents, it is worth noting how these individuals and organisations act as useful containers in which racism can be deposited and how these exceptions often act

2 *Introduction*

as an alibi for broader silences. Isolated events and individuals act as convenient moments in which to account for racism without dragging the rest of society into a relationship with them. Hence, the students approach a contemporary sociology course as if it is a history lesson and one that is abstracted from their own lives.

Understandings of race and racism are currently undergoing a re-examination. Across Europe and the US there is a growing momentum to reflect on the history of theorising race and to rethink how this helps us understand how race continues to grow and affect day to day life (see, for example, Meer and Nayak, 2013; Winant, 2006). The way in which race has been written out or silenced in public debate is fast becoming one of the key concerns in academic work (see, for example, Amin, 2012; Lentin and Titley, 2011; Goldberg, 2009; Winant, 2006), as is the way that the post-racial has itself become a racist expression and an organised embedded feature of social life (Goldberg, 2015). So far, these studies have importantly drawn attention to the structures and relations that obscure racism. What is perhaps lacking, however, is research that examines the effect and lived experience of the disjuncture between rhetoric and reality; between people's lived experience (of discrimination, racism and unequal treatment) and a discourse that says race no longer matters. I suggest that it is particularly pressing to think about the pertinence of these new expressions of racism for young adults who are often imagined as epitomising the future of multiculturalism, but must grapple with these contradictory processes as they leave education and peer-group settings and enter broader social spheres, including labour and housing markets.

In this book I reflect heavily on how these contextual features shape the way racism is recognised, understood and articulated to provoke thinking about how we might attempt to unravel some of these features and challenge the logics that underpin them.

Working with young people aged 20–30 years old – a similar age group to the students above – I consider the relationship between racism, generational identities and how young adults make and navigate the city in which they live. In doing so, I analyse some of the contradictions that prop up many of the contemporary understandings of racism and consider them in connection to people's everyday lives and where they are situated. I highlight how, and in what ways, race remains a salient dimension of social experience. But this is not an abstracted enquiry. It is driven by an anti-racist rationale and thus is equally determined to think about how racisms are negotiated and resisted. There is a lot to be learned from the stories presented here about how we can challenge racism and support young people in their determinations.

In this chapter I offer an overview of the key debates and bodies of literature that motivates and taps into this research, before going on to outline the design and methods used. In order to explore the relationships between race, place and young adulthood, my enquiry takes motivation from a number of sources. Principally, it takes its cue from work that engages with a politics of difference (Hall, 1992) and raises questions about what it means to be black and what it means to be British, as well as a literature that argues for the need to consider the spatial and temporal logic of race (Amin, 2010). I am interested, for example, in how meanings given

Introduction 3

to race are 'placed, positioned, situated' and contextualised (Hall, 1992: 257) in order to incorporate a range of social and cultural experiences (see, for example, Coombes and Brah, 2000; Back, 1996; Alexander, 1996). Of particular interest is the way in which these approaches have highlighted how the lived experience (rather than politics) of race can challenge essentialised features and borders of exclusion. These studies have problematised prior notions of homogenous communities, groups and boundaries (Ali, 2003) that shape so much dominant understanding about how we live with difference, by arguing for an understanding of hybridity that takes account of 'multiply inflected forms of social identity' (Back, 2002: 7). This work therefore provides a useful point from which to think about what forms of difference are recognised and how terms of visibility are secured within a particular locality, like Manchester. Race is not reproduced in the same way everywhere, and 'we all experience race in a contradictory fashion' (Winant, 2006: 996). With this in mind, I also take note of research that reflects on how the way difference is managed in places has the potential to exclude people from being considered a part of the fabric of a place, or as 'agents of restructuring and rearticulating a city.' (Glick Schiller and Schmidt, 2016: 7). These are processes of exclusion that are deeply entrenched in a collective history and are pertinent for young people when they negotiate their own identities. They are also central because they shape and are shaped by the material conditions of the city and affect how people encounter the city, confront other bodies and live in a place. Hence, the framing of this research is also influenced by the understanding that in order to recognise how race comes to matter in spatialised encounters we have to think of the multidimensional way in which space is produced through both its materiality and forms of representation (Lefebvre, 1991).

Much of the work on race and place has been written as a critical response to a series of policy agendas that position integration/segregation at the centre of concerns for multicultural cities. How we live with multiculture has become an object of fascination, intrigue and often alarmism. Within a policy context it is a question that is often fuelled by a set of fears and anxieties predicated on culturalist ways of seeing difference – the political establishment and mainstream media's damaging obsession with 'migrants' is certainly testimony to that. Subsequently, from a policy perspective, much of the emphasis on living with diversity remains on its push for assimilation – to smooth out differences (see, for example, Cantle, 2001; Commission on Integration and Cohesion, 2007; Casey, 2016). This push for assimilation in the UK is somewhat perversely predicated on the idea that we live separately, even whilst the statistical bases for imagining segregated lives and the reasons people have come to live where they do have been directly and successfully challenged (Finney and Simpson, 2009). Notably, these discussions are driven within existing culturalist paradigms that shape so much understanding about how we live with difference. Indeed, in targeting only ethnically diverse neighbourhoods, these areas and the people that live in them are put at risk of becoming ghettoised as social initiatives and imagined as the 'sinks of society' (Amin et al., 2000; Burgess, 1985). And, people who are racialised as non-white are continually interrogated with regard to how much they 'integrate' in order to

4   *Introduction*

justify their presence. These matters, and the ways in which race and racialised difference takes on a territorial dimension, are worth bearing in mind here because issues of integration and cohesion circle around precisely the kinds of neighbourhoods in which the young adults live and work. These neighbourhoods are often overdetermined by race, a problem exemplified by the way that they are often described in simplistic ways as, for example, "white", "black" and "Asian" (Hartigan Jr., 1999; Amin, 2002). As Valluvan (2016) notes, culturalist paradigms that underlie integrationist thinking about places also allow for race to circulate without recognising racism. In fact, they rely on the failure to recognise racism to work. Put crudely, they offer an 'acceptable' means to construct identities and define decisions about the allocation of resources, like housing, and in doing so, allow racism 'to take place' (Lipsitz, 2011).

This book is interested in how the multiple stories of a city relate and how they are re-articulated in the mundane to shape young adults' lived experience, including how they talk, do and negotiate race. Exploring these overlapping narratives allows us to begin to open up an exploration of how race is reproduced through its different layers. Manchester, as elsewhere, assumes a status that marks it as a future-facing global city, representing an economic base that espouses liberal values of cultural diversity. But Manchester has many faces, and I am interested in how its various spaces are configured around conflicting notions of racialised difference. The different parts of a city, I argue, provide a means to investigate competing discourses of race and their effects on people's everyday lives. Their intricacies are discussed in detail in the following chapter to think through how space can be conceptualised as political (Keith and Pile, 1993) and as a location in which multiple conditions come together and affect social and cultural practices in ways that reflect how difficult it can be to disentangle the range of experiences (Tizard and Phoenix, 1993). This discussion is driven by the understanding that the corresponding ways that race is mapped onto the city, allows it to form a location from which to observe how the management of difference plays out. It is where race, gender and class are mutually constituted and articulated together in different spaces. This is most visible, perhaps, in representations of the inner city that are often articulated with blackness, masculinity and crime and in gentrified neighbourhoods that are often imagined as white middle class 'cultural quarters' with particular relationships to gendered domesticity (Sassen, 1991). This relentless process of differentiation also has an effect on 'relations between bodies, things, and spaces' (Swanton, 2010: 2334). Hence, I analyse how these discourses, and the material conditions to which they refer, shape how the young adults talk race and resist processes of identification and racism, and how they negotiate and produce difference in their everyday social interactions.

In race studies, the shift in emphasis to the everyday has partly been motivated by the need for a critical response to the political agenda that scrutinises how people live with difference. Here I draw from studies of the everyday that reveal how race 'functions as a local matter' (Hartigan Jr., 1999: 13) and intersects with historical and global processes to 'give meaning to living with diversity' (Amin,

2002: 976). I am conscious of calls to divert the focus of our attention away from abstracted notions of identity towards everyday experience (Harris, 2009; Nayak, 2003) to consider how identities are lived and experienced through everyday interactions. Moving away from a descriptive approach, there has been a growing body of work that considers the ways in which exploring the lived experience of race more broadly (i.e. not confined to acts of racism) offers up a possibility to think about how people negotiate structures and relations that organise social life. This work has resonance with a notion of everydayness that De Certeau (2011 [1984]) and others motion towards (although usually not through the lens of race). For example, rather than 'reveal' racism, this work acts to unravel complicated processes and has been important for thinking through how race is made and functions, presenting us with more nuanced understandings of identities and social relations and the interactions between them. This work has thus moved us away from a focus on race, primarily as a question of epistemology and interpretation, that was particularly prevalent in the 2000s and which has been described as having a 'deadening effect' on our understandings of race (Swanton, 2008). And, since this work has focused on complicated and fluid interactions and negotiations, it has also importantly, directly and indirectly, challenged static notions of identity which have dominated more popular understandings of racialised everydayness that remain oriented around dichotomous questions of segregation/mixing, in-group/out-group, belonging/not belonging and so on.

Studying the lived experience of race can thus help avoid the kind of 'meta-theoretical reification' that Back (1996) cautions against, by attending to the way race intersects with other transforming social processes and is 'done' in different spaces and by taking account of how all forms of culture are related to each other (Rutherford, 1990). Thinking about race from such a position makes a good deal of sense since the meanings of race are always shifting and the ways in which they are negotiated as a consequence is complicated and messy. Thinking about the everyday as unruly also gives us space to consider how rules and norms are resisted, corrupted, negotiated and renegotiated. I am interested in how, within such a context, the young adults make the city and how they are positioned and position themselves as part of its fabric. Pertinent to this enquiry is the way in which new urbanism and a multicultural future is typically given a youthful texture (Amin, 2010), and how young people become perceived as emblematic of change. Specifically, I am interested in how, in making the city, young people deal with the responsibility of representing a particular vision of the future (James, 2015) and struggle to have their lived experiences recognised.

Young adulthood is generally overlooked (Blatterer, 2010) and is most apparent in sociology in studies that focus on youth transition (see, for example, Thomson et al., 2004). Yet, people aged in their twenties are at an interesting lifestage worth examining. The lives of young adults give us access to different levels of experience that can explain how positionings shift and are negotiated across different thresholds. 'Moments of mobility' and transition that young adults experience can be exploited because they offer a threshold between 'the habituation of home, school, and neighbourhood on the one hand, and that of work, family, class, and

6 Introduction

cultural group, on the other hand' (Amin, 2002: 970). Thus it represents a stage in which, typically, the lifespace is in a process of expansion as people begin to interact with different and more varied spaces that no longer necessarily revolve around the peer group. This is also, as has been noted above, an age group that has grown up in multicultural environs and within a political context that has endeavoured to divert attention from the historical legacy of race, including repressing references to colonialism (Hesse, 1999). This work thus sits alongside some of the important work on new ethnicities, urban multiculture, and education that has been important in bringing to life everyday practices of young people, but contributes a much-needed focus on young adulthood that reaches beyond interactions within the peer group and in a specified location, such as the school or neighbourhood where the youth club is situated. Much of what makes up young peoples' lives certainly represents convivial relations in which people live multiculture in an 'unremarkable' way (Gilroy, 2004), or have a sense of 'indifference to difference' (Amin, 2013). However, as Back notes, these new forms of expression are 'equally being met by multiply accented forms of popular racism that sometimes operate inside urban multiculture and at other times prey on these fragile forms of dialogue from outside' (Back, 1996: 7). Taking these contradictory processes into account, I unravel how encounters are embedded in a series of wider socio-political encounters to think about how the young adults reconcile multiple layers of experience. In focusing on how young adults talk race I pay attention to how they recognise racism and how they resist and negotiate its terrain when constructing their identities and negotiating their encounters. As I noted above, the stories that they tell are important for understanding how racism is recognised and resisted. But they also prove how, whilst policy approaches to integration and youth make little sense, the kind of rhetoric they employ nevertheless has an enduring effect on how people negotiate their encounters and talk race.

The research

In this section I offer a brief explanation of the methods used. As noted above, the research took place in Manchester, and it principally centred on three neighbourhoods (Gorton, Longsight and Moss Side) that border each other and the city centre. In Chapter 2 I detail the sites of the research and offer an analysis of how they fit within the Manchester context and are shaped by their national and global connections. But it is perhaps worth briefly noting here that, because of their proximity, the young people participating tended to know them all to some extent and were fairly mobile between them. The overall purpose of the research was to examine the relationship between racism, place and identities. To address this I made use of a combination of methods, which I outline below.

The stories presented throughout the book have been collated over a ten-month period and are drawn from a series of ethnographic encounters, photographic diaries and more formalised interviews. In total 32 people were interviewed, 24 of whom also completed a photo diary – one also elected to supplement this with a written diary. I interviewed a roughly even number of people in each of the three neighbourhoods (9 in Gorton, 10 in Longsight and 13 in Moss Side). There was a great deal of diversity within the group. They identified with a range of ethnic identities and class backgrounds (although the majority would describe as working class) and represented a broad range of educational and employment backgrounds, social interests and so on. Some were single and lived alone, others had partners and some had children. Conscious of criticisms that much of the work on the everyday is dominated by masculinities (Ali, 2003), I endeavoured to recruit a roughly even number of women and men (17 women and 15 men). The majority lived in the neighbourhood I met them in, whilst the remainder were linked through work, friends and leisure activities. Since the research was not a study of the neighbourhood, per se, it was not a concern that they did not live in the neighbourhood or knew it particularly well. I was not looking to get a true account of what it is to live in a place. I was interested in their perceptions of neighbourhoods and in their encounters in place, rather than obtaining some sort of 'authentic' account of what it is like to live there. I was also aware that some people may have vested interests in offering a particular representation (Gunaratnam, 2003). This did not make those accounts less interesting or less meaningful. They only raised questions about how such a story was produced and why.

I visited each of the three neighbourhoods on a regular basis over the research period. I met the young adults through a variety of means during these extended visits, most often on the street, in cafes, the launderette and in market places, but also at community based events and at children's services such as toy libraries and mother and baby classes, or through knocking on people's doors in residential areas. I met up with the young people on multiple occasions and chatted to other people, including friends and associates, who do not make up the formal interviewing sample. Our relationships were negotiated over time because I spent extended periods of time with the young people before interviewing them. This benefited the quality and extent of the material collected, but also helped me to situate their stories within a lived practice. Certainly our relationships reflect how the way we read each other shifted and was renegotiated. My position as a white woman researcher forms part of this negotiation and this is reflected on in the analysis.

I approached people solely based on whether I perceived them to be aged between 20 and 30 years old. Most of the people that I approached were those that I met from hanging around in local markets and launderettes and sitting in cafés. In Moss Side I went to a café regularly, so much so that I sometimes got a free cup of tea. I also went each week to a toy library that was situated in a community building that offered training and advice services to local residents. I would often run into people that I had met in these more formal settings later in the street or in the park and it was often through these random encounters that our relationships were developed. In Longsight I spent two weeks working as a volunteer in a warehouse sorting deliveries for a charity and became a regular at a café on the industrial estate, even after I finished working there, as well as at one in the market nearby. The launderette in Longsight was also a fruitful place to run into people and there were always people hanging outside chatting if the weather was fine.

8 *Introduction*

In Gorton, I inadvertently joined a drumming group for six months after meeting Paul and Andrew in the market one weekend, when they were playing. The particulars of this are discussed elsewhere in the book, but beyond the relations with the group it is worth noting here that my participation also gave me the opportunity to meet a range of people from the local community when we played at local festivals and fun days.

I wrote a fieldwork diary during the course of the research that contained descriptions of a series of observations I had made. These were overwhelmingly made within the neighbourhoods themselves, but also include some instances on public transport travelling to and fro. These notes incorporated descriptive data of interactions within locations in which the research has been conducted as well as incidental conversations that I have overheard and been part of in the course of the fieldwork. My participation in various activities on which these notes are based helped me get some grounding in these places. These activities were intended to make me more familiar with the neighbourhoods, as well as to give me access to different spaces and increase my contact with a range of people. The amount of time I spent in the three neighbourhoods benefited my understanding and feel for these different places. At times my presence was met with scepticism, but this tended to be from older members of the community who I met in passing. I was cautioned for example on three separate occasions by the receptionist in a training centre, a worker at a parenting group and by a hairdresser that '*young* people' would not want to talk to me.

There was also occasionally some confusion about what I was doing and my presence occasionally led to speculation about what I was 'really' doing. This was usually due to some other external influence. In Longsight, for example, I flyered a street on the same day a 30-year-old man was shot dead in the street parallel. When I returned three days later to knock on doors, people assumed that what I was doing somehow related to the shooting and to crime levels in the area. When I explained that my project was not related to this incident this often fell on deaf ears and I consequently found myself stood on doorsteps listening to stories about crime and "the trouble with society". Similarly, in Moss Side, I attended a local boxing club on several occasions, and it became clear that I was understood to be someone who was interested in young men from 'deprived' areas. One young man, who was not from the local area, made this explicit when he told me that he knew "exactly what I was looking for". When I asked him what he thought I was looking for, he said it was "obvious" that I was interested in "deprived young men" and he could not help because he was a university student. There was an understanding from the coaches too that I wanted to speak to young men from areas that had bad reputations and had been caught up in criminal activity but had 'done good'. I was summarily presented with a 13-year-old boy who was a wrestling champion and then met with disappointment when I explained that he did not fall within the age group of people I wanted to speak to. These instances tell a story of their own in terms of how the role of social research is perceived, but they also tell us about how these neighbourhoods are often over-determined by a status of deprivation.

Introduction   9

In addition to hanging out more informally, I invited those people I met to participate in a photo diary exercise and an interview. Those who agreed were asked to take photographs over a seven day period of places they went and the people they spent time with, using their phone or a disposable camera that I supplied. The interview was then framed around a discussion about the content of the photographs, with an emphasis on their relationships to places and the people they spent time with. Presenting the idea of taking photographs as a 'photo diary' was useful because the young people readily interpreted it as a means of reflecting their day to day life. The first part of the interview involved a discussion of their photos. Having the photographs for people to leaf through allowed the interview to take on a more 'natural' turn. They were able to construct a story about themselves and the people in the photos using the tangible object they were holding as the reference point. Crucially too, they enabled a description of mundane activities that would otherwise have been difficult to elicit. Several people commented on how they were surprised by how much they did in a week and had their memories jogged by the photos of one-off events that they had forgotten about. This was perhaps best illustrated by the interview with Amir who had done a photo diary but had forgotten to use the flash (a consequence of using disposable cameras with a generation more used to digital technology) and so we had to do the interview without. The interview took place at his flat. I asked him to describe to me the places he went, but he could only think of the city centre. I reminded him that I had met him in Gorton, but he could not add to that. Similarly, when I asked him who he hung out with, he told me he did not have many friends. In the living room of his flat we sat on the floor drinking tea. I made fun of him for not knowing how to work the camera and he laughed and explained he had a good camera with which he enjoyed taking photos. He put up a slideshow of his photos on the large flat screen TV in the corner and as we watched them he talked about where they were taken and who was in them. It emerged that he had a number of friends, including one close friend with whom he had recently been on holiday to Paris, and a group of more casual acquaintances he met regularly in a square in the city centre with whom he went to parties. Most of the photos were taken in the city centre and in his flat, which opened up a discussion about why, after being the target of a series of racist attacks on the estate where he lived, he did not go out much. The city centre, which was a short bus ride away was his central meeting point and, it emerged, a place where he felt safe.

Once the young people had gone through them, I left the photos out and we were able to refer back to them during the course of the interview. The interview itself was very loosely based on a set of topics and was, in practice, guided by the flow of conversation. I encouraged people to talk about their experiences of places and their relationships to other people and to draw on reputations, as well as personal experience. I also asked the young people about their experience of different spaces in the city. Most people had a broad network of friends and acquaintances they had made since leaving school, including colleagues accumulated from a series of jobs, friends from college, friends of friends and people they had met through activities, such as sport or music. These relationships opened up other

10 *Introduction*

spaces to them and I was interested too in how friends and places were related. For example, why they spent time with friends in some places but not in others. These conversations encouraged discussion about the way that the young adults negotiated multiple subjectivities, particularly when they reflected on their encounters in different spaces.

The final part of the interview introduced a quite different element. This moment was used to get an understanding of how the young adults perceive the relationship between their understandings of identification and the production of race. To do this, I presented the participants with an equality monitoring form, which replicated Census categories on age, gender, ethnicity, religion and national identity. I took this opportunity for two principle reasons. Firstly, on an instrumental level, it was helpful to get people who had been talking in coded references about religion, class, gender and race to confront these. This was uncomfortable for some, but using the form allowed them to externalise these constructions. Second, there is surprisingly little qualitative research about these kinds of forms and the categories they contain despite their prevalence in the UK. Everyone living in the UK is familiar with these forms and they are distributed in many different contexts, as they are attached to job applications, college applications, health and leisure service registration and so on. They are typically employed under the premise that they monitor equality by gathering data on a range of categories. In my interview I did not ask the participants to categorise their experiences using the form. Rather, I framed the conversation about how they felt this form might be used and what they thought of its use. This was helpful in getting the young people to identify contradictions that can arise from using analytical categories. The form was only introduced at the end of the interview and, therefore, did not interfere with the initial open narrative approach. As the ensuing discussion will illustrate, this part of our conversations was often very impassioned and it was clear that many of the young people, especially those racialised as non-white, were frustrated with these kinds of forms and had a lot to say.

The book

The book is set out over seven chapters. Chapters 2 and 3 offer a sense of the contextual backdrop to the research, whilst Chapters 4 to 6 give more focus to the lived experience to consider the relationship between racism, identities and encounters. The following gives an overview of the themes covered and an indication of how they relate to each other.

To begin, Chapter 2 sets the scene of the research by introducing the multilayered and conflicting narratives that make up Manchester's various spaces. I draw on work that emphasises the territorial dimension of race and offer a sense of place by exposing how meanings, particularly those given to difference, vary and are employed in multiply inflected ways across the city. As such, Manchester is introduced as a medium or subject through which to consider the emergence of social identities, relations and organisation and as a site through which to explore how people do and make sense of their everyday lives.

One of the central concerns of this book surrounds the tension recognised in race studies between wanting to move beyond race and recognising the multiple ways in which racism manifests. With this in mind, the chapter explores the paradox that becomes apparent when the contemporary city is imagined as a tolerant multicultural space, i.e. *beyond* race, and yet is nevertheless a place through which racism is clearly reproduced. I am particularly interested in how the neoliberal machinations of a city can allow for diversity to be conceived as simple plurality to brand the city as harmonious and celebratory, whilst the inner city becomes the signifier of difference and racialisation and imagined as if outside the core economic base. The chapter analyses the relationship between these two divergent views of a city and considers how they are shaped by their national and global connections. It is suggested that how people talk about the city provides a useful avenue for exploring how social processes are reproduced in its spaces. Hence, this is not a study of a place, but rather a study in place. Also perhaps worth noting is that, whilst the research is set in Manchester, much of the ways in which the city configures around race will resonate with post-industrial cities elsewhere. Indeed, I draw on literature from across Europe that illustrates how claims to uniqueness are common, as are the terms on which these claims are made.

Leading on from the geographical backdrop to the research, Chapter 3 pays attention to the extent to which the young people find appeal in the liberal notions of tolerance and 'forward thinking' that epitomise the brand of neoliberal cities like Manchester. I examine how they weave these stories into a narrative to construct a sense of a generation for themselves. I am particularly interested in how, in doing so, the young adults position themselves in relation to post-racial imaginaries. This discussion is framed in the knowledge that young people are often readily called upon as representatives of the future of multiculturalism. I offer a critique of some of the ways in which the young adults find appeal in the myth of sameness when they construct a sense of a generation. However, I also approach this discussion by couching it in a broader understanding of how they come to make these claims. Their narratives are therefore read against the broader context in which they are situated, namely the culturalist and integrationist frameworks that underpin so much of the discourse on how we live with difference.

Chapter 4 discusses how the young adults recognise and deal with diversity in their day-to-day lives, and especially on how race shapes their encounters. It examines how the young adults describe a set of competencies for dealing with difference, which, they claim, is learned through growing up and living in multicultural urban spaces. But, the chapter pays attention to the way in which difference is produced through encounters in multifaceted ways, often depending on where and when they occur. In many ways this chapter sits in juxtaposition to the narratives that draw on the idea of the post-racial generation when it draws out the complexities of the relationship between encounters and the spatial configuration of the city that throw up a set of contradictions. I explore how the young adults talk about their interactions by drawing on a body of literature that examines the affective qualities of encounters. This discussion will bring attention to some of the

12 *Introduction*

anxieties and frustrations experienced as young people anticipate race and anticipate being positioned as different within their encounters.

In Chapter 5 I address questions of identity by engaging with the young adult's
routine experiences of being positioned as 'different'. This discussion points to the
limitations of understanding how race works without taking account of how people
are positioned. It will draw on the research presented in the earlier chapters to
consider, in the first place, how individuals are forced to locate themselves in
particular ways and are associated with some spaces more than others. As such, it
illustrates the connection to the ways in which neighbourhoods are associated with
strong, fixed identities. Here I look at the ways in which the identities the young
adults want to lay claim to are spatialised and intersect with these crude narrations
of place. I consider the challenges faced by people who are positioned as 'Asian'
and 'Black' and who must make claims to, and demand recognition for, a multi-
faceted identity, as opposed to a normatively prescribed representation. However,
the chapter is ultimately concerned with how the young people manipulate and
resist processes of identification and (mis)recognition. I highlight the different
expectations that people are under when creating an account of themselves without
losing sight of the power the young adults express when they direct attention to
their multiple subjectivities and undermine processes of racialisation. A large part
of the focus in this chapter thus falls on the ways racialised identities are manipulated and resisted, rather than accommodated.

Chapter 6 explores how racism is defined and recognised as a feature that
structures the young adults' everyday lives. I begin by reflecting on some of the
ways that definitions of racism have narrowed to assume a status that marks it
as a historical phenomenon and yet one which is abstracted from its historical
roots. The discussion engages with the growing literature that critically engages
with post-racial imaginaries and places this in the context of some of the key
debates that shape the way that the young people talk about the city and the
neighbourhoods in which they live. I examine how post-racial logics that represent an embedded feature of society create a challenging environment in which
to name racism. The chapter gives focus to the way the young adults struggle to
talk about racism in their own lives and consider what we might learn from their
experiences when trying to challenge and overcome racism. In particular, the
chapter considers the implications of discourses that silence race for how people
can talk about their own experiences, and the challenges this presents for being
able to name racism when racialised difference is widely conceived as if absent
of meaning. I suggest that it is important to bring these experiences in to the
contemporary collective consciousness of British society as well as place them
in a broader historical context in order to challenge the way in which race continues to structure everyday life.

In Chapter 7 I offer some final reflections on the research and how it contributes
to some of the key debates that have been introduced. In conclusion I also offer
some thoughts on how some of the significant ideas presented throughout the book
might be helpful in addressing how racism is understood in multiple ways in order
that we might challenge some of these processes.

References

Alexander, C. (1996). *The art of being black*. Oxford: Oxford University Press.

Ali, S. (2003). *Mixed-race, post-race: Gender, new ethnicities and cultural practices*. Oxford: Berg.

Amin, A. (2002). Ethnicity and the multicultural city: Living with diversity. *Environment and Planning A*, 34(6), 959–980.

Amin, A. (2010). The remainders of race. *Theory, Culture and Society*, 27(1), 1–23.

Amin, A. (2012). *Land of strangers*. Cambridge: Polity Press.

Amin, A. (2013). Land of strangers. *Identities: Global Studies in Culture and Power*, 20(1), 1–8.

Amin, A., Massey, D. & Thrift, N. (2000). *Cities for the many not the few*. Bristol: Policy Press.

Back, L. (1996). *New ethnicities and urban multiculture: Racisms and multiculture in young lives*. London: UCL Press.

Back, L. (2002). The fact of hybridity: Youth, ethnicity and racism. *In:* Goldberg, D. T. & Solomos, J. (eds.) *A companion to racial and ethnic studies*. Boston, MA: Blackwell.

Blatterer, H. (2010). The changing semantics of youth and adulthood. *Cultural Sociology*, 4(1), 63–79.

Burgess, J. A. (1985). News from nowhere: The press, the riots, and the myth of the inner city. *In:* Burgess, J. A. & Gold, J. R. (eds.) *Geography, the media and popular culture*. London: Croom Helm.

Cantle, T. (2001). *Community cohesion: A report of the independent review*. London: Home Office.

Casey, L. (2016). *The Casey review: A review into opportunity and integration*. London: Department for Communities and Local Government.

Commission on Integration and Cohesion. (2007). *Our shared future*. London: Commission on Integration and Cohesion.

Coombes, A. E. & Brah, A. (2000). Introduction: The conundrum of 'mixing'. *In:* Coombes, A. E. & Brah, A. (eds.) *Hybridity and its discontents: Politics, science and culture*. London: Routledge.

De Certeau, M. (2011 [1984]). *The practice of everyday life* (Vol. 3rd Edition). Berkeley: University of California Press.

Finney, N. & Simpson, L. (2009). *Sleepwalking to segregation? Challenging myths about race and migration*. Bristol: Policy Press.

Gilroy, P. (2004). *After empire: Melancholia or convivial culture?* Abingdon: Routledge.

Glick Schiller, N. & Schmidt, G. (2016). Envisioning place: Urban socialities within time, space and multiscalar power. *Identities: Global Studies in Culture and Power*, 23(1), 1–16.

Goldberg, D. T. (2009). *The threat of race: Reflections on racial neoliberalism*. Malden, MA: Wiley-Blackwell.

Goldberg, D. T. (2015). *Are we all postracial yet?* Cambridge and Malden, MA: Polity Press.

Gunaratnam, Y. (2003). *Researching 'race' and ethnicity: Methods, knowledge and power*. London: Sage.

Hall, S. (1992). New ethnicities. *In:* Donald, J. & Rattansi, A. (eds.) *'Race', culture and difference*. London: Sage.

Harris, A. (2009). Shifting the boundaries of cultural spaces: Young people and everyday multiculturalism. *Social Identities*, 15(2), 187–205.

Hartigan Jr., J. (1999). *Racial situations: Class predicaments of whiteness in Detroit*. Princeton, NJ: Princeton University Press.

14 *Introduction*

Hesse, B. (1999). Reviewing the western spectacle: Reflexive globalisation through the black diaspora. *In:* Brah, A., Hickman, M. & Mac an Ghail, M. (eds.) *Global futures: Migration, environment and globalisation.* New York: St Martin's Press.

James, M. (2015). *Urban multiculture: Youth, politics and cultural transformation in a global city.* Basingstoke: Palgrave Macmillan.

Keith, M. & Pile, S. (1993). Introduction: The place of politics. *In:* Keith, M. & Pile, S. (eds.) *Place and the politics of identity.* London: Routledge.

Lefebvre, H. (1991). *The production of space.* Oxford: Basil Blackwell.

Lentin, A. & Titley, G. (2011). *The crises of multiculturalism: Racism in a neoliberal age.* London: Zed Books.

Lipsitz, G. (2011). *How racism takes place.* Philadelphia: Temple University Press.

Meer, N. & Nayak, A. (2013). Race ends where? Race, racism and contemporary sociology. *Sociology,* 49(6), 3–20.

Nayak, A. (2003). *Race, place and globalisation: Youth cultures in a changing world.* Oxford and New York: Berg.

Rutherford, J. (1990). The third space: Interview with Homi Bhabha. *In:* Rutherford, J. (ed.) *Identity: Community, culture.* London: Lawrence and Wishart.

Sassen, S. (1991). *The global city.* Princeton: Princeton University Press.

Swanton, D. (2008). Everyday multiculture and the emergence of race. *In:* Dwyer, C. & Bressey, C. (eds.) *New geographies of race and racism.* London: Routledge.

Swanton, D. (2010). Sorting bodies: Race, affect, and everyday multiculture in a mill town in northern England. *Environment and Planning A,* 42(10), 2332–2350.

Thomson, R., Holland, J., McGrellis, S., Bell, R., Henderson, S. & Sharpe, S. (2004). Inventing adulthoods: A biographical approach to understanding youth citizenship. *The Sociological Review,* 52(2), 218–239.

Tizard, B. & Phoenix, A. (1993). *Black, white or mixed race? Race and racism in the lives of young people of mixed parentage.* London: Routledge.

Valluvan, S. (2016). What is 'post-race' and what does it reveal about contemporary racisms? *Ethnic and Racial Studies,* 39(13), 2241–2251.

Winant, H. (2006). Race and racism: Towards a global future. *Ethnic and Racial Studies,* 29(5), 986–1003.

2 The conflicted city

In this chapter I introduce the different ways in which the city of Manchester and three of its neighbourhoods are represented and talked about. In doing so, the chapter sets the scene of the research by introducing the multi-layered and conflicting narratives of Manchester's various spaces. The intention of beginning in this way is to offer a sense of place by exposing how meanings, particularly those given to difference, vary and are employed in multiply inflected ways across the city (Young et al., 2006). This is an initial step in developing an understanding of how the young adults in the research make sense of their own subjectivities and experiences and how they can contest and negotiate space and identifications in relation to where they live.

There is a wealth of literature in race studies that explores race through a located study and this breadth suggests a confidence in such an approach. Nevertheless it is always useful to reflect on what it is we are doing when we situate our research in a place and what this can tell us about the processes we seek to explore. Notably, there has been a significant shift in focus and method since the early work of the Chicago School and related neighbourhood studies in Britain, including Young and Wilmott's (2011 [1957]) study of East London and Rex and Moore's (1969) study of Sparkbrook, in Birmingham. This earlier body of work was concerned with how race shaped, and was shaped by, the city. Its interests lay particularly in the spatial arrangements of, for example, housing, education and employment. Critiques of this work have since detailed the manner in which focusing on place in such a way only over-emphasises the limits of place and risks reproducing an ecological fallacy that links places to sites of 'community' (Back, 2005), or 'unwitting essentialist representations of race' (Nayak, 2011: 550). Indeed, related to this, Massey (2004) cautions against taking the usefulness of place-based research for granted and against imagining that in some way places provide us with accounts that are more real, authentic and earthy. This caution seems particularly wise to heed here because, as cities are becoming increasingly diverse (Centre on Dynamics of Ethnicity, 2013), they are also the nucleus from which broad and often nebulous claims about the essence or quality of that diversity can stem.

More recently, there has been a turn to think about cities and their neighbourhoods as something more than just 'places' that are bound by various arrangements. This marks a shift away from thinking about the urban as having explanatory

16　*The conflicted city*

potential; an idea that is problematic when cities are the culmination of so many different social, economic and political processes (Agnew et al., 1984). Cities can also be understood as sites through which people *do* and make sense of their everyday lives (De Certeau, 2011 [1984]). It is following this tradition that this book takes its cue. In particular, it aligns itself with ethnographic approaches that take an urban locality as its base through which to explore the lived experience and production of race. The city is not brought in as the object of study, nor is it imagined that place is able to *explain* the phenomena that is being explored (Agnew et al., 1984). This is not a study of place, but a study *in* place.

In this chapter the city is introduced as a medium, or subject, to enable consideration of the emergence of social identities, relations and organisation (Holston, 1998). The multiple and often conflicting stories presented here are introduced to reflect how the city is always in process (Castells, 1996), but also to reflect how these stories render the city as a site of negotiation of multiple and conflicting identities and experience. Cities are, after all, 'spaces of difference' (Sennett, 1992), and they allow us to see the multiplicity of cultures (Sassen, 1999). Subsequently, the spaces within a city are also useful sites to interrogate how processes of racialisation and 'difference-making' link people, politics and culture. In short, the city taken in its entirety 'provides the site through which racial difference is potentially erased (assimilated) or reproduced' (Keith, 2005: 58). For example, the following discussion will illustrate how image-making forms part of attempts to market the city centre to attract investment (Peck and Ward, 2002), whilst leaving the representations (and the conditions) of other parts of the city, particularly those outside of the economic base and those that do not 'fit' with the acceptable face of the city, out of the limelight (Young et al., 2006).

The chapter starts by looking at how a dominant narrative of the city is produced. The city in this respect is reinvented to be a site of celebration of diversity and revolves around its economic base. This is a celebration of diversity that pays little heed to the meaning or salience of multiculture beyond its commercial value. Second, I introduce the three neighbourhoods in which I did the research. Here we see difference is managed quite differently as if dislocated from the core brand/message of the city. Difference (notably not diversity) is manipulated to pathologise the 'inner city' and the people living within. The focus on these three neighbourhoods shows another face of Manchester but it also gives attention to that which is otherwise silenced elsewhere. Finally, the chapter considers how these two means of managing difference relate to broader forms of representation beyond the boundaries of the city, including its salience to the national.

The multi-layered city

A city can be many things. It is the site of different modes of production, the site of urban living and, here, of course it is the site of research (Sassen, 1996b; Agnew et al., 1984). It is also simultaneously a global, local and national location. The narratives of a city can therefore be both epic and everyday (Holston, 1998), and they represent numerous layers that often overlap and conflict with each other.

Hence, 'knowing [a city] is always experimental' (Holston, 1998: 37). The aim here is to detail the different narratives to understand how processes of inclusion and exclusion map onto the city, and produce what Sassen refers to as 'analytic borderlands', as well as to think about the nature of the dynamic that connects them (Sassen, 1996b: 24). This is an important first step before going on to explore how they then shape people's experience of these places.

Taking on the multiple layers of a city carries the risk that the scale of analysis might collapse into a 'scalar mush' (Jones and Fowler, 2007: 339), or that the tension produced by the 'fixity and flow' in everyday life (Amin, 2007) will be somehow lost. Somewhat perversely, perhaps, part of the aim here is to reflect just how fixed and limited the different spaces of the city can appear to be. I am nevertheless alert to the ways in which places can be interpellated in a whole variety of ways in order to emphasise or avoid particular qualities to meet political and economic expectations in the management of 'difference' (Harries et al., forthcoming), hence, 'their status is always in a process of fraught negotiation' (Nayak, 2011: 553). At no point is it presupposed that the lived experience cannot 'shake up' and corrupt the way in which certain political questions are formulated. Indeed, how this can be achieved becomes the focus in the rest of the book.

The city

Greater Manchester is the third largest metropolitan area in the United Kingdom with a population of more than 2.5 million. It is made up of ten metropolitan boroughs: Bolton, Bury, Oldham, Rochdale, Stockport, Tameside, Trafford, Wigan, and the cities of Manchester and Salford. The research took place in the city of Manchester itself, which is the fastest growing local authority area in the UK outside of London.[1] Despite its ranking as third largest (this includes all boroughs – taking the city borough alone would rank it fifth[2]), Manchester is often found vying for recognition as the UK's 'Second City'. Much of these claims draw on the political, economic and cultural legacies that Manchester has produced historically. Look for a popular book about Manchester and it will invariably discuss the city's position as a postmodern 'radical' city, particularly through its historical connection to the labour movement, co-operative, suffragette and other social movements,[3] or more latterly through its contribution to an 'alternative' UK music and creative arts scene.[4] Since the 1980s, Manchester's identity as a radical city has become somewhat more difficult to cling onto in an increasingly post-industrial economy and in light of the City Council's shift from a socialist to a neoliberal position (Peck and Ward, 2002). However, these historically bound forms of representation nevertheless live on through the narration of the city, albeit perhaps for different ends.

What we see today is a rearticulation of 'radical' that weaves a selective history with an imagined potential to *imply* progressive practices and attitudes towards marginalised groups in the present, rather than to necessarily point to any real progress; an ideal that is harder to sustain. Citizenship ceremonies in Manchester, for example, promote the 'welcome' that Manchester has given historically to

18 *The conflicted city*

migrants, with only a narrowed history of racism (Byrne, 2014: 99). Research also illustrates how the history of Manchester's LGBT 'community' is manipulated to make broader statements about the status of the city. The City Council, for example, describes 'the community' as 'an important part of the social and cultural history of the city and the North West'. Yet, whilst social and cultural contributions are hailed as symbolic of the city's tolerance, Binnie and Skeggs (2004) rightly point out how, in the process, gay, lesbian and transgendered people are largely excluded from this story except as *objects* of fetishisation. Here I consider how the idea of the 'radical city' is reinterpellated, to meet contemporary liberal concerns around 'ethnic diversity' and 'multi-culture' rather than around any close approximation to progressive thinking on the politics of race and inequality. The foregrounding of this way of thinking here will be salient to succeeding chapters, which will examine how the physical, material and discursive interrelate to produce a particular kind of lived experience and produce multi-faceted forms of negotiation and resistance amongst the young adults in making sense of their own subjectivities and experiences.

In order to compete within a global market, the ways in which cities reinvent themselves is such that the emphasis falls on the financial and associated sectors at the expense of other key elements of the economy and society (Massey, 2007; Sassen, 1999). This becomes visible and audible in the physical environment and the discursive repertoires the city has to offer, as well as in the ways in which the two interlock. Again, Binnie and Skeggs' (2004) work is useful here. They demonstrate how the commodification of gay spaces in the city centre of Manchester has become a vital component of the marketisation and management of difference. As part of this, the 'LGBT community' is presented (irrespective of how clunky and ambiguous the term community is) as a metaphor for the success of the city's liberal values and openness to difference. Certainly, the claiming of this success is bluntly illustrated in the heading of the City Council's LGBT source guide in which they declare, '*We* have been championing LGBT equality for well over 25 years', thus succinctly claiming the work and overriding the efforts of gay, lesbian and transgender activists in the process.[5] This reformulation of historical processes implicitly suggests that the city has bestowed on its citizens the accommodation for equality policies to emerge, rather than an understanding that persistent inequalities have stimulated activism and struggles against them. There are resonances in this work with the ways in which 'ethnic spaces' and 'ethnic communities' have been fetishised and these will be drawn out at more length in the chapters that follow. It is useful, nevertheless, to reflect here on the manner in which cities take advantage of and rework characteristics from the past. This can involve reworking the political struggles of marginalised groups to be claimed by the authorities that stood against them, and it can involve reworking symbols and relics of empire that are 'mined to shore up the legitimacy and the social cachet of the new' without addressing contemporary concerns (Massey, 2007: 46). We might also think about how some cities across the UK have offered up responses to the ongoing migrant crisis to support the 'refugees welcome' campaign to appeal to populist demands to do so, and yet, do not in practice act on racism and inequalities. Piacentini (2016), for example, cautions against seeing refugee solidarity projects as a means to contribute to the myth that there is no racism in Glasgow, or Scotland more broadly. Hence, post-industrial cities typically represent a paradoxical space – the site of celebration of difference, but also sites that bear witness to racism and forms of injustice (Uitermark et al., 2005; Wilson, 2015).

Looking at the ways in which Manchester (or at least a particular segment of Manchester) presents itself as a diverse, tolerant and progressive city seemed an obvious starting point when I began the research. I had not long been living in the city and had felt the weight of this marketing strategy when I started to look for work and housing. It had a pulsating effect. The way in which people I met 'sold' Manchester to me felt exciting, and that effect is felt too among the young people I did the research with, as I will go on to discuss. The populist appeal of 'multiculture', as a cultural asset, allows for narratives that champion diversity to be continuously repeated and reinforced, without pausing to reflect on what that means. These narratives circulate above the city in its entirety but find a more tangible connection to the city's strategic economic base in the centre, as opposed to its informal economy (Sassen, 1996a) and parts of the inner city. It also made sense to look at the institutional emphasis on tolerance and diversity which is produced alongside and not disconnected from populist narratives. Notably, in the same year that the research was carried out, the City Council came to the end of their ten-year programme 'Agenda 2010', which aimed to 'tackle inequalities for BME communities' in Manchester. In its final summary, Agenda 2010 cited a project that helped 148 people find employment as its biggest achievement. Yet, 2011 Census data on employment show that ethnic minorities in Manchester are still more likely to be unemployed than white British people.[6] The Council's strategy has since been one of 'mainstreaming', which effectively dissipates the need to focus on particular modes of inequality, and instead foregrounds the needs of 'all' at the expense of the most marginalised.

Somewhat perversely perhaps, 'Agenda 2010' came to an end in the same year in which the British National Party won one of their two seats in the European Parliament in the constituency that incorporates Greater Manchester. This was also the year that the Council launched their 'Cultural Ambition' report bin which the Council describes Manchester in the following way:

> A passionately local and global city, its diversity and tolerance will be reflected in the richness of the city's experience, economy and the warmth of its welcome.[7]

Here, repeated terms like ' richness', 'tolerance' and 'passion' take on the tone of cliché. They are conjured in order to give us a particular vision but without explanation of what they mean or how they are given value. Diversity and tolerance remain unspecified throughout the document. They are touted as positives but it is up to us to interpret why and how they are conceived of as such (Harries et al.,

20 *The conflicted city*

forthcoming). Koller (2008) points to the irony of the way much of a city's marketing focuses on its potential through semantics of the future (as in 'will'); ironic because they suggest that we are 'not quite there yet'. It is useful to put this idea alongside the ways in which a historical legacy (we have *always* been like this) is drawn upon to 'transform an unwanted present' (Holston, 1998: 40). The future vision, I would suggest, is employed to capture our attention away from the workings of a city which others have, perhaps more poetically, described as that which 'hum with the sum of resonances from the past' (Amin, 2007) or lay quiet like ghosts (Pile, 2005). In this way, the process of reinvention not only reshapes how we think about the past, but also enables us to ignore what is happening in the present. This will have particular significance for the young adults in this research who confidently mark a break with their time and that, which 'may have', come before. The repetition of these narratives means that our attention is steadfastly drawn to the *potential* and to the desire for the future to be realised in spite of limited action being taken to make it so.

So why does Manchester (and other cities) draw on the nebulous concept of diversity to reinvent itself in such a way? Certainly we can see prominent examples of this practice elsewhere. For example, in the ways in which diversity formed part of the reimagining of the city in London in its bid for the Olympics (Winter, 2013; Evans, 2016) and in Cardiff in its bid for WOMEX in 2013 (Harries, 2015). Indeed, it is apposite that the marketization of diversity in Manchester is almost entirely connected to the rejuvenation of the city centre, whilst drawing on the economic success of *local* people. Part of the role of this reinvention is to situate the city as a 'World city', to participate in global neoliberal economy (Massey, 2007) and to place it in competition with other global corporate brands, to secure investment, tourism and a workforce (Koller, 2008). At the time of the research, in Manchester, 'multiculture' was being advertised as a key asset through advertising hoardings in prominent positions surrounding the Central Library and Town Hall as they underwent renovation work for a further four years:

Adverts from Manchester City Council

> 'Multicultural Manchester is a city of opportunity'. Jazz, restaurant owner, Northern Quarter.
>
> 'I've always felt Manchester is a place of opportunity. People are open to new cultures'. Yemi Adetone, winner of Business and Women Award 2010.
>
> 'As a born-and-bred-Mancunian, I am very proud to live and work in a constantly evolving city like Manchester'. Nicky Davison, lives and works in Manchester.

The text and images on the advertising hoardings emphasised 'openness' to and 'pride' in an evolving multicultural city, but more specifically they told *the* story of the city as one that does not belong to the subjects themselves. They are used to reinforce a collective imaginary but one that is not directed by the subjects of the

Figure 2.1

Figure 2.2

22 *The conflicted city*

Figure 2.3

images. 'Opportunities', we are told, are provided *by* the Council and 'the city' *to* racialised minorities. Note the way that the image of the white male does not have to account for his position in the same way. He is just 'born and bred' Nicky – he is not required to justify his position beyond these two facts, and there is no entrepreneurial success that he is required to attribute to the city. In these branding exercises the success of the selected few becomes the rule rather than the exception. They act as a means to ignore the ways in which the multiculture alluded to is profoundly racialised (Young et al., 2006), whilst simultaneously constituting ethnic minorities as 'other' (Sassen, 1996a). Crucially though, these images do not reflect the more mundane experiences of people's daily lives. It is only a particular form of representation of diversity that is conveyed – the success of the entrepreneur – and conceived of as assets of the city. What is more, the 'successes' of these individuals are then claimed by the city rather than related to individual or political struggle for recognition. These kinds of universalising messages are reinforced through the repeated mixture of well-worn clichés (Mommaas, 2002) and in the city's attempts to position itself as unique and individual (Koller, 2008: 446).

Perhaps unsurprisingly, given the strength of the narratives, the way in which the young adults' start to tell the story of Manchester emulates the kinds of narratives of the city described above. They are introduced here briefly to forefront how these narratives work in people's everyday talk to say something about the status of race and racism in the city. The city is imagined as a tolerant multicultural place constructed by the young adults as an "open" and accessible space that is free of racism. This depiction, as the book will go on to show, is typical across all respondents, including those whose experiences (as will be discussed later) contradict such images, such as those presented here by Maz and Nasreen, who both describe themselves as British Asian:

> That's what I love about Manchester cos you can go anywhere and just feel comfortable, it's like home, you know you don't find many problems here in terms of like racism and stuff like that, it's quite open, everyone gets along with everyone.
>
> (Maz)

> I can't think of any racist experience that I've had maybe, from white or black people, I can't think of anything like that.
>
> (Nasreen)

I want to turn now to think about who is excluded from the city by looking at its 'other' face. This provokes thinking about how citizenship comes to be defined and in whose interest it is that difference is *managed*. And, with this in mind, it is to an alternative form of difference management that I now turn.

The 'other' side of the city

The repetition of the 'celebratory' narratives described above happens alongside and not disconnected from those which construct the city's 'other' face. This is its 'inner city' that is, perhaps somewhat ironically, far more diverse. This 'other' face is that which adversely endures through its own fetishised appeal. It is what Sassen (1996a) describes as the space 'of the amalgamated other', distinct from the core narrative of 'the city'. If we can understand the city as a space that claims *diversity* as celebration whilst ignoring difference in experience, then the inner city is where *difference* is made central and its constituent parts are bundled together as 'other'. These are locations that have typically missed out on the same level of investment as the city centre and wealthier suburbs (Jones and Wilks-Heeg, 2004: 356–357). The inner city is produced as if 'an alien place, separate and isolated, located outside white, middle-class values and environments'(Burgess, 1985: 193). It is invented as the sites of moral panic and social problems (Wacquant, 2008), and their residents are constructed as operating outside the boundaries of the city,

24 *The conflicted city*

dislocated from its socio-economic context, and its moral limits. Consequently, different sites within a city, such as the 'ghetto', the suburb and the gentrified neighbourhood, make visible different sorts of multiculture and 'mediate demographic categorisation' (Keith, 2005).

Difference, outside of the city centre and Manchester's economic base and in the poorer parts of the inner city, is constructed in such a way as to draw on the very same forms of histories of racialisation that are excluded from the dominant city narrative. Neighbourhoods instead become known locally in different ways and are associated with different kinds of characteristics. These are then given labels to distinguish the 'posh', the 'ethnic', the 'dangerous', the 'pretentious', the 'dirty' and the 'bobo' from each other. The commodification of diversity described above as part of a city's assets jars against the ways in which residential neighbourhoods outside the centre's limits are typically constructed in ways that suggest (dangerous) ethnic concentration, which belie their heterogeneity. This seems somewhat absurd when we understand these areas as those that *are* actually diverse. The city centre itself is 68 per cent white (including 'white British' and 'white Other') with only one ethnic minority Census group represent over ten per cent. Paradoxically, this group is the 'Chinese', which made up 13 per cent of the city centre population according to the 2011 Census but is rarely represented in liberal conceptualisations of British multiculture beyond the 'Chinatown' (Barabantseva, 2016). Instead, inner city neighbourhoods that lie on the peripheries of the city centre are crudely racialised and become known locally through simplified tags such as 'Asian', 'Black', 'Chavvy', 'Irish' and 'Jewish'(Amin, 2002). In the UK (as elsewhere) much of the formation of these different forms of identification can be linked to post-war processes of migration and patterns of settlement. Settlement patterns of migrants to the UK from India, Pakistan, Bangladesh and islands in the Caribbean Basin during the post-war period, for example, have been explained partly in terms of proximity to sources of employment and housing discrimination, but also through poverty and hostility to migrants which forced people into the poorest housing in the inner city (Peach, 1998; Phillips, 1998). However, the way that neighbourhoods continue to be 'known' suggests that a much larger and more homogeneous ethnic minority population exists in parts of Manchester's inner city. This is also evident when looking at patterns of Jewish migration from the late 19th Century onwards to parts of north Manchester. The areas to which these flows of Jewish migration originally settled continue to be associated primarily with Jewishness, even though the neighbourhoods are far more diverse than the label suggests and many Jews with these historical ties have since moved to other areas (Williams, 1976).

I want to now turn to look more closely at the neighbourhoods in which the research happened. The narratives presented here integrate the voices of the young people alongside, where relevant, cultural products that reference these places.

Gorton, Longsight and Moss side

The descriptions of the three neighbourhoods in which I met the research participants presented here are intended to give the reader a snapshot of the spaces in which the research, for the most part, took place. It is also worth noting however that, whilst the interviews primarily centred on a discussion of the three neighbourhoods described here, they were not restricted to them. Many of the young adults drew on their experiences of other places including those located outside of the city and often did so as means to form comparison and as a way of relating a sense of mobility. It is also important to bear in mind when reading these descriptions that they are based on generalisations, stereotypes and reputations and should be treated as such. Neighbourhood statistics reveal not only how the heterogeneity of the local population in terms of ethnicity is often forgotten, but also how recorded crime levels do not equate with popular representations, particularly when placed in the broader context of Manchester and the UK. Later chapters will go on to explore how respondents represent quite different positions in relation to these representations. For the moment, it is important to stress that they were not always passive recipients of these forms of representation, and how they negotiate stereotypes and representation are critical. This does not always happen in the ways we might expect, and we should, therefore, also heed the warning given by one of the young adults when we approach these descriptions:

> We read too much into the way areas affect people, or the way you expect an area to have affected a person and stuff.
>
> (Ian)

It is notable that these descriptions are driven by how they are framed by the young adults, and it will become clear that the ways in which the neighbourhoods are racialised is not always obvious in these initial descriptions, but rather centre on the gendered and classed dimensions of commonality. I problematise this universalising discourse and how it avoids the intersections with race in later chapters. Nevertheless, in order to contextualise the discussion, it is salient to note here that the three neighbourhoods are given quite different crude racialised identities, as 'Asian', 'black' and 'white working class' within the broader Manchester landscape. These are identities that are imagined as discrete because the areas are constructed as having homogeneous populations. Longsight, for example, is understood as an 'Asian' neighbourhood, although the percentage of people living in Longsight that describe themselves as 'Asian' is just 50 per cent. Moss Side is understood as a 'Black' neighbourhood and, as the following chapters will discuss, this is typically constructed as 'Black-Caribbean', but only 35 per cent of the local population describe themselves as 'Black' and only 10 per cent as 'Black-Caribbean'. Gorton is divided into two wards (North and South) and is typically described by respondents as white and 'chavvy'. This is the only one of the three neighbourhoods that does have a majority population of an ethnic group that squares with its image. Ninety per cent of the population in Gorton North and 77 per cent of Gorton South describe themselves as white.[8]

Regardless of where they stand in relation to reputations, all the young adults maintain that Gorton, Longsight and Moss Side are typically articulated with

26   The conflicted city

working classness and deprivation,[9] and they all do rank quite highly on the index of multiple deprivation.[10] The three neighbourhoods are also all imbued with negative images that centre on similar notions of criminality, such as drugs, street gangs and violent crime. Drawing these kinds of similarities between the three areas is, perhaps, made easier because they are close to each other geographically and roughly equidistant from the city centre – they all fall under the label of 'inner-city'.

The three neighbourhoods are said to have their own street 'gangs' that are depicted as marking territory and allowing for border areas to be referred to as, 'like the Gaza strip' (Simon). Physically, the areas look similar. They constitute similar housing, largely red-brick Victorian terraced housing built in the late 19th Century, and are at various stages of regeneration. As Nicky says:

> If you didn't know both areas and you drove round them you'd struggle to distinguish between [Longsight and Gorton], very similar lay outs with estates and that.
>
> (Nicky)

Criminal activity was said to dominate the way in which these 'inner city' neighbourhoods were represented from the 'outside', especially through the media. They have all, for example, been depicted and referenced in the national media through associations made to TV shows such as The Wire, Shameless and the book 'Gang War: the inside story of the Manchester gangs', by Peter Walsh (2005). These products were all referenced on several occasions in interviews.

Moss Side and Longsight are described by the young adults as the worst neighbourhoods in terms of crime levels in the city. The media focus on Moss Side as a dangerous crime area is said to contribute to this and it is one that has allowed Moss Side to attain an iconic status nationally (see Fraser, 1996 for a discussion on this). However, local statistics for 2010–11 compiled by Greater Manchester Against Crime (GMAC) on behalf of the City Council reveal that in both Moss Side and Longsight incidences of crime and anti-social behaviour are lower than that of the city average.[11] The young adults maintained that the negative reputations and associated criminal activity almost entirely associated with young men in their teens and early twenties that live there, and this certainly matches local media portrayals of crime. Stories about the three neighbourhoods thus featured largely gendered and youth oriented accounts of criminality. For instance, one respondent Pete, (a 25-year-old white male), explains that people, usually those who live 'elsewhere', imagine that the "youth culture" in these three neighbourhoods allows people to work on a different moral compass to the rest of society and gives them free rein to do anything, where "drugs are knocking about all the time, and people are always on the rob". The hooded teenage boy in particular is often presented as an archetypal resident that causes trouble and invokes fear. Hamid (who is 23 and describes himself as English and Somali) explains that young people in these areas are readily associated with certain behaviours and assumed to be 'gang-bangers' based on their age and the way they walk, talk and dress; codes that we will see in later chapters unravel to also represent various forms of race, gender and class.

> You are more likely to get stopped because of your age and technically I don't get stopped as much as I used to and I still dress the same. . . . When I was younger we used to get sconced [stopped by the police] once a day for nonsense reasons but now I hardly get stopped . . . I don't fit the profile of a kid that'll be a young gangbanger.
>
> (Hamid)

Moss Side was also reported to be commonly blamed for crime beyond its own boundaries. Tony, who unlike the other respondents often challenges the dominant narrative, recalled a recent stabbing that was reported in the press as having happened in Moss Side. However, he says, the incident happened several streets away and in a different neighbourhood. When I asked Tony why this differentiation occurs he argued that all areas, even wealthy ones, have their "hood", but they have "less of a reputation" ostensibly because they are less black. Unlike other neighbourhoods, Moss Side, he explains, is *always* associated with blackness and with being criminalised:

> Everybody knows that Longsight has a mix of, it's not like Moss Side, they're primarily black in Moss Side. . . . Moss Side's always got the reputation for being, even when things don't go down in Moss Side, they'll say, ooh it's in Moss Side.

Indeed, the black community in Moss Side were said to be represented as leading the way in terms of criminality and gang culture in Manchester. Several of the young people talk about a sort of trickledown effect of crime that emerged in 'black' neighbourhoods and has since affected 'Asian' and finally, 'white' areas. Stories about the 'leaking' of 'immorality' and criminality invoke ideas about 'contagions' (Swanton, 2008) and 'contamination' that are associated with fears about transgressions of social orders (Douglas, 2001: c1966) through which white people have been imagined as at risk of *becoming* black.[12] For instance Nadia, a 27-year-old woman (who describes as black, African and British) who works in Moss Side, explains how drug and gang activity is, for her, predominantly associated with black people in Moss Side, and whilst it is not something she has associated with the Asian community in the past, she says it may be "coming up".

> Looking at Moss Side, there's quite a lot of like black people around and the activities they get involved in and the drugs and gangs and things, there's more . . . I've not really heard many Asians saying that they're involved in gangs. Maybe it's coming up now.

28 *The conflicted city*

These narratives reflect the way in which blackness and 'black' spaces have come to be associated with moral panics and second class citizenship (Keith and Cross, 1993; Gilroy, 2002).

The role of the media in facilitating these associations was emphasised when I asked why these reputations prevailed in light of doubts over their veracity. 'Media hype' and popular preference for bad news over good were often held to account. Despite mocking the media hype, several young adults also admitted that they had accepted this view, particularly before moving to or working in the area, as evidence of how persuasive the stereotypes are. For example, Mina, (a 23-year-old who describes herself as British and Pakistani) describes her own fear of hoodies and acknowledges that much of this has come from watching Crimewatch, a TV series that appeals for public help to solve crimes. She says:

> You know when you have hoodies and stuff, people on bikes and stuff. You probably think I'm a scaredy cat or something, but I'm scared of them, people on bikes. That's why I don't go out. I refuse to go out at night time and like obviously it goes dark now doesn't it [at this time of year] quickly innit. And I've heard so many things that I just get scared. . . . You know what it is, I watch Crimewatch a lot.
>
> (Mina)

It was generally determined that those most likely to believe negative media portrayals were those living in 'posher' areas, 'southerners' (i.e. those from the south of England) and 'the closed-minded', all who apparently knew no better. Pete explained how he reasoned that people "like" to portray these areas in a bad light because then they can be sure that they live in a better area, "With their heads up their arses". These descriptions depicted a representation of class distinction, differentiating between what was said to be a local working class and lower middle class population and a middle class and upper middle class population that lived elsewhere. Consequently, at times, the young adults drew parallels between the three neighbourhoods and other parts of Manchester that were inscribed with similar class characteristics and contrasted them with largely middle class neighbourhoods, often located in the outskirts of the city, which map onto formations of most British cities.

There was some attempt to formerly redress these stereotypes through the promotion of 'good' news stories. Negative stereotyping, in this context, was broadly discussed as a problem that the neighbourhoods faced in terms of a sort of image crisis. During the process of the research I was invited, on several occasions, to observe celebrations of 'the community' in Gorton, including the launch of a book about Gorton, entitled 'Best viewed from within'. I was also asked to report on positive activities taking place in Moss Side and Longsight by contributing to a community newsletter and a housing association report. All of these events and ideas were intended to counteract negative stereotyping. These invitations also perhaps say something about the way in which I was perceived as someone with some power through connection to the University to get this message out to that very audience that is perceived to be likely to pathologise these areas; to other academics and public institutions. Notably, these invitations and suggestions came from community groups and social care organisations that I came across in the course of my fieldwork rather than from the young adults and, therefore, also likely represented particular interests around funding and public support for local individual initiatives (Harries et al., forthcoming). The young adults instead often drew upon stereotypes and reiterated many of the ways that places and the people living in them are pathologised, before going on to challenge them in other ways. Simon (a 30-year-old who describes himself as mixed race and English), for example, recommended the Peter Walsh 'Gang war' book to me, as a means to help me understand how these reputations have become "immortalised". He ridiculed the label 'Gunchester' that Walsh applies to Manchester and said he was amused by Chris Grayling, MP's reference to Moss Side as a scene from the US TV series 'The Wire', a series he said he refuses to watch.

> What was going on [in Moss Side] at the time was nothing short of an urban war. . . . It's the world of the drama series 'The Wire'.
>
> (Chris Grayling, MP, 25 August 2009)

Humour and mockery was a common means to respond to media representation and is, perhaps, best summed up by the title of a Facebook group page entitled 'I lived/live in Moss Side and survived!!'

The young adults' challenges to processes of pathologising focused less on rebranding or marketing the neighbourhood and concentrated instead on a critique of those 'small-minded' enough to believe the hype. Typically, these can be understood as challenges to the weight of meanings granted to stereotypes. In other words, they do not necessarily negate the presence of crime, but they refute the broader implication that this behaviour is endemic to the neighbourhood and the people who live there. In doing so, they point to the multiple layers and effects of practices of representation. Nadia (a 27-year-old woman who identifies herself as Black and African) does this here:

> When you look at a lot of things that are said about Moss Side it's always about like, someone got shot, there are a lot of gangs and everything else and it does happen. A lot of things they do say about, they do happen really and truly, but I think most of them, there is a reason behind it, there's no this and that happening to someone just randomly. . . . You know what, one time I was just walking down and then there was this guy who was like, "Is this Moss Side". I was like, "Yeah" and he was like, "Oh my god, I can't believe I've not been shot". That's really the reputation that Moss Side has. Someone thinks that they can just walk down Moss Side and someone will just come out with a gun and shoot you, just because you're in Moss Side [laughs]. I mean seriously, I couldn't believe this guy.

30 *The conflicted city*

What becomes clear from the interviews and from the media representations that the young adults draw on more generally is that these neighbourhoods appear to belong to another place to the city described at the outset. What is significant too is that, whilst diversity is celebrated in the city centre, there is nothing here to be 'celebrated' by a mainstream commercial audience. In these initial descriptions, racialised difference is only hinted at alongside other images of difference only in superficial labels, thus opening up a space of ambiguity to allow for the articulation of blackness, Asianness, white working classness with crime, deprivation and so on.

The discussion so far has explored the contrasting and conflicting ways in which difference is produced across the city. The city is not static in its representation although if we spend too much time focusing on one reading it can seem to be the case. Indeed, the above discussion can illustrate how paying too much attention to a particular form of representation can have a seductive allure – through different appeals to difference. Taken together, however, the various forms of representation allow us to explore conflicting modes of difference and contrasting ways in which this is managed. In the chapters that follow I will consider how these different discursive repertoires present different avenues through which people can talk about race and racism and negotiate their own subjectivities. Before moving on to do this however, I want to place the discussion within the broader context to consider how these local narratives connect beyond the city.

Beyond the city

The consequence of talking about forms of representation, no matter how illuminating they might be, is that they run the risk of reproducing a kind of stasis. To a great extent, I am interested in the relationship between the production of certain types of talk and how it jars against and connects with lived experience. This relationship will become more evident in the chapters that follow as the discussion shifts to explore how the young adults negotiated different spaces in their daily lives. It is worth reflecting first on the effects of imagining a city in a sort of stasis, rather than being more accurately depicted as a process that is shaped by global connections and information flows (Castells, 1996: 386).

The re-interpellation of Manchester's identity has been described above in part as one that can be understood as a strategy through which cities position themselves in a diversifying global political and cultural economy (Peck and Ward, 2002). However, whilst a range of actors and institutions make use of a particular kind of 'diverse' and 'progressive' identity to position Manchester in a global market, we fail to get a sense of the very movement that has enabled this sought for status. It is somewhat paradoxical that we are presented with competing visions of multiculture as if they are new formations that 'we' are dealing with in the present when cities have always been diverse. What perhaps is more novel is that the global forces that bring about diversity are rarely acknowledged. As Sassen points out, immigration and ethnicity are seldom thought of in the same frame of international as, say, global corporate markets

(Sassen, 1996b). Diversity (as it is articulated in the city) and racialised difference (as it is articulated in the inner city) have taken on new meanings that are embedded in the postcolonial melancholia that Gilroy (2004) describes and trapped in the confines of immigration debates that are removed from their global elements to be conceived of as if produced *from* nowhere, but *in* the local (Sassen, 1996a: 190). It is precisely because of this that racialised minorities continue to be seen as 'immigration communities' rather than people that are part of the internationalisation/globalisation process (Sassen, 1991). This kind of formulation gives the impression that it is the local that has produced the social context, rather than seeing the social as a changing space produced by the people in it. This was reflected in the advertising hoardings described above where racialised minorities were seen as recipients of the city's welcome, rather than the constituent element of that welcome and of that city. These elements together are worth noting because they will raise pertinent challenges for how the young adults can make claims to the city and have their experiences heard. We need to pay attention to how 'categories of difference and concepts of diversity exclude people from consideration as city-makers and agents of restructuring and rearticulating a city'(Glick Schiller and Schmidt, 2016: 7).

The way in which Manchester (as elsewhere) positions itself as 'unique' requires us reflect on its relationship to other scales. Each place is after all constituted through its relations to other places (Massey, 1994). The above discussion gives an indication of how the central narrative of the city relates to bordering neighbourhoods and vice versa. Yet, how do they relate to a broader context? Writing about a place becomes an exercise in purposeful concentration on what else is necessary to add for the reader to grasp the picture that is being conveyed. Always a partial view, narratives of place often appear more complete than they are because they exude a sense of familiarity that stretches beyond local registers and can encourage us to (not always accurately) fill in the blanks. For example, readers do not need to *know* Manchester to be familiar with the ways in which post-industrial cities in the UK, and indeed elsewhere, have been redeveloped/reimagined in their physical and discursive manifestations to be increasingly suggestive of the idea that their 'spaces, languages, positions or structures are neutral' (Puwar, 2004: 135), which can and does include the suggestion that they are absent of racialised meanings (Clayton, 2008). It is precisely because of these familiarities that we can find parallels in the way that Manchester reinvents itself in a somewhat paradoxical fashion with the way in which, say, Amsterdam (Uitermark et al., 2005) or Birmingham (Wilson, 2015) present themselves. Indeed, it is precisely because they are not entirely so that means they can be recognised and tell us about something beyond the city. Yet, in spite of these overlaps, it is somewhat ironic that each of these cities presents itself, as Wilson says of Birmingham, as 'contained, distinct and unique' (Wilson, 2015: 588). This latter contradictory phenomenon is set to deepen in UK cities as a result of policies driven by a localism agenda. Devolution in Greater Manchester has, for example, meant that some of the representations discussed above have become more pronounced, as the city feels compelled to justify its newly devolved status by more

32 The conflicted city

deeply carving out its uniqueness. Time will tell how these policy shifts will affect the local-national-local relation. For the moment it is worth approaching any suggestion that they will mark a big shift with caution, since devolution represents only a 'thin form' of neoliberalism so long as the majority of powers and 'ideological control' remain centralised (Peck, 2001: 452).

In spite of the limitations to its power, and perhaps because of it, the city can also be a site in which alternative forms of citizenship to that of the national can be negotiated, as Bauböck (2003) and others argue it can. Patriotism can be contested even when civic pride and the uniformity of a city is not. This is precisely because the city is offered as if a counter-narrative, especially by those who seek to use the city to develop or imagine a progressive agenda. Thus it is, perhaps, that whilst there has been a long debate about how national governments respond to multiculturalism 'the city is becoming increasingly salient as a site for generating, managing, negotiating and contesting cultural and political identities' (Uitermark et al., 2005: 622). Nevertheless, the histories that are imagined in Manchester are not only local histories, they are *a part* of a national history, including those that are hidden (Hesse, 2000). The city's position is not separate from elsewhere, as its unique representation might suggest, but is produced in dialogue with this process. Yet it would be a mistake to assume we must first understand the nation in order to understand the local (Confino and Skaria, 2002: 9). What is produced as local is really 'a set of practices which emerges in intimate relationship to nationalism, which in some ways even sustains nationalism' . . . and which, 'continues to live, in the era of nationhood, not so much outside the national, but beyond and alongside it' (Confino and Skaria, 2002: 10). In short, the city's narratives are not only produced in response to nationalist messages but also carry the potential to shape them (Jones and Fowler, 2007: 336). What is more, the representations detailed above are not simply the products of elite and centrally produced thinking; they also reflect populist demands, and they are reproduced and reworked in people's lives to make sense of their own lived experiences. Although the two broad sets of narratives detailed above are told separately, it is nevertheless necessary to remind ourselves that they rely on each other in their production and their borders are not fixed. Just as bodies cross these discursive spaces the narratives themselves can become merged or separated to meet different ends. To illustrate this, here, for example, we see the two converge as Maz (a 23-year-old who identifies as British and Pakistani) draws on the city narrative to distinguish Longsight, the neighbourhood where he lives, from other cities and towns that are synonymous with an 'Asian' label.

Maz: The Bradford community is totally different as well to maybe Manchester or other areas.

Bethan: How do you mean?

Maz: I don't know, I think just the Asian community is totally oblivious to what's happening out there in the real world.

Bethan: Right.

Maz: Yeah.

The conflicted city 33

Bethan: So do you go into the community while you're there? Or where do you get that feel from?

Maz: Just from speaking to people and being around them, you know [coughs] it's a bit of a shame really, but yeah, I just don't think that [people in Bradford] are particularly aware of what's going on around and it's very like . . . they like know everyone down their street, they've got their corner shop, corner mosque and to them that's their life, you know that little proper, little circle, you know that's the community, that's them and they're happy with that, but they don't like know people in the opposite streets or from different areas or how to interact with you know different types of people from all different walks of life.

A key word to note here is that of 'community'. Maz is comparing the 'Asian community' in his neighbourhood of Longsight to 'the community' in the city of Bradford, in the north-west of England. To do this, however, he does not dwell on local representations of the neighbourhood but draws on the Manchester narrative of tolerance in order to say something about nationalist imaginaries, and at the same time asserts his own right to, and membership of, the city.

Maz is not alone; several young adults describe direct and indirect experience of nearby towns, including, Bradford, Burnley and Oldham. They depict these towns as multi-ethnic, but rather than 'celebrating' the diversity and multiculture in these spaces, they are instead described as synonymous with what Maz calls "racial tensions". These contrasts draw on wider discourses, which have gained currency since urban unrests in 2001.[13] Indeed, it is through these kinds of negotiation that we can see how 'the local [can] mark the limits of the national' (Confino and Skaria, 2002: 10). The young adults draw upon narratives that conflict with each other in order to use them as comparisons. In doing so, they highlight the multiple possibilities of constructing and relating to the national through different forms of the local. The somewhat paradoxical relationships to the national that these simultaneous narratives represent pose interesting questions. As such, further consideration of how the young adults make sense of these conflicting narratives forms a basis of discussion in the next chapter as I turn to explore what we can already see emerging as the reimagining and distortion of place and time. This is indicated when the difference described in nearby towns is accounted for by the way in which these places are both spatially distant and imagined as if belonging to another era.

Conclusion

This chapter has set the scene of the research. It has illustrated how the city is a useful lens around which to frame research on the lived experience of race because the city acts as a location in which racialised difference is imagined in conflicting ways; simultaneously as a site of celebratory diversity and superficial difference and as a location that is inherently problematic. We saw above how diversity in 'the city' is imagined as 'simple plurality'; as harmonious and celebratory. These

34   *The conflicted city*

narratives are produced as part of the city's 'delight' and ignore 'the relations between the elements of this diversity, relations which mutually construct the different elements, that perhaps set them in conflict'. (Massey, 2007: 88). In contrast, inner city neighbourhoods become signifiers of processes of racialisation. They also act as locations of other local processes of identification including those related to class, gender and urban culture. In the chapters that follow I want to explore how the conflicting narratives that are produced in and about different spaces can, therefore, help to draw out multiple subjectivities (Majumdar, 2007) and allow for an examination of when and how race is done and comes to matter. I am concerned with examining the relationship between how people negotiate physical, social and political spaces and how people negotiate the ways in which they are positioned in these different spaces. First, however, I want to turn to consider how much of the narratives described above work with a temporal reference. The discussion continues by exploring how time and place interrelate, the salience of which will be demonstrated when the young adults describe themselves as being both of a place and of a particular historical moment, or 'generation'.

Notes

1 According to the Office of National Statistics figures from the 2011 census, www.ons. gov.uk/ons/dcp171778_270487.pdf. Accessed 12 April 2016.
2 The city of Manchester's population was said to be 503,000 according to the 2011Census.
3 See, for example, http://radicalmanchester.wordpress.com/for a collection of 'radical' writings on Manchester.
4 From the punk and post-punk periods of the 1970s and 1980s to what became known as the 'Madchester' scene of the 1990s.
5 Manchester City Council. *Manchester city council LGBT source guide.* www. manchester.gov.uk/info/448/archives_and_local_history/520/lgbt_source_guide Accessed 07 April 2016.
6 Local area data profiler available from www.ethnicity.ac.uk/research/data-sources/
7 Manchester City Council & Manchester Cultural Partnership. (2010). *Reframing Manchester's cultural strategy.* www.manchesterculturalpartnership.org/wp-content/ files_mf/culturalambition.pdf Accessed 07 April 2016.
8 These statistics are taken from the Office for National Statistics and are based on 2001 census data, which is the most recently available data at neighbourhood level.
9 How these articulations are formed in different ways will form part of the later discussion.
10 Gorton South and Moss Side are ranked in the top one per cent of most deprived areas in England and Wales. Longsight is ranked fourth in Manchester, whilst Gorton North is seventh, Moss Side is ranked eleventh and Longsight is fifteenth.
11 Available from Manchester City Council's. *Research and intelligence website.* www. manchester.gov.uk/info/200088/statistics_and_census_information/438/research_and_ intelligence/3 Accessed 12 April 2016.
12 In an interview on Newsnight on BBC Two on 12 August 2011, David Starkey (historian and broadcaster) said that riots across England were indicative of how "the whites have become black".
13 Oldham, Burnley and Bradford have been portrayed as the epitome of self-segregation and the principal targets of community cohesion agendas. The urban unrests in 1995 and 2001, that were portrayed as race riots, and the Rushdie affair in 1989 during which

copies of the Satanic Verses were burned in Bradford are often drawn upon to substantiate such claims. (For a critique of these representations see, for example, Alexander, C. (2000). *The Asian gang: Ethnicity, identity, masculinity*. London: Berg., or Phillips, D. (2006). Parallel lives? Challenging discourses of British Muslim self-segregation. *Environment and Planning D: Society and Space*, 24(1), 25–40.

References

Agnew, J., Mercer, J. & Sopher, D. (1984). Introduction. *In:* Agnew, J., Mercer, J. & Sopher, D. (eds.) *The city in cultural context*. Boston: Allen & Unwin.

Alexander, C. (2000). *The Asian gang: Ethnicity, identity, masculinity*. London: Berg.

Amin, A. (2002). Ethnicity and the multicultural city: Living with diversity. *Environment and Planning A*, 34(6), 959–980.

Amin, A. (2007). Re-thinking the urban social. *City*, 11(1), 100–114.

Back, L. (2005). 'Home from home': Youth, belonging and place. *In:* Alexander, C. & Knowles, C. (eds.) *Making race matter: Bodies, space and identity*. Basingstoke: Palgrave Macmillan.

Barabantseva, E. (2016). Seeing beyond an 'ethnic enclave': The time/space of Manchester Chinatown. *Identities: Global Studies in Culture and Power*, 23(1), 99–115.

Bauböck, R. (2003). Reinventing urban citizenship. *Citizenship Studies*, 7(2), 139–160.

Binnie, J. & Skeggs, B. (2004). Cosmopolitan knowledge and the production and consumption of sexualized space: Manchester's gay village. *The Sociological Review*, 52(1), 39–61.

Burgess, J. A. (1985). News from nowhere: The press, the riots, and the myth of the inner city. *In:* Burgess, J. A. & Gold, J. R. (eds.) *Geography, the media and popular culture*. London: Croom Helm.

Byrne, B. (2014). *Making citizens: Public rituals and personal journeys to citizenship*. London: Palgrave Macmillan UK.

Castells, M. (1996). *The rise of network society*. Cambridge, MA: Blackwell.

Centre on Dynamics of Ethnicity (2013). Does Britain have plural cities?, 4 July 2016. Available from: www.ethnicity.ac.uk/census/869_CCSR_Bulletin_Does_Britain_have_plural_cities_v7.pdf.

Clayton, J. (2008). Everyday geographies of marginality and encounter in the multicultural city. *In:* Dwyer, C. & Bressey, C. (eds.) *New geographies of race and racism*. Aldershot: Ashgate.

Confino, A. & Skaria, A. (2002). The local life of nationhood. *National Identities*, 4(1), 7–24.

De Certeau, M. (2011 [1984]). *The practice of everyday life* (Vol. 3rd Edition). Berkeley: University of California Press.

Douglas, M. (1984 [1966]). *Purity and danger: an analysis of the concepts of pollution and taboo*. London: Routledge

Evans, G. (2016). *London's Olympic legacy: The inside track*. London: Palgrave Macmillan.

Fraser, P. (1996). Social and spatial relationships and the 'problem' inner city: Moss side in Manchester. *Critical Social Policy*, 16(49), 43–65.

Gilroy, P. (2002). *There ain't no black in the Union Jack* (2nd Edition). Abingdon, Oxfordshire: Routledge.

Gilroy, P. (2004). *After empire: Melancholia or convivial culture?* Abingdon: Routledge.

36   *The conflicted city*

Glick Schiller, N. & Schmidt, G. (2016). Envisioning place: Urban socialities within time, space and multiscalar power. *Identities: Global Studies in Culture and Power*, 23(1), 1–16.

Harries, B. (2015). Empire, transnationalism and multicultural Wales *A tolerant nation?* University of South Wales, Cardiff, 22 October 2015.

Harries, B., Byrne, B., Rhodes, J. & Wallace, S. (forthcoming). Diversity in place: narrations of diversity in an ethnically mixed, urban area. *Journal of Ethnic and Migration Studies*.

Hesse, B. (ed.). (2000). *Un/settled multiculturalisms: Diasporas, entanglements, transruptions*. London: Routledge.

Holston, J. (1998). Spaces of insurgent citizenship. *In:* Sandercock, L. (ed.) *Making the invisible visible: A multicultural planning history*. Berkeley and Los Angeles: University of California Press.

Jones, P. & Wilks-Heeg, S. (2004). Capitalising cutlure: Liverpool 2008. *Local Economy*, 19(4), 341–360.

Jones, R. & Fowler, C. (2007). Placing and scaling the nation. *Environment and Planning D: Society and Space*, 25(2), 332–354.

Keith, M. (2005). *After the cosmopolitan: Multicultural cities and the future of racism*. London: Routledge.

Keith, M. & Cross, M. (1993). Racism and the postmodern city. *In:* Cross, M. & Keith, M. (eds.) *Racism, the city and the state*. London: Routledge.

Koller, V. (2008). 'The world in one city' Semiotic and cognitive aspects of city branding. *Journal of Language and Politics*, 7(3), 431–450.

Majumdar, A. (2007). Researching south Asian women's experiences of marriage: Resisting stereotypes through an exploration of 'space' and 'embodiment'. *Feminism & Psychology*, 17(3), 316–322.

Massey, D. (1994). *Space, place and gender*. Cambridge: Polity Press.

Massey, D. (2004). Geographies of responsibility. *Geografiska Annaler: Series B, Human Geography*, 86(1), 5–18.

Massey, D. (2007). *World city*. Cambridge: Polity Press.

Mommaas, H. (2002). City branding: The necessity of socio-cultural goals. *In:* Affairs, U. (ed.) *City branding: Image building and building images*. Rotterdam: NAI Publishers.

Nayak, A. (2011). Geography, race and emotions: Social and cultural intersections. *Social and Cultural Geography*, 12(6), 548–562.

Peach, C. (1998). South Asian and Caribbean ethnic minority housing choice in Britain. *Urban Studies*, 35(10), 1657–1680.

Peck, J. (2001). Neoliberalizing states: Thin policies/hard outcomes. *Progress in Human Geography*, 25(3), 445–455.

Peck, J. & Ward, K. (2002). Placing Manchester. *In:* Peck, J. & Ward, K. (eds.) *City of revolution: Restructuring Manchester*. Manchester: Manchester University Press.

Phillips, D. (1998). Black minority ethnic concentration, segregation and dispersal in Britain. *Urban Studies*, 35(10), 1681–1702.

Phillips, D. (2006). Parallel lives? Challenging discourses of British Muslim self-segregation. *Environment and Planning D: Society and Space*, 24(1), 25–40.

Piacentini, T. (2016). Refugee solidarity in the everyday. *Soundings: A Journal of Politics and Culture*, 64, Winter, 57–61.

Pile, S. (2005). *Real cities: Modernity, space and the phantasmagorias of city life*. London: Sage.

Puwar, N. (2004). *Space invaders: Race, gender and bodies out of place*. New York: Berg.

Rex, J. & Moore, R. (1969). *Race, community and conflict: Study of sparkbrook*. London: Institute of Race Relations.

Sassen, S. (1991). *The global city*. Princeton: Princeton University Press.

Sassen, S. (1996a). Analytic borderlands: Race, gender and representation in the new city in King. *In:* King, A. D. (ed.) *Re-presenting the city: Ethnicity, capital and culture in the 21st century metropolis*. London: MacMillan Press.

Sassen, S. (1996b). Rebuilding the global city: Economy, ethnicity and space. *In:* King, A. D. (ed.) *Re-presenting the city: Ethnicity, capital and culture in the 21st century metropolis*. London: MacMillan.

Sassen, S. (1999). Whose city is it? Globalisation and the formation of new claims. *In:* Beauregard, R. (ed.) *The urban moment: Cosmopolitan essays on the late 20th century city*. London: Sage.

Sennett, R. (1992). *The conscience of the eye: The design and social life of cities*. New York: W. W. Norton & Company.

Swanton, D. (2008). Everyday multiculture and the emergence of race. *In:* Dwyer, C. & Bressey, C. (eds.) *New geographies of race and racism*. London: Routledge

Uitermark, J., Rossi, U. & Van Houtum, H. (2005). Reinventing multiculturalism: Urban citizenship and the negotiation of ethnic diversity in Amsterdam. *International Journal of Urban and Regional Research*, 29(3), 622–640.

Wacquant, L. (2008). *Urban outcasts: A comparative sociology of advanced marginality*. Cambridge: Polity Press.

Walsh, P. (2005). *Gang war: The inside story of the Manchester gangs*. Preston: Milo Books.

Williams, B. (1976). *The making of Manchester Jewry: 1740–1875*. Manchester: Manchester University Press.

Wilson, H. F. (2015). An urban laboratory for the multicultural nation? *Ethnicities*, 15(4), 586–604.

Winter, A. (2013). Race, multiculturalism and the 'progressive' politics of London 2012: Passing the 'Boyle Test'. *Sociological Research Online*, 18(2), 1–7.

Young, C., Diep, M. & Drabble, S. (2006). Living with difference? The 'cosmopolitan city' and urban reimaging in Manchester, UK. *Urban Studies*, 43(10), 1687–1714.

Young, M. & Wilmott, P. (2011 [1957]). *Family and kinship in East London* (Vol. Routledge Revivals). London: Routledge.

3 The imaginings of a 'post-racial' generation

> I think a similar generation would have a similar view, I do think that.
> (Nasreen, 28 years old, 'British-Muslim-Bangladeshi')

This chapter explores how the young adults position themselves within the city and as part of its fabric. It pays particular attention to the extent to which they find appeal in the liberal notions of tolerance and forward thinking that epitomise the brand of Manchester and weave these into a narrative to construct a sense of a generation.[1] I therefore continue to consider how articulations of diversity and progress shape the way the city constructs itself but, more specifically, I focus on how they are employed by the young people in order to distinguish how race and racism is conceived in the present (by their generation) and how it has been dealt with in the past. I argue that the young adults find a certain appeal in the post-racial narratives of the city. They often work with the reimagining of a historical narrative to suggest a process of improvement or maturation (Brown, 2006) that are nevertheless part of an ongoing process of reworking and responding to new forms of difference and new forms of race-making.

The chapter begins by critically engaging with the concept of being a post-racial generation. It suggests that whilst post-racial logics are problematic, they have purchase in the national imagination and have particular consequences for young people that are worthy of exploration. I then go on to explore the means through which the young adults construct themselves in relation to post-racial imaginaries by presenting themselves as being of a particular moment that is shared through their age and their city. I am interested in how ideas of the post-racial take form and why they have appeal for the young people. Hence, I examine two discursive frameworks through which the notion manifests. Firstly, I consider how racism is compartmentalised as if it belongs to another period of time and to places that are constructed as if distant from Manchester and its brand of tolerance. Second, I go on to consider how the young adults emphasise ways of knowing difference and, in doing so, tap into dominant discourses of 'mixing', 'integration' and 'cohesion', rather than rely on their more convivial relationships that might have more success in overcoming race by virtue of their indifference to difference (Amin, 2013; Valluvan, 2016).

40 *The imaginings of a 'post-racial' generation*

There is something particularly useful about exploring these ideas with this group of young adults. We can describe this cohort as one which has grown up within a political context that continues (rather than begins) to divert attention from the historical legacy of race, including, or perhaps especially, through the repression of references to colonialism (Hesse, 1999). It is a context in which the idea of being post-racial, no matter how dubious, has traction in the popular imagination both nationally and in Manchester where the research took place. And finally, it is also a setting in which the language of race has become increasingly diffuse (Song, 2014) and has moved towards individualised 'explanations oriented around psychologized concepts of bias and prejudice', rather than 'socially meaningful acts' of racism (Ambikaipaker, 2015: 2056). At a more mundane level, it is also worth noting how the young adults are in the process of expanding their lifespace. Since leaving school they have entered work that takes them to different parts of the city. They are becoming familiar with a wider range of institutions that they would have been previously limited from, including job centres, employment agencies and housing institutions. This also means that they form new relationships and develop their cultural and social lives well beyond the boundaries of their neighbourhood, schools, youth and community centres. This work therefore compliments previous research on youth which has often centred on the peer group or been centred on a specific location, (see, for example, Alexander, 1996; Back, 1996; Dwyer, 1999; Nayak, 2003; Kim, 2014; James, 2015; Hollingworth, 2015; Kulz, 2014), but opens up the discussion to think about how these broader spaces produce contradictory effects and tensions that shape the way the young adults navigate the city in which they live.

There is a long tradition of observing how race shapes young lives and youth cultures. However, whilst research with young people that centres on issues of race and racism remains prevalent in cultural studies, education and sociology, it is perhaps telling that in youth and young adult studies race has become primarily 'conspicuous only in the production of its very absence' (Harries et al., 2016: 2).[2] The absence of race in youth studies is symptomatic of a broader shift in social sciences in which issues of immigration, diversity and identity are examined as if they are detached from politics, history and power relationships (Alexander, 2002; Alexander et al., 2012; Back, 2015). As Alexander et al argue:

> Issues of inequality, discrimination and racism have fallen off the academic map completely or have been replaced with an obsession with culture and cultural identity which focuses on difference at the expense of the broader social, political and economic context in which difference matters and is made to matter.
>
> (Alexander et al., 2012: 4)

What we witness in the discussion that follows might be described as the fall-out of the ways in which these issues have dropped off the map – what is happening in academia is itself a reflection of broader social trends. The ways in which the young adults describe themselves as being 'post-racial', 'race-less' and 'beyond'

The imaginings of a 'post-racial' generation   41

difference must therefore be read alongside the broader context that led to this point. Their narratives therefore do not and should not serve as a rejoinder to integration debates or assessments of the quality of diversity, even when they tap into these very discursive repertoires in order to construct themselves in a particular way.

A 'post-racial' generation?

Chapter 2 reminds us how race can be mapped onto the city, but it also points us to another key aspect of race that we know to be true – it is always in process and historically contingent. The meaning of race shifts over both place and time and we therefore need to take account of how 'racial practices are (re)constructed at different historical moments and places' (Wilson, 2002: 32). Over the last 15 years or so, a growing body of work has begun to address the ways in which an overall trend has developed in Europe and the US that conceives race as an outmoded, atavistic concept and a relic of the past (Winant, 2001). Whilst the resurgence of far-right politics might, on the face of it, appear to destabilise this conception, post-racial debates nevertheless continue to have significance. Principally, this is because far-right populist movements still tend to be treated as discrete phenomena, rather than a result of embedded racist structures that are integrated in mainstream politics and thus have further reaching effects. Subsequently, it is worth casting a lens onto the continuing salience of the post-racial. I would suggest that it is particularly pertinent to do so here in light of the way that the young adults often identify with a liberal position that posits itself against anything resembling discrete phenomena, such as the nationalist ideologies of UKIP, the British National Party or English Defence League, but do find appeal in the city's depiction as a site of progress and tolerance even whilst the neoliberal machinations of the city function to distort a racial past and present.

In its simplest and crudest form the term 'post-racial' suggests a chronological understanding of the emergence and transcendence, or submergence, of race. The notion of being 'post-racial' is therefore sometimes employed to hint at the way that racism is expunged from the present and envisaged to have no salience for the future. In this way racism is conceived as if locked into being a thing of the past, although this past also remains somewhat obscured (see, for example, Lentin, 2008 for a discussion on this). However, under these terms the prefix 'post-' falsely indicates a sequential process and its (mis)use can risk failing to contextualise the practice of silencing and denying race into a much longer history, as Hesse (2011) is quite right to alert us to. Hence, although the prefixed '_post_-racial' gestures towards the future by marking a break in history, it is somewhat a misnomer. We are, after all, always in a moment in which history is being reworked. The tenacity of the post-racial thus lies beyond the disavowal or silencing of racism and in the way in which it organises and reproduces structures of domination to imagine a particular kind of future and one that obfuscates the realities of racism historically and in the present (Goldberg, 2015). In this chapter I am interested in how these narratives take hold. I argue that the idea of being post-racial has a particular allure

42 *The imaginings of a 'post-racial' generation*

and takes hold in the imagination, not solely because it relinquishes the need to deal with a racist past, but also because it embodies what Bhabha describes as a 'restless and revisionary energy' (Bhabha, 1994: 6). Indeed, the effect of this energy is illustrated in the seductive appeal of the narratives of the post-industrial city, in spite of, and perhaps because of, the way that they are crudely and hurriedly pieced together to make a coherent story of reinvention.

Part of Manchester's reinvention relies on managing racialised difference in conflicting ways in different parts of the city through a range of discursive mechanisms that shape boundaries of exclusion. The construction of these narratives depend on certain depictions of past, present and future. Manchester might seek to reinvent itself as if it is something new, but there are nevertheless patterns and repetitions in the reproduction of its narratives that rely on the past and its continual reworking. This process of reinvention has a sense of youthful vibrancy at its core when it encourages us to look towards the future. And so, just as the city is conceived like 'the phoenix rising from the ashes' (Keith and Cross, 1993: 8), its young people are imagined to hold the potential to offer us something better than before, and these two things are mutually constituted. Of particular relevance here is the way that young people are not only called upon as representatives of the future, but also as the future of multiculturalism and living with diversity (James, 2015). Indeed, young people are often imagined as symbols or markers of tolerance and a tolerant Britishness (Amin, 2010) in similar ways that new forms of urbanism are said to mark change. Understanding this helps us to comprehend the allure of the post-racial for the young adults. There is, after all, a certain appeal to be found in being regarded as part of, or constituting, a period of progress or change. I suggest that this goes some way to explain why so many of the young people were keen to describe Manchester as a place in which racism no longer features even though, as later chapters go on to illustrate, this is repeatedly contradicted.

It should also be noted that the notion of being post-racial can also hold a less cynical appeal in that it can also speak to attempts to 'develop an anti-race anti-racism' (Titley, 2016). This too is, of course, likely to have significant appeal for the young people and certainly any attempt to drive an anti-racist agenda should be heeded (Valluvan and Kapoor, 2016). The difficulty is that the young adults' calls to a kind of universal humanism that might seek to overcome race are articulated here in somewhat naïve ways, even when they are borne from optimism. As I will go on to show, there is often too much reliance on crude understandings of what counts as 'non-racial', rather than anti-racism, particularly through attempts to erase difference altogether by over-emphasising sameness. This has the misguided effect that the young people fail to acknowledge the way in which race structures and organises their lives, even when they are aware that it does. Arguably then, these efforts often do not meet up to the realisation of 'anti-race anti-racism'. However, paying attention to how these failures materialise and how a post-racial logic that obscures race takes precedent instead might help us to understand how a clearer expression of anti-racism can be developed. I begin by thinking through how the myth of sameness is developed as a generational phenomenon.

The imaginings of a 'post-racial' generation   43

The myth of sameness and the fantasy of non-racism

There is a considerable amount of literature that examines how the myth of sameness, or colour-blindness, reproduces white privilege because it comprehends race in an ahistorical way (see, for example, hooks, 1992; Bonilla-Silva, 2014). This work explains the prevailing understanding that it is sufficient 'not to subscribe to crass prejudicial views about racial minority groups' to move beyond race, without thinking through what racism is and from where it originates (Bonilla-Silva, 2015: 1359). What I am interested in specifically is how a sense of sameness is assumed through the shared identity of being young and from Manchester, in order to create the illusion of non-racism. This happens in the narratives across the group of young adults as part of the way in which they imply a generational shift. However, their claims to sameness silence the way they do not share the same experiences and are positioned in differentiated ways.

Statements about the lack of racism are common among the young adults. Maz for example says that you "don't find many problems [in Manchester] in terms of like racism". Statements like this, as the rest of the book will go on to illustrate, are regularly contradicted. Nevertheless it is worth thinking about why they are there in the first place and question the purpose they are intended to serve. It is certainly notable that they are often placed within a historical frame (albeit an inaccurate one), and as such the young people do not solely reproduce a narrative of tolerance in the city, but also mark a generational shift in the way the city (their city) is today and how it was/may have been previously. In the following quote from Anna we can see how this takes form when she explains how negative representations and stereotypes about black people in Manchester are no longer 'a thing' for her generation:

> I think it's a generational thing largely because err, probably [my husband's] parents and his parent's generation, the same as my parents, they're very small-minded, they grew up with certain stereotypes and they're very reluctant to let go of them and even though they may have work friends, or family friends even who are Asian or black or other background, they still can't see that they're just the same as them.
>
> (Anna, 26 years old, Czech/usually read as 'Eastern European')

This is a common sentiment shared across the participants in the research and one, as I said above, that will be repeatedly contradicted. Leaving that aside for the moment, what I want to draw attention to is the way that by putting racism into the past, Anna (and the other young people) also creates a sense of a 'we'; that is a sense of a generation that suggest that "we are all just the same". Indeed, a key point reiterated in many of the conversations I had with the young people centred on how "we are all the same" and we are all "human", both common iterations expressed across all the young people, irrespective of how they are racialised, although with different things at stake. And, whilst we might interpret these claims

44 *The imaginings of a 'post-racial' generation*

in multiple ways, their effect is extended to suggest that *being* black and *being* white amount to the same thing. But, whilst these are often presented as if led by an anti-racist logic this fails when they instead tend to deny racism and reflect narratives that historicise race and racism without thinking through their broader salience. Hence, Steve, who is white, is able to conclude the following when I ask him to clarify whether he also understands that this means that people have the same experience:

> You know if it was just me, but with black skin, I don't think it would make a difference walking down the street, so I don't think it makes too much of a difference, in my own experience anyway.

Steve seemed genuinely baffled by my question and his answer suggests that he does not recognise differentiated positionings or recognise why it might be an issue of any concern.

Zoe, who is white, also suggests that she understands blackness and whiteness to be without meaning beyond superficial appearance. This comes across even more problematically when she claims that it is easy to adopt any identity by, for example, changing hair styles and getting a tan:

Zoe: You can be what you want. If you want to be black you can be black, if you want to be white you can be white. . . .
Bethan: Can you be black if you're white?
Zoe: Well, like you can tan a lot and get braids, do you know what I mean? I know, that's going like over the top, but I don't know, cos Michael Jackson went white didn't he, and he was black.

The lack of attention to (or denials of) the ways in which people are differentially positioned in the young peoples' narratives is reminiscent of some of the discussions that have surrounded name calling in sport and institutional racism in the police. These debates are frequently limited to labels, rather than the historical roots and legacies of race that construct meanings and are embedded in the everyday (Song, 2014), and in doing so, they deny that 'categories are effects and they have affects' (Ahmed, 2004: 10).

Zoe continues:

> My sister is getting married and she's only invited one black person and this is what she said, 'We need to invite another black person cos it looks odd otherwise' [laughs]. And me and my mum were like, God [sister], don't be ridiculous, but she was really conscious of that, yeah. She said this woman said that this woman had said that she was aware when she was the only black person, whereas it's nothing, it's not something that really affects me. I don't think, oh, I'm the only white person, but that's an attitude that people have.

The imaginings of a 'post-racial' generation   45

Here then we get to the crux of the problem more acutely. In this story, Zoe disregards the concerns expressed by a black woman about being in an all-white space. She describes the concern as 'ridiculous' based on her own experiences as a white woman, as if their positionings are synonymous. When she adds that 'it's not something that really affects' her, she draws our attention to the absence of any recognition of the privilege of whiteness. Zoe's account is located firmly in the understanding that 'these days' there is no difference between black and white people, but more specifically, no difference between being black and being white. Thus, she reasons that complaining or voicing concern about being black in a white space can be put down to 'an attitude' of an individual, rather than a symptom of structural hierarchies and dis/advantage. When white young people like Steve and Zoe 'choose not to recognise' or 'refuse to understand'(Foucault, 1978), they reflect the broader tendency to demand assimilation/silence rather than recognise marginalisation. Hence they speak directly to, rather than challenge, an integrationist logic and its mode of exclusion.

The black young adults also repeatedly stress how, as Laurence puts it, "we are all the same":

> We're all the same, no matter if you call yourself that and I call myself this and that, actually everyone's born and everyone dies really so what we class ourselves as while we're here is just kind of that really.

And it is clear that there are also concerns about how to talk about how to identify difference. Jameela who identifies as Asian British, for example, succumbs to a literal silence when I asked her to describe Moss Side, when she mouths:

> [Moss Side] is mostly like black people [mouths silently] going there and stuff.

Tony who is black also offers a sense of universalism when he reflects on how Manchester has changed. We were discussing how the pub and club scene had changed in Manchester when he concludes that "nowadays" you can go where you like because people are more accepting and have merged identities of blackness and whiteness:

> Back in the day, do you know, it was literally, you dressed black, you dressed white or whatever, everything was associated with probably your colour or something like that. Since Kanye West, since these people, black people wear skinny jeans, black people have straight hair, white people have Afro hair, white people have stuff like beards, black people have beards, people wear big thick glasses cos it's alright to be a geek now . . . But now it's alright cos everything's slimmed down and trainers cost £10 now and nobody's bothered about the sweat shops no more, do you know what I mean? . . . I think people now are more accepting.

46 *The imaginings of a 'post-racial' generation*

This description of racialised dress codes implies a common understanding that there is a way of dressing/being black and a way of dressing/being white (Ifekwun-igwe, 1999; Alexander, 1996). But Tony suggests that "back in the day", these distinctions were more clearly marked. He speaks enthusiastically when he imagines that he and his friends occupy a post-racial moment that is, again, explained through a historical trajectory to imply that the city and levels of tolerance are better than before. Later, Tony goes on to contradict this statement when he begins to reflect on the way that he is positioned as 'black' and acknowledges there are places in Manchester that are for him no-go areas. And whilst there is undoubtedly something credible in his description of shifting cultural identities, it is in placing them in dialogue with non-racism that is problematic. In doing so, he is reflecting back the way in which racism has so often been reduced to labels and to appearance, rather than more fundamental structural constraints. I argue that it is because of this false link between cultural sameness and non-racism, rather than anti-racism, that convivial qualities that convey an indifference to difference described elsewhere (see, for example, Valluvan, 2016) are limited in the way they can be conveyed as having potential to overcome difference.

To overcome some of these potential problems certainly it is worth stressing then that, whilst the young adults do all tend to access shared repertoires, their orientations towards these discourses do not represent a shared experience. It is therefore worth taking time to reflect on how generation, as it is constructed by the young adults, might be better conceptualised. The original intention to sample people from this cohort was based on the premise that they would have most likely completed full-time education, have an expanded 'lifespace' and be able to draw on a shared history. It is important to note here that despite the sense of shared history implied through the emphasis on a particular place and 'moment', I do not want to risk over emphasising commonality within the 'group', even when the young people do. Indeed this has been a criticism of work that seeks to define cohorts according to adult stages – as in 'emerging adulthood' (see Bynner, 2005; Bynner, 2001 for a critique of this) or in generations as, for example, in the tradition of Mannheim (1952). The individuals within this study can be differentiated in the way in which they are oriented towards certain social experiences. They identify in different ways across social categories. They experience race, gender, class and presumably sexuality (although this is never mentioned) in different ways. They include people who have/do not have children, are unemployed, work part-time, have chosen a 'career', returned to education, are married, are single and have not had or do not want a long-term relationship. Significantly, they do share a common historical location and one that is spatially located within Manchester. Of the 32 participants that were interviewed, three were not born in the UK, but had come to live in Manchester when they were teenagers, two were born in the UK and had spent part of their teenage years overseas and two had only recently migrated to the UK. All of the young adults were alert to discourses that centred on the neighbourhoods in which they lived[3] but have different experiences of those same spaces. Consequently, when the young adults talk about being a generation, it is useful to think not of a

The imaginings of a 'post-racial' generation   47

'generation' as some sort of tangible or concrete entity, but rather in the sense suggested by Reulecke (2008):

> Generation and generationality are, in the end, not tangible entities but rather mental, often very zeitgeist-dependent constructs through which people, as members of a specific age group are located or locate themselves historically, and accordingly create a we-feeling.
>
> (Reulecke, 2008: 119)

What I want to reiterate here then is that, whilst shared discursive repertoires and geographical and historical locations can present the possibilities of a 'we-feeling', they do not represent a coherent 'we' that shares the same conditions or experiences, as many of the young adults are prone to suggest. Nevertheless they do carry significant weight and to deconstruct them more need to know more about how they operate. In the following I explore two discursive frameworks that make use of and help reproduce the myth of sameness. These are, notably, two frameworks that dominate public and policy debates on how we live with difference. The first examines how the young people make use of historicising narratives to think about how articulations of diversity and progress that shape the way the city and a generation constructs itself are employed to distinguish themselves from 'other' places that can then become sites in which race and other modes of problematised difference can be contained, whilst the city itself is allowed to flourish. Second, I reflect on the way that integrationist perspectives dominate the discursive frame through which to talk about how people live by over emphasising ad hoc forms of 'mixing' and 'contact'. I argue that the young people are compelled to defend themselves on the wrong terms. Rather than articulating their convivial relationships, they tend to instead speak directly to integrationist demands.

Other times and 'othered' places

Manchester might seek to reinvent itself as if it is something new, but there are nevertheless patterns and repetitions in the reproduction of its narratives that rely on the past and its continual reworking. It is notable that what is presented to us are two convincing means of dealing with race in the city. At its heart we are presented with the image of the liberal future-facing global city that has shrugged off the weight of its past and treats diversity as a celebratory emblem of this image. In the process, the city is imagined as a diverse space, but it is one created as if in a political and historical vacuum. On the other hand, the bounded inner city is imagined as being its opposite, the heart of problematic difference and associated malfunctions that are articulated with race. Within these dual narratives we witness plenty of temporal metaphors. The city's branded diversity is considered to be part of a vision of progress, whilst the inner city is imagined as if belonging to a different era and one that has not 'caught up' with the more appealing image of the city. Moss Side, in particular, received a lot of negative attention that was disjointed from the city's liberal tolerant brand. It is a neighbourhood that is often

48 *The imaginings of a 'post-racial' generation*

represented in the media at a local and national level as the "worst" neighbourhood in Manchester with a high level of violent crime. Crime and gang culture are depicted as if embedded and difficult to shift, and there was a sense that these issues were innate to the area because its problems date back a long way. This historical legacy gave the young people a means to explain representations of Moss Side without always getting caught up in the way they are articulated through race. When Paul (a 20-year-old who is white and English) is asked why, as he has said, Moss Side gets more negative publicity, he responds by saying:

> It's just cos back in the day, like years ago, really bad stuff used to happen in Moss Side, like shootings weekly.

Hence these representations are given foundation as if they are based on something that is/was real, but in a way that leaves out the way in which they are articulated with race. To illustrate this further we can reflect on how Gorton and Moss Side are characterised. Alice, who is white and lives in Gorton, tries to explain why Gorton is not as "infamous" as Moss Side. She recalls a recent shooting in Gorton in which a young woman was killed that did not receive any national publicity. Alice explains that she is certain it would have received more media attention if it had happened in Moss Side. I asked her why she thought this might be and in thinking through this disparity, she concluded that the focus on Moss Side must be because, "it has been going on for longer". These kinds of narratives thus provide an avenue through which the young people can construct their story about their relationships to different places and to racism.

The comparisons made between different places across the city reflect a form of racial historicism that Goldberg (2001) otherwise describes at a national level in which areas with relatively high ethnic minority populations, that are also typically poorer neighbourhoods, are represented as 'backwards' and out of step with liberal ideals. This depiction puts the young people in a somewhat awkward position. They live and work in these neighbourhoods, and so in reconciling these two issues, they have to juggle embedded representations whilst they also seek to maintain their sense of commonality and non-racism across these divides. Doing that, however, requires them to look beyond the localised narratives and tap into other scales, particularly the national.

When young people like Maz and Nasreen explain that things have changed to the extent that there is no racism in Manchester any more, it is the articulation of both time and place that is prescient. Both aspects of a shared location help them to create a sense of a 'we' (in the here and now) that is distant (somewhere else and from another time). In contextualising this in relation to discourses of race and racism it is worth reflecting on the ways that we know that racism is often compartmentalised to suggest that it is something that belongs to the past (Winant, 2006), or it is associated with individuals or groups that are perceived as 'backwards' or living in the past. We can witness the latter, for example, when certain pathologising depictions of the white working class are both imagined as being uncivilised and articulated in ways that are 'emblematically racist' (Haylett, 2001).

The young people also compartmentalise racism but, having said that Manchester is devoid of racism, they have to look beyond its boundaries, and they do not look very far.

The young adults often formed comparisons between Manchester and other towns in the North West of England in order to distinguish between particular ways that difference and racism is managed. In considering these narratives more closely I want to highlight how in doing so they made distinctions between the here (Manchester) and now (this cohort) and towns that they described as 'other' and 'elsewhere' in both time and place. Places that the young adults construct as 'other' are located at a physical distance and work as a heuristic device to draw attention away from their neighbourhood to other places that have become known for their difference. In particular, it is smaller towns in relatively close proximity to Manchester that have diverse populations and that have some purchase in the national imagination that are brought into the discussions by the young adults, such as Bradford, Burnley and Oldham. These towns have been the subject of national debates on multiculturalism and self-segregation for decades, but particularly since the urban unrests in 2001. They are drawn upon by the young adults in order to offer a comparison as something 'worse', which allows for attention to be drawn to somewhere else, rather than confronting the stigma attached to their own neighbourhood. What I am interested in here is how, in the process, the young adults fix these 'other' places in the past through racialised historicised narratives and make use of national discourses that racialise and problematise multiculture – the very same issues they are imagined to be beyond.

Bradord is perhaps the most cited case in this respect. Maz, for example, describes Asian people in Bradford as insular and less "developed" than people in Manchester. Bradford Asians are imagined as if, as Nasreen says elsewhere, they are stuck in a "time-warp". Maz suggests that this then has implications for how people can(not) deal with difference in the way people in Manchester can. In doing so, the problem of race and racism is imagined as lying somewhere else further afield and at a distance from the tolerant brand of Manchester. Simon, who describes himself as mixed race and grew up in Manchester and went to live and work briefly in Bradford, makes a similar analogy:

> Uhhh, [Bradford's] a world away from Manchester, a world away from a lot of places. You know it's quite, well when I was there it was quite divided and segregated and . . . [breathes through teeth] well there was a lot of tension still.

Simon's description of Bradford as being of another world suggests a geographical and historical gulf between it and the imagined 'tolerance' of cities like Manchester. In doing so, he draws attention away from his home neighbourhood of Moss Side in Manchester and towards negative ideas of segregation and racial tension that resonate with national discourses of problematic multiculture and racialised 'communities' elsewhere in the north of England. In this way, towns such as Bradford become the depository of difference. When they are constructed as

50 *The imaginings of a 'post-racial' generation*

"backwards" and insular they are also constructed as if far removed from the Manchester brand.

Placing this series of narratives alongside each other allows us to see multiple layers and multiple contradictions that emerge at different scales. I suggest that by locating some people at a distance and as historically 'backwards', the young people pave the way to construct themselves as being of a tolerant/less racist city and as being more tolerant/less racist than what has gone before, as if this can be accurately quantified and as if such a comparison matters more than thinking about how the meaning of race and racism has shifted over time. In later chapters I will draw out some of the contradictions such a position presents when they then try to explain their experiences of different forms of racism and racialisation in the very places that they claim to be beyond difference.

Mixing ≠ multiculture

In public debates about what it means to be British we have seen a growing emphasis on the notion of mixedness through the rhetoric of integration and community cohesion and superficial signifiers of multiculturalism and regional identities that are co-opted to imagine a 'collective identity' (see, for example, Cameron, 2011). In the recent government review into 'opportunity and integration' (Casey, 2016) emphasis was given to the way in which so-called ethnic divisions, that were clearly labelled as the responsibility of already marginalised communities, could be ameliorated by social mixing. In many ways, this latest review, authored by Louise Casey, has repeated previous iterations of cohesion through assimilation that have been made by successive governments. However, arguably this latest policy guidance represented a closer accommodation of right-wing values and many of the liberal niceties that may have been included in previous versions were heavily criticised for being too 'soft'.[4] It is particularly significant to this discussion that special mention was given to young people in the review. In addition to the recommendation to introduce lessons on British values in schools, the report contained a section devoted to encouraging young people to 'mix' and 'cluster' socially. We are told that:

> If our children grow up playing and learning with people from different backgrounds, they will be less prejudiced, more understanding of difference, more confident and more resilient living in a globalised and connected society.
>
> (Casey, 2016: 58)

The Casey review was not novel in suggesting this, although the recommendations were presented with a more authoritarian edge. Indeed, young people's lives are often drawn upon to illustrate the possibilities of multiculture because they live and have grown up in in increasingly diverse environs. However, it is not typically the complex and interesting convivial relations that emerge in these contexts and those which can unsettle fixed notions of culture and identity that are brought to

The imaginings of a 'post-racial' generation   51

our attention. Instead, young people are called upon as examples not of conviviality, but rather as symbols or markers of tolerance (Amin, 2010). This latest review only consolidates this practice.

Mixing is presented as if it is a process that has no need for any sense of dynamism and is articulated in ways that leave marginal identifications intact. One must, according to the likes of Casey, mix in order to assimilate to a certain way of being British to which other identifications may then be supplemented. This has particular salience for young people who are often caught up in rhetoric that positions them as if caught between two 'cultures' (Gilroy, 1993; Back, 2002). Young ethnic minorities are often imagined as trying to consolidate their 'traditional' and fixed ethnicness with a Britishness that has the potential to give them 'values', as Casey and others recommend. These ideas are currently perhaps most often evoked in relation to the positioning of young UK-born Muslims who are depicted as inhabiting the crossroads of the extreme limits of these two identities. Young Muslim women in the UK have, for example, typically been represented through gendered, classed and racialised assumptions that denote them as 'oppressed' and 'powerless' (see, for example, Dwyer, 2000). However, increasingly, we hear of the ways in which young women are resisting these apparent forms of oppression through their association to Britishness. Stories of young women being 'forced to lead double lives' are reproduced as examples of the ways in which they perform Britishness or Europeanness (Balci, 2011) as if an antidote to their 'Other' selves. But such representations not only risk reproducing culturalist tropes, but they are also disingenuous and misrepresentative of the way people live. The use of 'mixing' thus may appeal to a pragmatic ideal that something can be done to ameliorate division, but in fact it does nothing to challenge racism, unsettle identities or even disrupt normative ideas of what it is to be British. It is instead indicative of the kind of multiculturalism that 'tolerates' and 'bestows rights' on the 'Other', but does nothing to demythologise the 'Other', or engage with the needs of minorities (Amin, 2010).

Inside the academy, the interest in 'mixing' extends into naïve conceptions of understanding ways to overcome race by allowing mixedness to allude to non-racism. Allport's (1979 [1954]) work on contact is perhaps the most well-known example of this but it also persists when social scientists attempt to measure 'inter-cultural' contact and people's relationships to, and with, 'difference' in order to draw conclusions about levels of integration or racism (see for example Ford, 2014 for a discussion of an association made between levels of racism and public 'acceptance' of 'mixed' relationships). The emphases on sameness, together with a somewhat simplistic understanding of cross-cultural contact, fails to give adequate consideration to inequalities and relations of power that shape the effects of encounters (Wilson, 2016). This resonates with what Ash Amin (2012) warns against in thinking about how policy and academic work has focused too much on what he calls the 'inter-human'. Amin argues that this kind of framing of the social has pushed back the critical work of queer, feminist and

52 *The imaginings of a 'post-racial' generation*

postcolonial theory to re-emphasise instead narratives of common life (rather than common cause) through imagining social ties and reduced or reconciled difference. Indeed, arguably there is an excessive focus on simplified ideas of mixing or contact in the media and across policy and academic work (Amin, 2012). This is problematic because these enquiries remain detached from history and politics, as noted above. Such a focus relies instead on crudely constructed groupisms that flatten and simplify social life and therefore perversely cannot adequately grapple with the very questions around integration and racism that they themselves pose.

Despite the clear problems with the emphasis on mixing this notion is nevertheless conveyed as if attractive because it has a pragmatic quality in that it appears to be doing something – even if the so-called problem and solution are understood the wrong way round. Here I look at how the young people gravitate towards these kinds of narratives, even when their lived experiences offer far more complex and nuanced understandings of living with difference. I am interested in how these ideas take hold in the young people's imagination when they talk about themselves and their relationships, and I suggest that for them the possibility it offers to self-construct an identity of a generation that is better than before adds to the allure. As suggested by Alex:

> For my parent's generation, I guess maybe more, because society was maybe less used to this idea of more mixed community of different races . . . the ways things generally seem to work in this country, it's more mixing now . . . So for my parent's generation society wasn't quite as mixed up and culturally . . . [long pause].
>
> (Alex, 25 years old, white British)

On the whole, the young people do have diverse networks of friends and colleagues, and these are no doubt more diverse than the relationships of their parents. However, it is not the complex and nuanced intricacies of these relationships that come to the fore here. Instead they draw on crude and often staged forms of 'mixing' that meet the expectations of integrationists but do little to disrupt this logic.

It is perhaps worth reiterating again here that this research was not presented to the young adults as having a particular focus on race and ethnicity. They were responding to questions about their day to day lives, including who they interacted with and where, during the course of a typical week. The following discussion illustrates the extent to which emphases on racialised difference become the focus of their examples and ways of talking about their relationships as a means to infer tolerance and negate racism. One immediate way into this emerged when I asked them about changes in their social lives since leaving school. They described themselves as more mobile, accessing more and varied spaces through work and social lives that took them beyond the peer group and beyond the neighbourhood. But, most young people also started by remarking on how, since leaving school, they "mixed" with a broader range of people of different "backgrounds". This way of mixing was said to significantly differ to earlier social networks, which were said to be prescribed by

The imaginings of a 'post-racial' generation 53

neighbourhood and school demographics. What is of interest here is how, unprompted, race and ethnicity formed a central thread in these stories:

> I think because I lived in Moss Side so, when you go to school, most of your friends are the ones that you kind of live nearby and most of them are black.
>
> (Nadia)

> Cos of going to school in like Central Didsbury, where a lot of the children are white middle class, you sort of just integrate with what's there really [laughs], so yeah.
>
> (Carina)

In contrast to previous social networks their current social lives were described as knowing "a bit of everything", as Nadia puts it. This 'everything', however, is invariably confined to interactions that are defined as different in ethnic, racialised and religious terms. Class is identified as a mode of difference that they go beyond only when it is, articulated with race. And gender and sexuality differences are never noted as significant.[5] As Nadia says in describing her close group of friends:

> The three of us, there are like three in a group, one is Hindu, one is Muslim and I'm a Christian so there's kind of like a bit of everything there.

A broadening lifespace was said to have had, not only an impact on expanding personal and social relationships, but also on the way they thought about difference. This manifests, almost entirely, through notions of cultural, ethnic and racialised difference. For example, Steve, who is white, explained that he would describe himself as less "naïve" since leaving school, because now he says he is more comfortable with talking to people of "different ethnic backgrounds". Laurence, who is black, explained how since he started work he has made friends with people who he describes as "totally different".

> I mean like when I was in school, it'd be mainly the people in my school, the people who lived around the area where I lived and I'd just associate with them, but as soon as I entered the world of work . . . I'd always end up making a friend with someone who's just totally different to me. Like the first job I had, um, I was working for a windows and doors company in Oldham and um . . . the closest friend I had there was this skinhead white guy from Salford . . . I wouldn't say he was racist, I think he was a bit ignorant in terms of his views on certain things and stuff but we still managed to get on, you still find things to talk about and you just find common ground.

Laurence draws attention to a point that many of the young adults want to convey – that it is the capacity to identify common ground, in spite of difference that is important. And, it is this in particular that was said to characterise their relationships and interactions. This competency was said to define their cohort.

54 *The imaginings of a 'post-racial' generation*

Nasreen, for example, who describes herself as Asian and British, here describes the similarities she shares with a friend "even though" she is white because of their shared spatial and temporal references:

> I think people from the same age group would have similar experiences . . . I was talking about this [news story] to one of my friends and she is like from . . . she's white, same age as me, been brought up in a different area, yet that same thing had a significant effect on us really. . . . That's why I think that people from a similar age cos it's the same influencing factor in terms of you know, I think, would bring a lot of similarities perhaps, yeah. . . .

Not all relationships to people produced as racially and ethnically different were invoked in the same way. Whilst many of the young people talked about close friendships, some of the white young people had to rely on more casual encounters at work, with neighbours and with parents of their children's friends to construct a similar identity. Narratives that depended on casual encounters tended to be presented in hurried and apologetic ways toward the end of the interview when I asked them to talk about their attitudes towards the categories on the equality monitoring form. It became clear that there was an understanding that having multi-ethnic networks should be an important facet in the production of their own identifications. This was acutely revealed in narratives when some of the white young people became aware that inter-ethnic encounters had not featured in their stories so far, and they were then quick to respond by adding on irregular or casual interactions with people they described as different to them. It is therefore notable that, when some of the white young adults were unable to call upon intimate relationships with black and Asian friends, they inferred that they were concerned they might then be read as intolerant. Casual encounters were then quickly mentioned as if to provide proof of non-racism. Zoe, for example, described casual encounters with black people in her neighbourhood and expressed concern that the absence of closer relationships might sound "bad":

> All my friends are white English, I do like have a good chat with the (black) lads in the launderette but no, all my friends are white English, my family as well . . . I haven't got any black or Asian friends, so that sounds bad don't it . . . I haven't got many friends anyway.

Alex also expressed concern that I might interpret the life he presented in his photo diary as devoid of 'mixing', because it contained only images of white people. He joked at the end of the interview (once the recorder was switched off) that if he had known when he took the photographs that I was interested in what he thought about racism and ethnicity he would have taken a photo of himself with his arms around "people from different racial backgrounds" to emulate an advert for the United Colors of Benetton. These kinds of concerns led the white young people to apologise because they inhabited predominantly white spaces that did not facilitate encounters with racialised difference. And at this point, they reached beyond the

The imaginings of a 'post-racial' generation   55

everyday to draw upon structural factors as if constructed outside their lives to deliver explanations for this. As Sarah says:

> I only have a couple of friends who aren't white, um, not . . . it's just the way it happens isn't it, it's not like um . . . you don't tend to, it's a shame really, but society isn't as integrated as we'd like it to be.

These explanations certainly infer a shared understanding that it is 'correct' to know and mix with people who are produced as racially 'different'. Yet beyond this there is also a compulsion to lay accountability for their own lack of mixing to societal factors outside of their own lives, since they refer to structures built (in the past) and in a way that 'we' do not like. Doing this allows them to maintain the idea that their generation is some way more tolerant without confronting their own lived practice. This is perhaps particularly important to do to prevent potential questions about the currency of racism in their present lives.

It is also notable that casual interactions were often embellished with closer details about the nature of the relationship, and it is often the most acute examples of difference that are offered up as evidence of tolerance and as a means to negate racism. This is illustrated when Petra, who describes herself as white and Czech, does not draw on her marriage to someone of a different nationality when exemplifying what she describes as generational differences in levels of tolerance. This is presumably because her husband is white and British. Instead, Petra talks at length about the interactions she has with her "Asian" neighbours.

> They're fine, we mainly talk about arranged marriages, that's quite different because I have to . . . we have a very different culture and sometimes it's difficult for me to not judge how they live and I'm sure it's the same for them, you know, I lived with my husband before we were married and I think a lot of them found it difficult and it was just a way of sort of ignoring that and pretending that he wasn't my boyfriend.

When Petra describes "them" as "fine" she not only reiterates 'difference' between her and her neighbours, but also suggests a need to comment on how that relationship works, in spite of this. Yet, in doing so, she reiterates how "they" are different by drawing upon common-sense representations of Asian women in the UK (see Brah, 1996 for discussions on this; Dwyer, 1999). Subsequently, when Petra maintains that she mainly talks about arranged marriages with her neighbours she points to the fragility of these relationships, and it becomes clear that they are not ordinary or unremarkable. Instead, they resonate with a 'politically correct' means of narrating the 'other' (Donald and Rattansi, 1992: 2), and whilst this might be crudely read as serving an anti-racist function, the emphasis on racialised difference is often employed to allude to an idea that they (as individuals) are not racist and, by association, their everyday lives are absent of racism. In other words, the idea of anti-racism is replaced with individualised claims to non-racism. This hints towards the sense of white superiority that Douglas (1984 [1966]) talks of, most

56   The imaginings of a 'post-racial' generation

particularly because, by individualising their social experience they draw a boundary around themselves and their everyday to distinguish their means of dealing with race as civilised and dislocated from any other interpretations of social life.

Paradoxically then, whilst multiculture or 'mixing' was invoked to suggest the meaninglessness of race, young people's narratives drew attention to the significance of race through these explanations. Contradictions emerge, because whilst these interactions form an integral part of the construction of the 'post-racial' generation they nevertheless make use of culturalist stereotypes and racialised signifiers. This is evident when Ian, for example, talks of his "multi-racial" friendship group, giving weight to the diversity of the group by naming them in terms of ethnic and racial "origins". He is critical of any suggested meaning given to such labels when it comes to their use on equality monitoring forms, but when talking about the football team he plays in he uses these categories to draw upon biological and physical stereotypes:

> I think we did benefit from having this kind of big multi-racial group cos um, X was mixed race, X was mixed race, X was black, X and his brother X were black, you know and we had a few others who were Jamaican black, whereas we had a couple of black African as well, so we had a nice kind of mix and then we've got a few friends who are from Asian origins and from oriental origins as well, so, um, we kind of get a nice mix in there of different perspectives as well, and even with football as well, we used to play in a 5-a-side league and it was quite funny cos we used to come across either a fully white team or a fully black team and we were kind of like the only inter-racial team within the league and I think that eventually put . . . it did do as well, because we kind of had the best of both really, you know in terms of the styles in which both kind of races play and the physical aspects as well and stuff and eventually we won the league, which was a great bonus to us cos we were also the youngest team as well.

Ian's story is more complicated. It is complicated because, from the broader context he provides, we know that Ian's friendships are not casual encounters that are hurriedly conjured from nowhere and they do have a convivial quality in that, mostly, they are unremarkable ordinary relationships. Nevertheless, we witness him getting caught up in a series of dilemmas when explaining how they 'work' together as a group. Indeed, he is driven to using the same categories he speaks so passionately against at other moments in our conversations. Closer attention thus reveals complex negotiations of identities, identifications and navigations of space and failing to take account of the nuanced and more complex convivial relations risks over-simplifying young people's lives. We see similar difficulties in Sarah's account. Here the United Colors of Benetton advertisement campaign is used again. This time by Sarah to exemplify her "mixed" group of friends:

> I do sometimes joke at [the social club], you know with [my two friends] that we're like the United Colors of Benetton and as well, when I'm at

[work] when I'm with [four friends] who are all from like a kind of black or various backgrounds, or mixed, or mixed race or whatever and I'm like the white one [laughs] it is quite funny cos I do like stick out like a sore thumb, but we don't really comment on it, I've just noticed it, like I've just, I've been aware of it like you say, but I don't, it doesn't bother me, it just kind of makes me laugh . . . yeah.

Her story suggests that her mixed friendship group is not always permitted to be 'unremarkable', even when it might be. Whilst Sarah maintains that ethnic and racial difference does not matter, she says that she is "aware" of sticking out. This is apparently difficult for her to articulate because she makes fun of her own observations when she explains their meaninglessness. This is not about questioning whether difference has meaning for the quality of Sarah's friendships, but it is important because it points to a wider significance evident in Sarah's need to explain herself in this way. The use of the United Colors of Benetton adverts that have, over the years, drawn attention because of their portrayal of multi-racial groups, indicates that Sarah's group of friends is not interpreted as 'mainstream' and warrants attention. The controversy around Benetton's promotional campaigns is indicative of a shift in representations of race from one generation to another, because they were interpreted as 'original' and 'ground-breaking'. The adverts are thus arguably invoked to reflect contemporary attitudes to mixing and to mark a distinction from the past. But her story also makes us question why this is necessary. For all the problems we can identify in the casual encounters discussed above, it is arguably the relationships that cross imagined boundaries that have a harder time being considered for their everydayness. This is in part because they do not fit quite so easily into the paradigm of crude understandings of 'mixing', ironically by virtue of having meaning in and of themselves.

Conclusion

This chapter has paid attention to the way in which the young adults imagine themselves to be part of a post-racial and tolerant 'generation' as a consequence of living in a diverse and multicultural city. This is produced in marked contrast to preceding generations who are imagined instead as less tolerant. In particular, the chapter explores how the notion of being post-racial is imagined and mediated through different competencies, largely associated with age, life stage, class, multicultural networks and knowledge and experience of the inner city.

The young adults present a shared knowledge when they construct a unifying 'generation' narrative that disavows racism through the emphasis on similarity, in spite of difference. Tolerance becomes a key means to do this and is emphasised through interactions with racialised and ethnic difference, often referred to as "people from different backgrounds". To do this, the young adults employ

58 *The imaginings of a 'post-racial' generation*

the notion of age, or life stage, class and inner-city location to assert their own 'open-mindedness' through their relationships to those they produce as different to themselves. This works through the construction of a historical narrative, which suggests a process of improvement or maturation (Brown, 2006), in the same way that the city is imagined in a process of betterment. To reinforce the authenticity of their representations, the young people emphasised their relationships with a range of actors and people from a range of "backgrounds", even when these are quite peripheral relationships. They also often employed 'acute' examples to enforce the notion of tolerance. They did so to emphasise similarity even in the face of the acute differences that they themselves constructed. The emphasis that the young adults place on knowing people, who they produce as racially and ethnically different from themselves, therefore confirms that difference is rendered significant even when it is denied. The context in which these knowledges are produced is important. It is necessary to read them as part of the broader changing social and political context. For example, much of the narratives of tolerance produced by the young people reflect discourses of multiculturalism but also colour-blindness when the presence of mixedness is offered as evidence of a lack of racism. That is not to say, however, that many of the young adults do not live multiculture in more dynamic ways. Indeed, many of their relationships have a convivial quality, which is founded on a general 'indifference to difference'. However, these relationships become difficult to articulate in a context that depends so heavily instead on crude and often staged forms of mixing that speak directly to integrationist and post-racial logics. I continue this line of argument in the next chapter in which I consider in more detail how encounters with difference are lived and narrated.

Notes

1 As a point of note – throughout this chapter I use the term 'generation' only in so far as the young adults make use of this term. They construct what is for them a 'generation' by aligning certain cultural configurations to their peer group.

2 I am hugely grateful to Sumi Hollingworth and Malcolm James for our conversations that have informed this discussion.

3 The narratives of the two young people who recently migrated to the UK are included in the study, but the different ways they interpret spaces indicates that they are less familiar with some of the normative discourses about Manchester that commonly emerge in the other narratives. Where these differences emerge, they are discussed by taking account of this context.

4 Casey specifically criticises the 'saris, samosas and steelband' approach for being too soft and liberal. This was an approach that was of course criticised in the 1990s for failing to challenge ethnicist and culturalist discourses through simplistic celebrations of diversity. See, for example, Donald, J. & Rattansi, A. (1992). Introduction. *In:* Donald, J. & Rattansi, A. (eds.) *'Race', culture and difference.* London: Sage.

5 Notably gender and sexuality is entirely absent from these representative practices. This is particularly interesting given the emphasis in Manchester City Council's branding on the city's LGBT 'community' (see Chapter 1).

References

Ahmed, S. (2004). Declarations of whiteness: The non-performativity of anti-racism. *Borderlands*, 3(2). www.borderlands.net.au/vol3no2_2004/ahmed_declarations.htm

Alexander, C. (1996). *The art of being black*. Oxford: Oxford University Press.

Alexander, C. (2002). Beyond black: Rethinking the colour/culture divide. *Ethnic and Racial Studies*, 25(4), 552–571.

Alexander, C., Raminder, K. & St Louis, B. (2012). Identities: New directions in uncertain times. *Identities: Global Studies in Culture and Power*, 19(1), 1–7.

Allport, G. W. (1979 [1954]). *The nature of prejudice*. Reading, MA: Addison-Wesley.

Ambikaipaker, M. (2015). Liberal exceptions: Violent racism and routine anti-racist failure in Britain. *Ethnic and Racial Studies*, 38(12), 2055–2070.

Amin, A. (2010). The remainders of race. *Theory, Culture and Society*, 27(1), 1–23.

Amin, A. (2012). *Land of strangers*. Cambridge: Polity Press.

Amin, A. (2013). Land of strangers. *Identities: Global Studies in Culture and Power*, 20(1), 1–8.

Back, L. (1996). *New ethnicities and urban multiculture: Racisms and multiculture in young lives*. London: UCL Press.

Back, L. (2002). The fact of hybridity: Youth, ethnicity and racism. *In:* Goldberg, D. T. & Solomos, J. (eds.) *A companion to racial and ethnic studies*. Boston, MA: Blackwell.

Back, L. (2015). Losing culture or finding superdiversity? *Discover Society*, 20. Available from: http://discoversociety.org/2015/05/05/losing-culture-or-finding-superdiversity-2/ (accessed 8 July 2016).

Balci, G. (2011). Forbidden Love: Taboos and fear among Muslim girls. *Der Spiegel*, January 6, 2011.

Bhabha, H. (1994). *The location of culture*. Abingdon: Routledge.

Bonilla-Silva, E. (2014). *Racism without racists: Color-blind racism and the persistence of racial inequality in America* (4th Edition). Plymouth: Rowman & Leftfield.

Bonilla-Silva, E. (2015). The structure of racism in color-blind, 'post-racial' America. *American Behavioural Sciences*, 59(1), 1358–1376.

Brah, A. (1996). *Cartographies of diaspora: Contesting identities*. London: Routledge.

Brown, W. (2006). *Regulating aversion: Tolerance in the age of identity and empire*. Princeton: Princeton University Press.

Bynner, J. (2001). British youth transitions in comparative perspective. *Journal of Youth Studies*, 4(1), 5–23.

Bynner, J. (2005). Rethinking the youth phase of the life course: The case for emerging adulthood? *Journal of Youth Studies*, 8(4), 367–384.

Cameron, D. (2011). Prime Minister's speech at Munich security conference, 5 February. Available from: www.number10.gov.uk/news/pms-speech-at-munich-security-conference 5 February 2011.

Casey, L. (2016). *The Casey review: A review into opportunity and integration*. London: Department for Communities and Local Government.

Donald, J. & Rattansi, A. (1992). Introduction. *In:* Donald, J. & Rattansi, A. (eds.) *'Race', culture and difference*. London: Sage.

Douglas, M. (1984 [1966]). *Purity and danger: An analysis of the concepts of pollution and taboo*. London: Routledge.

Dwyer, C. (1999). Veiled meanings: Young British Muslim women and the negotiation of differences. *Gender, Place and Culture*, 6(1), 5–26.

60 *The imaginings of a 'post-racial' generation*

Dwyer, C. (2000). Negotiating diasporic identities: Young British South Asian Muslim women. *Women's Studies International Forum*, 23(4), 475–486.

Ford, R. (2014). The decline of racial prejudice in Britain. Available from: http://blog.policy.manchester.ac.uk/featured/2014/08/the-decline-of-racial-prejudice-in-britain/[Online].

Foucault, M. (1978). *The history of sexuality: Volume one*. New York: Vintage.

Gilroy, P. (1993). *The black Atlantic*. London and New York: Verso.

Goldberg, D. T. (2001). *The racial state*. Malden, MA: Blackwell.

Goldberg, D. T. (2015). *Are we all postracial yet?* Cambridge and Malden, MA: Polity Press.

Harries, B., James, M., Hollingworth, S. & Fangen, K. (2016). Reconstituting Race in Youth Studies. *Young*, 24(3), 177–184.

Haylett, C. (2001). Illegitimate subjects? Abject whites, neoliberal modernisation and middle class multiculturalism. *Environment and Planning D: Society and Space*, 19(3), 351–370.

Hesse, B. (1999). Reviewing the western spectacle: Reflexive globalisation through the black diaspora. *In:* Brah, A., Hickman, M. & Mac an Ghail, M. (eds.) *Global futures: Migration, environment and globalisation*. New York: St Martin's Press.

Hesse, B. (2011). Self-fulfilling prophecy: The postracial horizon. *The South Atlantic Quarterly*, 110(1), 155–178.

Hollingworth, S. (2015). Performances of social class, race and gender through youth subculture: Putting structure back in to youth subcultural studies. *Journal of Youth Studies*, 18(10), 1237–1257.

hooks, b. (1992). *Black looks: Race and representation*. London: Turnaround Books.

Ifekwunigwe, J. O. (1999). *Scattered belongings: Cultural paradoxes of 'race', nation and gender*. London: Routledge.

James, M. (2015). *Urban multiculture: Youth, politics and cultural transformation in a global city*. Basingstoke: Palgrave Macmillan.

Keith, M. & Cross, M. (1993). Racism and the postmodern city. *In:* Cross, M. & Keith, M. (eds.) *Racism, the city and the state*. London: Routledge.

Kim, H. (2014). *Making diaspora in a global city: South Asian youth cultures in London*. London: Routledge.

Kulz, C. (2014). Structure liberates? Mixing for mobility and the cultural transformation of 'urban children' in a London Academy. *Ethnic and Racial Studies*, 37(4), 685–701.

Lentin, A. (2008). Europe and the silence about race. *European Journal of Social Theory*, 11(4), 487–503.

Mannheim, K. (1952). The problem of generations. *In:* Kecskemeti, P. (ed.) *Essays on the sociology of knowledge*. London: Routledge and Kegan Paul.

Nayak, A. (2003). *Race, place and globalisation: Youth cultures in a changing world*. Oxford and New York: Berg.

Reulecke, J. (2008). Generation/generationality, generativity, and memory. *In:* Erll, A., Ansgar, A. E. A. & Nünning, A. (eds.) *Cultural memory studies: An international and interdisciplinary handbook*. Berlin: de Gruyter.

Song, M. (2014). Challenging a culture of racial equivalence. *The British Journal of Sociology*, 65(1), 107–129.

Titley, G. (2016). On are we all post racial yet? *Ethnic and Racial Studies*, 39(13), 2269–2277.

Valluvan, S. (2016). Conviviality and multiculture: A post-integration sociology of multiethnic interaction. *Young*, 24(3), 204–221.

The imaginings of a 'post-racial' generation   61

Valluvan, S. & Kapoor, N. (2016). Notes on theorizing racism and other things. *Ethnic and Racial Studies*, 39(3), 375–382.

Wilson, B. M. (2002). Critically inderstanding race-connected practices: A reading of W. E. B Du Bois and Richard Wright. *The Professional Geographer*, 54(1), 31–41.

Wilson, H. F. (2016). On geography and encounter: Bodies, borders, and difference. *Progress in Human Geography*, First published date: 13 May 2016, 1–21.

Winant, H. (2001). *The world is a ghetto: Race and democracy since World War II.* Oxford: Basic Books.

Winant, H. (2006). Race and racism: Towards a global future. *Ethnic and Racial Studies*, 29(5), 986–1003.

4 Anticipating race

Race and the recognition of difference in encounters with diversity

'Visual traces of others' lives accumulated through daily city navigation are important in how urban citizens navigate and understand their cities and those with whom they share them. Recognition and resentment begin from the signs of otherness inscribed on the city's (human and built) surfaces'.

(Knowles, 2013: 653)

How we live with diversity has long been an object of intense interest. It is a preoccupation that cuts across cultural and political spheres. It is as evident in the seemingly relentless record of policy-making that emphasises the need to get on (see, for example, Cantle, 2001; Commission on Integration and Cohesion, 2007; Casey, 2016), as it is in sections of the arts and media.[1] Increasingly, too, there is interest in the role of diversity, or what Puwar calls a 'hunger' for diversity, in institutions – including academia. And with it, a growth in local policy documentation that stresses the importance of learning how to deal with difference and encounter 'strangers' (Ahmed, 2000; Ahmed, 2014). Indeed, there is undoubtedly a never-ending supply of suggestions and policy advice that cross spheres of public and social life that we could draw upon to illustrate how the hunger for diversity and knowing how to live with it has become a key feature of our lives. This chapter focuses on how the young adults participating in the research recognise diversity and deal with difference in their day to day lives, and especially on how race shapes their encounters. This discussion leads on from the previous chapter, which examined the way the young adults constructed themselves as a 'generation' in relation to post-racial ideals. Indeed, by focusing on processes of differentiation, this chapter acts as juxtaposition to that earlier discussion and the way in which the young adults placed a great deal of emphasis on the role of sameness, under a somewhat hopeful but naïve sense of 'post-racial' humanism.

In light of the intensity with which we are asked to reflect on how we live with diversity, there has, alongside, been a long and vigorous critical debate about how processes of differentiation have come to matter. This book is shaped by those debates that attempt to reclaim race from ethnicist discourses within a new politics of representation and a politics of difference (Hall, 1992) and away from thinking only about identities and groupisms to take account

64　*Anticipating race*

of the ways in which meanings given to race are 'placed, positioned, situated' and contextualised (Hall, 1992: 257). Particularly salient to the aims here is the way in which that line of thinking has opened up avenues to rethink how attention to the lived experience (as opposed to politics) of race can effectively challenge absolute boundaries that mark difference. This work draws attention to the possibilities for 'genuine cultural syncretism' to reorient meanings of race and belonging (Back, 1996) and is therefore distinct from notions of simplified forms of common life that tend to expect too much from 'inter-human' contact to resolve social difference (Amin, 2012) but are so often advocated for in policy advice. It is significant too that much of this critical engagement has emerged from research on urban youth culture – often because young people have lived their lives in closer proximity to increasing diversity.

In this chapter I also take heed of the caution that, whilst approaches shaped by a politics of representation have considerable value in challenging how we understand difference and what that means, 'they often neglect the way in which these signs are imbued with emotion and affective intensities' (Nayak, 2011: 554). I therefore pay attention to work that attends to what race does and the affective qualities it possesses. Subsequently, this chapter works with the representational narratives introduced in earlier chapters but extends this discussion to account for how they shape and are shaped by social and material relations and the lived experience. This includes taking consideration of what Lorimer describes as the 'more than representational' (Lorimer, 2005), to think about the emotional intensities that encounters with difference can engender. In doing so, I hope to make a contribution to ongoing debates via the intersection of different approaches, as Nayak argues for in his critical examination of approaches to race across social and cultural geography (Nayak, 2011).

This chapter considers the various ways that the young adults experience and talk about their encounters with difference. Before doing so however it is worth noting that, for the most part, research on living with difference and on individual interactions tends to constitute that which focuses on the 'problem' with race. This is important, but it is nonetheless worth reflecting too on the potential that the encounter holds. We have to be careful as researchers that we are not producing differentiations in our ethnographies in ways that over signify difference or in ways that may not be salient. Indeed, there have been recent attempts to change the focus of attention away from how we interact with difference to think instead about the possibilities of becoming indifferent to difference through convivial encounters (see, for example, Amin, 2013; Gilroy, 2004; Valluvan, 2016). Knowles cautions that by focusing on geographies of resentment and exclusion' we 'may obscure important if small dynamics of inclusion and local connection' (Knowles, 2013: 662). And, Wilson reminds us that encounters have a transformative capacity, and this does not always result in hostility but can lead to an increased 'openness to the unknown'(Wilson, 2016: 15).

In what follows I begin by thinking through how difference and encounters with difference in the city have been conceptualised. I then move on to discuss the ways that the young adults talk about their own engagements with (including their avoidance of) difference. This includes a discussion on how those young adults, who are often perceived through a hegemonic lens to be 'different', make sense of their own encounters. The central argument that I want to make here is that the multidimensional ways that race and place come to matter establish a set of expectations of difference. These expectations then shape what kinds of difference are recognised and how that difference is then negotiated in everyday interactions. This is important to consider because who is recognised and on what terms are key questions inherently loaded with power.

Expectations of difference

As with cities elsewhere, Manchester's localities can be mapped along ethnic or racial lines. These processes of demarcation can then work to draw imagined boundaries around specific areas, and fabricate distinctive communities. The corresponding ways that race (and indeed its intersection with other categories of experience) is mapped onto the city allows it to form a location from which to observe how the management of difference plays out. This is visible, for example, in representations of the inner city that are often articulated with masculinity and crime and in gentrified neighbourhoods that are often imagined as white middle class 'cultural quarters' with particular relationships to gendered domesticity (Rose, 1993). Or, as illustrated in Chapter 2, the city centre can be imagined as the centre of openness and cosmopolitanism, whilst the inner city is burdened with pathologising tropes of criminality and dysfunction. These latter, 'problematic', localities are also often constructed as sites in which the segregated stranger is imagined to reside and can be sites of over-determination, where *everything* becomes about race. Places are, in this way, produced through the interrelation of the spatial and the political (Keith and Pile, 1993; Massey, 2005) and as locations in which multiple conditions come together and effect social and cultural practices in ways that reflect how difficult it can be to disentangle the range of experiences (Tizard and Phoenix, 1993). We see the social effects of these representations in the way in which the repetition of these stories enable the mobilisation of cultural and political ideas about legitimacy, entitlement, belonging and identity (Back and Keith, 1999: 138) and augment what Melamed describes as 'acceptable' and 'pathological' forms of difference (Melamed, 2006). This is indicated in the conflicting culturalist discourses about different parts of the city, in the form of the multicultural cosmopolitan versus the self-segregated 'stranger' (Keith, 2005). But, how then do these various forms of representation, which claim an ontological basis for understanding the process of differentiation, help us to understand how difference is recognised and dealt with in encounters with the city?

Places and experiences of place are multi-faceted, constructed as they are through competing political struggles over the form and meanings of space, but also through the possibilities that they open up (Lefebvre, 1996). Whilst the city is mapped out in particular ways, people develop their own sense of how to

66 *Anticipating race*

navigate its spaces through learned practices and knowledge developed in the local cultural and social context (De Certeau, 2011 [1984]). Hence, race does not only shape the discursive repertoires of place but also shapes how people can relate to and engage with their material surroundings. How race is produced by places and what race does is therefore mutually constitutive. Lipsitz (2011), for example, writes extensively about the ways in which 'racism takes place' by demonstrating how 'social relations take on their full force and meaning when they are enacted physically in actual place' (Lipsitz, 2011: 5). In doing so, he details how the movement of black people into white neighbourhoods can itself be seen as a transgression. As Puwar (2004) discusses, racialised bodies moving in such a way come to be signified as 'bodies out of place'. Indeed, there are numerous important examples that illustrate the way in which racism governs place. Gail Lewis (1985), for example, details how growing up in London she navigates the city to circumvent 'no-go' areas to avoid racism. Certainly, public spaces might assume a sense of freedom and openness, yet in practice, racialised (as with certain gendered or classed) bodies cannot always access public spaces on equal terms. Public space is therefore not always as public as we might imagine (see, for example, Massey, 1994; Rose, 1993; Ruddick, 1996). Furthermore, access is often very much dependent on how public space is articulated with race in the first place – the white cosmopolitan spaces of the city centre do not share the same notion of public as the park or playground in a racialised inner city neighbourhood – and access shifts accordingly (Ruddick, 1996).

In the 1990s and 2000s in particular, there was a series of attempts to create what policy-speak described as 'mixed' housing projects. Driven by a Putnam-esque understanding of social capital and integration, there was an idea put forward that, by mixing 'ethnic communities', residents of different backgrounds would start to interact (see, for example, Bailey et al., 2006). There was also a set moralising suggestions embedded in these ideas, such as that, in the presence of their new white wealthy neighbours, the poor and the racialised would raise their aspirations to attain things such as better education outcomes (ibid.). The spurious foundations for advocating this idea, which worked to further pathologise certain areas and their residents, were made despite the successful challenges to the bases for imagining segregated lives in the first place (Finney and Simpson, 2009), and evidence that ethnic minorities often have better education outcomes than their white counterparts in neighbourhoods considered to be 'diverse', even though this is rarely translated into employment opportunities (Harries et al., forthcoming). Crucially too, they failed to take account of long histories of racism and its territorial dimension. These policies did not only have poor underpinnings but were unworkable because ethnic minorities did not want to be (re)housed in areas which have histories of racism and were for them 'no-go' areas. Indeed, Becares et al. (2009) demonstrate how living in an area with higher ethnic minority density protects against racism and offers better health outcomes. Anxieties mediate how people navigate the city but also affect where people choose to live. Avoiding 'no-go' areas is a quite different and more rational expression of fear and anxiety than the fear of the racialised body on which many policies about how we live with difference are predicated.

The city is therefore not solely a physical manifestation or discursive space, but it shapes and is shaped by the ways in which its inhabitants negotiate and respond to its configurations. As such, the city can also be understood as 'a state of mind'(Park, 1925 cited in Pile, 2005: 1). And accordingly, to understand how race functions in place, our approach must also encompass the emotional and imaginary elements of urban life (Pile, 2005). Differentiation and the way difference is produced in encounters is certainly 'at least as much about relations between bodies, things, and spaces as it is about discourses' (Swanton, 2010: 2334). Exploring the powerful range of fears and anxieties prompted by racialised encounters can give us a strong sense of the interrelationship of discourse and emotion. Understanding how racialised bodies are perceived to transgress boundaries when they are encountered 'out of place' can be about exploring the ontological anxieties that this provokes (Puwar, 2004) – an anxiety driven by the desire to reorder, or tidy away what is considered to be disorderly, messy, dirty even (Douglas, 1984 [1966]). But encounters with difference can themselves be defined by the affect they have (Wilson, 2016). Drawing on the work of Fanon (1986); Ahmed (2014) importantly explains how, within an encounter, fear is not solely an emotion that is directed to an individual, but rather:

> Fear works to secure the relationship between those bodies; it brings them together and moves them apart through the shudders that are felt on the skin, on the surface that surfaces through the encounter.
>
> (Ahmed, 2014: 63)

Here then, Ahmed brings both bodies into focus to illustrate how difference is produced in the encounter and is as much about understanding the making and doing of race as it is about the performance of whiteness through the affect of becoming fearful (Swanton, 2010). Second, Ahmed reminds us that the relationship between bodies and their proximity to each other is important for understanding how race is made. The proximity between bodies can alter the intensities of fear of the racialised other and it is, Ahmed argues, the movement of the racialised subject and the potential that it possesses to become closer or pass by that fear becomes heightened. The intensity of racism and the ways in which it is expressed therefore changes as bodies move closer or pass each other, because increased proximity is translated as the 'possibility of future injury' (Ahmed, 2014: 67). This becomes of particular salience in the next section when I turn to look at how the white young adults recognise and deal with difference at various proximities.

In the following discussion I turn to look at the ways the young adults describe their own experiences of place. This marks a shift from earlier chapters in which I looked at how they thought neighbourhoods were represented and how they conceived of their peer group. In these earlier narratives the young adults were

68 *Anticipating race*

able to rely on ideas somewhat abstracted from their own lives, building a picture of the context, by retelling well-worn representations of place, or newly formed tropes that do not always fit with actual lived experience. That is not to say that these earlier narratives are not important. Indeed, as the following discussion will illustrate, they are integral to shaping the context from which to then make sense of how people interact with and negotiate difference. Important to note is that, whilst their experience often contradicts or troubles, in combination we learn a great deal about how race is produced and what race does.

No difference here

I want to start by considering what forms of difference are recognised. This question takes on a particular significance in light of the ways that the young adults have constructed themselves as a 'generation' which values sameness and universality when processes of differentiation were so powerfully at work in representations of the different parts of the city. In that earlier discussion it was noted that adherence to such a discourse of universalism had different resonances for white and black people. And, for similar reasons, the same can be said for how difference is recognised. This section begins by addressing how difference is dealt with by the white young adults. It is bell hooks that reminds us of the ways that 'whites have a deep emotional investment in the myth of "sameness" (hooks, 1992: 167), because to acknowledge difference is to recognise whiteness and white privilege with it. Indeed, it is in remaining faithful to that investment that the 'All lives matter' group appropriated the slogan of the Black Lives Matter movement, presenting a liberal argument for doing so and hence illustrated how engrained that myth is, even with evidence to the contrary.

When asked to talk about the neighbourhoods, the most common starting point for the research participants was to describe their physical characteristics. This is, perhaps, unsurprising since a request for a narrative of place might assume a geographical and physical focus. The point I want to highlight here is that often the focus on the material structure of a place dominates in their experiences of Moss Side and Longsight, crudely represented as black and Asian neighbourhoods, to the extent that these places appear uninhabited, or as places that people merely pass through. Furthermore, I want to illustrate how many of the young adults labour, sometimes excruciatingly, over bland physical descriptions to avoid describing their experience of and encounters in these neighbourhoods. To do this I present examples below that illustrate the different ways the white participants are made uncomfortable locating difference, which, in the process, disavows the presence of racialised bodies.

Andy works in a public sector role based in Gorton (he has requested more precise details of the kind of work he does be omitted to ensure confidentiality). In answer to a question about how he might describe his own experience of Longsight, Moss Side and Gorton (the three different neighbourhoods in the research), he gives a series of very lengthy descriptions of the physical attributes of the three neighbourhoods. Notably too, he frequently broadens the conversation to reference

Anticipating race 69

other parts of Manchester, or all of south Manchester – gaining distance from the question itself. For example, he says:

> In terms of facilities, I think they're all very similar cos again they all have the same . . . they're all from the same area pretty much and they all have the same amount of budget spent on them really and they've all got . . . like everything's standard built. Like our police station, apart from this one, if you see the new ones, they're all standard built and they're all built you know by the same company, so they look like identical versions of each other. So when you get the facilities round here now, wherever you get them, certainly in south Manchester, they're all identical. Like all the playgrounds are all identical, the sports halls will all look identical and the only difference is the name over the door really.

Andy continues in this way for *two* pages of the transcript. In our conversation he appears anxious, repeatedly pausing, hesitating with 'um's' and switching direction mid-sentence as he looks around him for ideas and occasionally at me as if stuck. This question, which was supposed to be a straightforward opening question, has made me feel like I am interrogating instead. He sighs and gives up. He says with a shrug that, 'I don't know how else to compare the areas really . . . I don't know, what do you think?' He looks again at me as if for help and, trying to help, I offer the reflection that he has not talked about people, or about his own experiences. In response, however, he quickly reverts back to the safety of discussing at length the buildings and facilities in each of the areas, always emphasising their sameness. Later he mentions the similarity in reputations for crime across the three neighbourhoods, and I ask him:

Bethan: And do people associate that crime in Moss Side with the same types of people as those in Gorton, or. . .?
Andy: Um . . . I would presume so, in my own head I would I think. It's still young males I think, sort of early teens through to about 30, something like that, so I would presume so in my own head but I'm not too sure what other people would perceive it as, but maybe people have got so many ways to check our crime statistics now.

Again we sense his anxiety in the speed through which he responds, whilst at the same time remaining keen not to give too much detail, or give a sense of where this idea comes from by way of an example. Whilst we should not risk assuming differentiation where he expresses none, it is his aversion to recognise how places are inhabited and that we learn nothing about his lived experience from these accounts that is remarkable. His interview stands out because of its monotony, and because he is uncomfortable with locating *any* difference. Throughout the interview race lingers between the cracks of his carefully constructed narrative. Race has bold significance in the places he talks about, but in Andy's interview it is the elephant in the room. It is audible in its silence, but also in each hesitation and

70   *Anticipating race*

nervous and hurried sentence, made more pronounced by his anticipation of my questions. His avoidance is amplified when, by pointing at the equality monitoring form, towards the end of the interview, I asked him if he thought people experience places differently, according to their ethnic background. In response, he looks directly at the form on the table beneath his gaze and then points to the boxes. Then, relying on the categories on the form he describes Moss Side as being "mostly B and maybe some D". Using the labelling on the form means he does not have to say 'mixed race' and 'black'. Again, no further explanation is offered to us and Andy keeps to his abstract descriptions.

Like Andy, Alex also labours over physical descriptions. He does, however, draw out some differences. Here he compares the three neighbourhoods:

> [Moss Side] . . . the fact that the Princess Parkway going past it, well at least it's got something going through it, whereas Gorton I didn't feel that maybe it had as many people going past it. I don't know why, maybe it has. In Longsight it was busy so yeah Gorton seemed the quietest of those two areas . . . I'm not sure really, there's the placing of the shops is quite different. Moss Side seems to have things on the outside for some reason in my head, to draw things in, whereas Gorton had just had more random placing of things. And then I guess Longsight seems very aware of the Stockport road going through it and seems very like, there's a road to leap on to, to get our businesses on, but there doesn't seem much room beyond that.

Most notably again, no people appear. We only get the sense that people are passing through. The busy-ness of Moss Side and Longsight that Alex describes is initially suggested as a positive attribute, offered as evidence of vibrant street life. The quietness of Gorton is, in contrast, imbued with negative connotations. Quietness is used as a contrast to suggest less things going on, though not in the orderly manner suggested in descriptions of middle class neighbourhoods. Gorton is too 'random' for that. Nevertheless, the distinctions he makes between 'noise' and 'quiet' are well-worn tropes for depicting racialised and gendered places and noise and busy-ness work as common metaphors with which to describe neighbourhoods that are represented as black and Asian (Watt, 2006; Blokland, 2003). But, Alex goes on to mix his metaphors when he tries to explain his experience of space. He begins by saying that, whilst he works in Moss Side, he would not want to live there because it is "too noisy". Concerned that his aversion to living in Moss Side might be interpreted negatively, he then describes it as "very quiet":

> It's more like multicultural and whereas [home town] was more white working class families, so that's a difference in terms of the population, erm, but like I find Moss Side more interesting for that reason.

The contradiction in Alex's narrative around noise versus quiet emerges as he attempts to reconcile his discomfort with criticising what he describes as "multicultural" areas, tempered by an emphasis on difference as an interesting 'quality'.

Anticipating race 71

This shift is also noted in his tone as he switches from a considered and hesitant tone to one that is more relaxed. Like Andy above, he fumbles to find the right words to explain how he feels in each neighbourhood and yet he becomes lighter and more comfortable as he talks in an abstracted way about the interesting side to multiculture. This switch in tone marks the shift in when he can talk about difference by embracing culturalist discourses. I return to think more closely about the use of culturalist discourses and that transition in tone later in the chapter. But first I want to think through how the young people talk about their experiences of Gorton, a white working-class neighbourhood.

Contrasted spaces: encountering the white working class

Chapter 2 explored how the representations of the three neighbourhoods in the research share a number of similarities. For example, the 'scruffy whites' or 'chavs' were constructed alongside ethnic minority groups through the way in which they are associated with criminality, drugs, gangs and other 'immoral' behaviours outside of the 'normal' narrative of the city (Rhodes, 2011; Nayak, 2009). This is spatialised so that 'ethnic' neighbourhoods and white areas are imagined as sites of these various behaviours (Rhodes, 2011). And, like the 'ethnic community', the white working class is also constructed as 'static, ahistorical and generally shorn of any subjectivity across time and space' (Carter and Virdee, 2008: 669). However, these similarities become less comprehensive when the young adults talk about their experience of these places, and it is this to which I want to bring attention. In particular, whilst Gorton, Longsight and Moss Side were all associated with working classness, criminality and so-called 'urban' or 'inner-city' culture, they are associated to differing degrees. For example, whilst Moss Side was represented as 'ahead' in terms of criminality, Gorton was represented as 'ahead' in terms of working classness and 'having and being of no value' (Reay et al., 2007: 1049). Indeed, Gorton was the only neighbourhood described explicitly as *working class*. Longsight and Moss Side, on the other hand, were typically referred to instead as "deprived", and these descriptions were imbued with sympathetic (albeit problematic) connotations in a way that working classness in Gorton was not. This reflects the different ways in which race and class are produced. Although blackness and Asianness are implicitly associated with deprivation and other sub-class indicators, it is *race* that works as the dominant signifier. In Gorton, however, class works as the dominant signifier when it is articulated with whiteness. As a consequence, most young people demonstrated little concern with regard to how their feelings about Gorton might be interpreted and apparently had free rein to explicitly associate white working classness with negative behaviours including a lack of community "values", violence and immorality.

Encounters with Gorton are as a consequence easier to talk about. In the discussion that follows it is also notable that Gorton is populated in their accounts. Indeed, at times Gorton seems somewhat over-populated. There is no attempt to disavow the presence of white working-class bodies in the way that black bodies were disappeared from view. Indeed, there are also no attempts to gain distance

72   *Anticipating race*

from the subject, and, rather than suggesting that they were reflecting broader generalised representations through the medium of 'reputations', young people who did not live in Gorton instead adopted crude stereotyping for the people living there, commonly using terms such as "scally", "chav" and "white trash". Here, for example, Karen describes her own encounters in Gorton where she works in health and social care, a job that sometimes requires her to make home visits. She explains how people in Gorton are "very different":

Karen: Whereas Gorton, again there's probably similar levels of deprivation as Longsight, maybe worse, but the characteristics of the people are very different and there's predominantly more white people living there I'd say, but I would sometimes feel a bit worried about the safety over my car and other things. It's not. . .

Bethan: What do you mean by the characteristics?

Karen: Rough, very rough [laughs] and the things and the stories that I hear people get up to, you know if I'm going in the house on my own I wouldn't necessarily bat an eyelid in Longsight, whereas going in to some of the homes I go into in Gorton I can feel a bit threatened.

Indeed, polite metaphors are rarely called upon to describe Gorton. For example, the tendency to use adjectives such as "busy" and "noisy" to suggest 'vibrant' representations of 'ethnic communities' do not emerge in narratives about Gorton. It is a neighbourhood, which is instead described as lifeless, not only lacking in "community", but, as depicted here by Karen, as devoid of anything apart from "unusual" people:

Bethan: What did you mean by the community spirit in Longsight?

Karen: Cos it's got a busy market there and everyone's always out of their houses, lots of people out and about on the street, you see families, you see kiddies walking around with their parents and it's just buzzing all the time, whereas when you walk round Gorton from what I've seen, the only people you see walking in the streets are looking a bit unusual, and maybe talking to themselves, maybe like with mental health problems.

Whilst the people of Longsight and Moss Side are often avoided altogether and the neighbourhoods depicted as being almost uninhabited, Gorton residents become the main subject of narratives, often crudely associated with rude and aggressive behaviour. White people living in Gorton are thus offered little flexibility in the way they are constructed, or as Damien, a market trader, puts it, it is just "how they are".

Bethan: And what about Salford, do you get any idea of what they think of you there?

Damien: Oh they just think everyone's scum and stuff, like last year I was doing [the market there] and I got kicked out and moved into my girlfriends. A couple of chavs were really rude, but that's probably just because that's how they are.

Anticipating race   73

These kinds of stereotypes are reinforced by the respondents when they call upon representations of white working class families on the TV series Shameless to illustrate their point. This has come to be a local referencing point because Shameless, when it first aired, was filmed partly on location in Gorton. And, Ian, who grew up in Gorton, explains how such popular representations have enforced the "scally" image without taking account of the diversity of the people living in the area:

> Obviously predominantly when you say Gorton and Salford, people will first of all think scallies and stuff. I don't think the show Shameless has helped as such because it kind of portrays this, that everybody in Gorton or Salford is that particular way with ASBOs [anti-social behaviour order] and stuff and you know, there's loads of kind of retirees around there, there's families, there's quite a few nice primary schools as well and you know.

The power and acceptability of this kind of image is reflected by Zoe, who pokes fun at people living in Gorton:

Bethan: [Shameless] is filmed in Gorton?
Zoe: Yeah it was, but they had to stop filming it there because people were wrecking the equipment [laughs].

Gorton also becomes a site through which the rough and respectable (Watt, 2006; Skeggs, 1997) can be distinguished. Steve, for example, distinguishes between *his* kind of working classness and chavs by drawing on popular tropes around work ethic that often fuel misunderstandings about poverty and welfare:

> You know I grew up in a working class background. I still work in a call centre, um, but there is, um, it's hard to put into words really I guess when it comes to . . . you know I hate to use the word chav, but it's become the applicable word I think these days.

Helen too describes herself as working class and distinguishes herself from her husband's family, who she describes as "scally" and lacking in similar levels of respectability:

> [My husband's family] are a bit kind of scally and my husband says the same thing, I'm not being awful, but I would . . . sometimes we might discuss things and I might act a bit differently, I don't know, trying to be a bit more similar and kind of like. . . . "Oh, did you watch X Factor last night?" Do you know what I mean, whereas with my friends I might say that if it was particularly good or something, but generally we're not really talking about X Factor.

Briefly, moments are captured in narratives when respondents express discomfort in telling their stories of areas like Gorton. This is typically when asked to explain

74 *Anticipating race*

how the area differs from a white middle-class area. Here, more comfortable narratives are called upon, often again through historical referencing. Nasreen, for example, talked about the inaccessibility of Gorton, but does not have the same impression of Chorlton. When asked why this is the case, she talked briefly about the affluence of Chorlton and then becomes stuck and switches to talk about how Gorton does not have a history:

> I think Chorlton's got that wow . . . I mean everyone talks about Chorlton being more affluent, south Manchester . . . you always hear about the more affluent south, bigger houses, the suburbs, I think that's why it's different to Gorton for example. Um . . . Didn't Gorton have that . . . oh I forget now . . . but I think Chorlton's always been an area that's been around whereas isn't Gorton an area of marsh land or something. . . . Maybe, I was thinking that there's more history associated with Chorlton so perhaps that makes it more.

This spatialised representation of class bears some resemblance to the cosmopolitan versus the criminalised racialised spaces discussed above. However, they are produced differently. Race, when it was conceived as blackness and Asianness, was always talked in a series of carefully constructed metaphors. In this way, stories of Gorton and other white-working-class areas not only reveal the acceptability of pathologising the white working class, but hint at the silences contained within narratives about black and Asian spaces. The 'acceptable' derogatory manner in which working classness is talked about can therefore act as a tool through which to mask racism more broadly. It is bearing this in mind that I now return to think about how racialised localities are imagined through culturalist discourses of community and so on.

Comfortable conceptions of difference

One of the enduring legacies of policies on integration and cohesion is the way in which they have contributed to the construction of the ethnic community. The most recent policy intervention in this area has come in the form of the Casey Review (*2016*), which makes mention of 'community' 184 times in its 181 pages. Like its predecessors, places and where people live are of central concern; although, notably only places identified as 'diverse' and where concerns can be raised about segregation feature. It is in such locations where everything becomes about race and the notion of diversity loses its potential to convey complexity. Casey claims that:

> We know that where communities live separately, with fewer interactions between people from different backgrounds, mistrust, anxiety and prejudice grow.
>
> (Casey, 2016: 8)

These kinds of sentiments have broader appeal beyond the parameters of policy-making and are widely repeated across public domains. And, neighbourhoods that

Anticipating race 75

are conceived of as diverse have been trapped in this reified status for decades. Indeed, by insisting on community we inevitably fail to recognise 'the subtle nuances that make up urban multiculture and [omit] possibilities of diversity beyond some crude ethnic groupisms' (Harries et al) and instead invite 'the risks associated with naturalization, genre, race, gens, family, and the nation' (Isin, 2012: 16).

In this research one of the key ways that the notion of community is carried through is via the emphasis on common values and kinship in relation to the 'ethnic community'. This emphasis, therefore, very much reflects a rhetoric, which seeks to divide the good and bad racialised minority. This is reflected here by Helen, a 28-year-old white woman living in Moss Side, who describes the community there with the vaguest means of othering by adopting the word 'they':

[In Moss Side] they've got like a massive kind of community. Well they're all extended family, all live together and all look after each other. I know a lot of them, when we spoke to people who lived there would say, "They'll never be lonely".

Helen's obscure comments about an unidentified community comes, as was common across the interviews, as an attempt to offer a 'positive' view of a place, which she has acknowledged is otherwise associated with negative behaviours. For example, this sentiment is expressed by Helen after she tells me that her family would not want to walk around Moss Side. It is because these two statements follow each other that we know that her family do not want to walk around the neighbourhood because of this 'community' and she perhaps tries to redress this by offering a somewhat romantic image even though, as I will go on to illustrate below, she herself physically avoids her local streets. These conflicting statements are driven by the anticipation of encountering difference. This is reflected in both her anxiety about a physical encounter with a stranger and her anxiety about acknowledging this in the interview itself.

It perhaps comes as no surprise that, related to these folkish conceptions of community, comfortable conceptions of difference also centre on the pleasurable aspects of living in, or more commonly visiting, a multicultural 'community' to eat and consume goods and services. Indeed, numerous studies have explored how white people can infer liberal practices through the commodification of ethnicity, including through the consumption of 'ethnic' goods (Reay et al., 2007; Hage, 1998; hooks, 1992). This kind of consumption and celebration of difference is spatialised and tends to centre around places that have 'symbolic and emotional importance' (Alexander, 2011) by virtue of the way in which they are designed. For example, in south Manchester, Rusholme – a neighbourhood that borders both Moss Side and Longsight – often becomes the key focal point for these kinds of ethnicised and community discourses, because it is an "ethnic" area known for its rows of south Asian and middle eastern restaurants, marketed in Manchester as the "curry mile". These kinds of spaces become sites where the young adults could talk about their experiences of place and express their own

76 *Anticipating race*

'open-minded' attitude whilst they safely avoid confronting uncomfortable narratives about race and unacceptable stereotypes. Crucially here, terms like 'ethnic' and 'ethnic community' are called upon to suggest diversity and conviviality in everyday life, even whilst these references are mostly missing in the less commercialised 'black' area of Moss Side and 'Asian' area of Longsight. The tendency to understand sites of difference through culturalist metaphors is therefore not arbitrarily implied. It is also dependent on *when* people access spaces. For example, whilst for the most part Moss Side is described as inaccessible, when people sit outside in summer it is equated by Caroline to a "carnival atmosphere". We might also want to think through how day and night alters access to the space. Certainly, like several of the white young adults, Steve is happy to walk around Rusholme at night but will get a taxi from there to his house in Moss Side ten minutes' walk away.

Steve lives in Moss Side although he often denies living there. He lives on the edge of the neighbourhood and takes advantage of being close to the border to say he lives on the other side of it, in Fallowfield. His story is useful in exemplifying how some sites of difference are easier to interact with, but also easier to talk about. When I ask him how it is to live in Moss Side, he begins by describing the neighbourhood as having "a haphazard mix". He does not explicitly say what he means by "mix" or "haphazard", but there is an unspoken gesture to the ethnic diversity of the area. He goes on to explain how he regularly shops for food on the main street running through Moss Side. And, later in the interview I asked him whether he thought his experience of this street might differ from that of black people his age using the same space. He replies by saying that, 'I haven't seen a great deal of black people walking about.' This is rather difficult to imagine. Even if he were to chance upon an empty street, it is hard to ignore that the majority of shops, cafés and takeaways cater to, and are run by, the local Somali and Caribbean population. But in making this statement he has denied their existence. His discomfort is palpable and becomes more audible when he talks openly about the "mix" of the neighbourhood of Rusholme. Defining what he means by mix here, he comfortably talks about how many "Asians" and "Muslims" inhabit Rusholme and how he himself visits the curry mile. Again, we see a switch in tone as he relaxes in to tell me about his ventures in the curry mile.

Whilst culturalist discourses are embedded in whiteness, their power nevertheless resonates too with black and Asian participants. For example, Usman, a 26-year-old 'Asian', distinguishes between Rusholme with its 'cultural' credentials by way of food and "bright lights" and his own neighbourhood of Longsight, which is conversely constructed as "rough", less "interesting" and less desirable than its neighbour. And, Carina who describes herself as "human", but is typically read as black, explains that she likes to go to Rusholme in "small doses" to see the "bright lights" and equates the experience with going abroad on holiday:

> You've got nearly ten different nationalities in the space of 100 metres and I just think for me that's really interesting because you can learn so much about other people and I think, I don't know, it's got that sort of . . . you know when

you go on holiday and it's like a fresh place and you're like wow, there's . . . you know you don't see the negative things, it's just like you see it for what it is, you see the pretty bright lights of Rusholme type thing. That's how I like to see it and, it excites me. I don't think I'd want to be there all the time, but in small doses I do.

There is a certain honesty in Carina's narrative as she professes that she only wants to pass through Rusholme. I want to suggest that there are various tensions at work in these kinds of narratives that reflect the conflicting anxieties that many of the young adults feel about their encounters. Like Helen above, Usman and Carina demonstrate concerns around encountering difference, but also about how to express their encounters without appearing overly concerned. More often than not, these efforts invoked a whole other set of stereotypes that fetishise difference and made those other silences more audible. Crucially too, these kinds of encounters do not necessitate an immediate encounter, as in the consumption of 'ethnic' products or foodstuffs (Ahmed, 2000), or they represent encounters that are arbitrated by the distance afforded through the relation of customer and vendor.

This relationship between difference and proximity in the encounter is important. Dealing with difference in spaces like Moss Side, where narratives of 'accessibility' are absent, I argue, is facilitated by the creation of a temporal or spatial distance from the subject under discussion. Put simply, just as respondents found it easier to talk about a racist past, rather than a racist present, they also found it easier to talk about difference when it was located elsewhere. Caroline was one of the young people who drew attention to the way that certain areas were racialised and made this association with levels of perceived criminality, by calling into question the notion of the UK as a "non-racist" society (see Chapter 3). However, in relation to her own encounters with the city, Caroline was reluctant to recognise whiteness and blackness. I met Caroline in Moss Side at a children's service that she would regularly access from home on foot. In the interview, she talked about her apprehension about walking through Moss Side, saying she was not comfortable because she "stands out". When I asked her what she meant by this, she said she was unsure and supposed it was because she does not have a purpose there, despite explaining that she goes there to access a specific service. Notably, these moments of discomfort emerged when describing moments where she was physically located within Moss Side herself, rather than talking about other people's experiences from the comforts of her own "mixed" (largely white) and middle class neighbourhood.

Helen lives on the edge of Moss Side in a relatively new apartment block that forms part of the regeneration of Hulme and Moss Side. She talks about her reluctance to walk around Moss Side, but cannot say why. After some consideration she says she supposes it might have something to do with the weather. At the same time, she acknowledges that there are few areas of Moss Side that she goes to. For instance, despite living a few minutes' walk from a large Asda supermarket, she instead drives several miles away to a more 'upmarket' supermarket in Didsbury, or even further to a Waitrose supermarket, half an hour's drive away in Cheshire.

78 *Anticipating race*

The reason for this, she says, is that the Moss Side supermarket is "too busy" – that busy-ness again! This is undoubtedly partly about constructing a classed identity through consumption choices, which is made implicit in Helen's choice of an upmarket supermarket, but it is also indicative of her more general resistance to any association with Moss Side. Here she explains how, such is her reluctance to be associated with anything Moss Side, that she sometimes lies about her address:

> Sometimes like I don't say I live in Moss Side cos like, people are going to think, "Oh God Moss Side". So I usually say Hulme cos it's easier . . . as soon as you say Moss Side, people are like, "Eugh".

Proximities to difference

I am interested in how, when we talk about race working as a 'local matter' (Hartigan Jr., 1999), this relates to when and how the local is inhabited. What we get are places that are described as more or less accessible than others. In the following discussion I want to explore how the way in which stories are constructed relies on the proximity of the narrator to the spaces to which they refer. Most obviously this includes how well someone claims to 'know' an area, thus a negative reputation can be reinscribed with the caveat, "I don't really know though" and acceptable stereotypes are delivered matter-of-factly often about 'known' places, but from an assumed outsider's perspective, using phrases such as "they do this. . . ." or "that's how it is". In addition, narratives change according to where the respondent situates themselves within the story. Thus, it is possible for the young people to distance themselves from racist representations and practices associated with a place whilst, at the same time, they struggle to define why personal experience of the same space invokes discomfort. In each of these cases, the distance created from the place under scrutiny acts not only to relinquish some responsibility for how stories are constructed, but also makes them difficult to dispute. The salience of this is explored below.

It was common for the young adults to say that they "have heard of" a place, or of a particular reputation. This allowed them to repeat stereotypes from a safe distance and maintain their independence from such constructions. When describing Moss Side, Helen for example, drew a link between "immigrants" and the association with the area being "rough". Whilst later she uses the term immigrant synonymously with black people, she distances herself from this representation of roughness by iterating that it is "probably true", she does not *really* know and it is only a reflection of what she has heard from other people. Helen does not want to be associated with this view, presumably because she thinks it would not be appropriate to portray herself in this way. However, it seems that she cannot tell the story without invoking these kinds of tropes:

> I think it's kind of generally seen as quite rough kind of people and think quite a lot of immigrants and stuff like that, which I think is probably true but I don't really know, but cos I don't really talk about it . . . but I guess that's what they

Anticipating race 79

presume, that it's all kind of foreigners and you know what people say and I'm sure I've heard people sometimes say, "Oh god, it's full of whatevers round there".

Helen tells this story via the voices of others. She does not explain who "they" are because "they" are only invoked in order to make it possible to tell a story about Moss Side. Helen used to live in West Didsbury, a relatively affluent and white neighbourhood and now lives on the edge of Moss Side. In comparing the two neighbourhoods, she says that she enjoyed living in West Didsbury because it is "cosmopolitan". She clarified what she meant by this term as an area that includes "people from all over the place". Earlier in the interview she had also described Moss Side as having "people from all over the place", and so I asked if she also thought of Moss Side as cosmopolitan. Here, she struggles to explain why the two areas are different.

Bethan: And would you say Moss Side is cosmopolitan?
Helen: Um, I guess it is really but in kind of . . . I don't know . . . I'm not sure . . . I mean obviously there's quite a kind of mix of ethnicities and things like that so it is cosmopolitan really in that sense, erm . . . yeah I mean . . . I don't know . . . I guess it is [laughs].

It emerges that she perceives the people in the two areas in very different ways. The quote above, interspersed with pauses and nervous laughter, reveals a reluctance to describe Moss Side as cosmopolitan. This is undoubtedly linked to the perceived differences in class composition of the two areas. 'Elites are cosmopolitan, people are local' (Castells, 1996: 415). However, it is also because she perceives that Moss Side includes people from a mix of ethnicities and from different countries. West Didsbury, on the other hand, she explains, has (white) professionals from different parts of the UK. Later in the interview, Helen equates the ethnic groups listed on the equality monitoring form, other than white, with "immigrants" and in the context of Moss Side, with migrants from Africa. When I ask her if she thinks that black people experience some spaces differently to her, she says:

I'm guessing that immigrants who maybe have just come over as well from wherever they've come from, they kind of like look around and think it's not very nice as well I'm guessing [laughs] . . . although saying that, I've been to like Africa and things and like they've not got anything there like, their houses are made of you know, they're kind of shacks and things like that . . . whereas I'm guessing that moving over here like, although the houses are nicer . . . just [laughs] you know, they've probably got more, like they've got tellys, you know they didn't have many tellys over there. I'm just thinking of . . . or even running water actually.

It is apparent from the above quote that Helen equates black people with immigrants, and her explanation for how her neighbours might then experience Moss

80   *Anticipating race*

Side includes a depiction of an archetypal 'African' living in a shack with no possessions. She imbues this account with a sympathetic tone and confirms her capacity to say such things, because she has personal experience of "Africa" from a holiday in Ghana. This association is clearly easier for Helen to make than to talk about the experience of black people in her own neighbourhood. The 'Africa' that Helen talks about is a less difficult space to talk about than that which is visible from the window she is sat next to whilst narrating this story. The distance at which Africa is at is not coincidental; it is a location which she temporally and spatially situates in the past. Crucially, we cannot go out the door and check whether Helen is 'right'; we have to rely on her having been there earlier (Lawler, 2002), and since we were not, her story becomes difficult to dispute within the terms of the conversation. What is more, the sympathetic tone here, together with the story of travel to 'Africa', can be read as suggestion of a 'tolerant' and 'open-minded' lifestyle. This becomes particularly pertinent when elsewhere she contrasts herself to her in-laws, who she describes as working class and insular. This suggestion reflects a tendency to consign racism primarily to a sub-class of the white working-class, or underclass, in order to claim a middle-class identification (Haylett, 2001; Reay, 2002).

Learned encounters: the "unspoken code"

Much of the work on encountering difference works from the perspective of understanding how marginalised bodies are encountered. In this final section, I want to reflect on how people who are racialised and/or live in racialised neighbourhoods explain how they have learned to negotiate their own encounters. For these young adults, having a broad lifespace that stretches far beyond their own neighbourhood is salient. They describe having learned how to negotiate both their own neighbourhoods, which are otherwise often perceived as being off-limits, as well as other parts of the city often perceived in more neutral terms. Unlike many of the young adults who make concerted efforts to talk about encountering difference at a distance as a means to infer their liberal credentials, these participants must instead negotiate their own encounters by taking into consideration the way in which they are positioned and how their locales are represented. I explore the ways in which the young people talk about how they perform certain roles in different spaces of the city based on their encounters with difference and of being perceived as 'different'. This in turn is said to enable them to mediate relationships across various spaces. Crucially, knowing how to deal with these encounters was said to be enhanced by increased contact with those they produce as racially or ethnically different to themselves and in spaces produced as racially or ethnically different to those they typically inhabit. The understanding that liberal cosmopolitanism is constructed as normatively white and middle class means that the young people who occupy a marginalised position, because of their perceived 'race' and class, are often denied such an identity. Nevertheless, they express more nuanced and deeper means of understanding how the city works.

Anticipating race 81

Hamid describes needing to know the "code" of Moss Side in order to read people in ways that have greater significance:

Hamid: The key thing round here is that you need to know what's what, you need to know who's who and the rights and wrongs. It's basically an unspoken code of what to do and what not to do.
Bethan: You don't get a manual?
Hamid: [Laughs] no you don't get a manual, it'd be a lot easier for some people if they did get a manual.

When Hamid talks about those who do not understand the "code" and might benefit from a manual, he refers to people who live outside of the area and who do not understand "what's what". This marking of people living outside the inner city becomes a common means to distinguish between those who are less competent at interactions within "ethnic" areas. Much of this is framed in terms of class. Zoe illustrates this when she turns the integration thesis on its head and describes the middle classes as "more repressed and keep themselves to themselves more". Different levels of competency are also typically articulated with place when respondents draw a distinction between working class friends in the inner city and those who live in towns outside of Manchester, as Ian does here:

If you're from anywhere in inner city Manchester, I'm talking Whalley Range, Hulme, Moss Side, Rusholme, Levenshulme, Gorton, Beswick, anywhere round there, you kind of know what it's like and how it is and stuff, anywhere from outside, around, so I went out with a girl from Stockport, I went out with, I had a friend from Blackpool who was staying in Bolton and coming to uni in Salford and you know, when you talk about the things that you talk about, they think they've lived a very sheltered life and that you've lived this really kind of depraved and you know horrid life and everything.

The distinctions made in perceived competencies are also emphasised through the way that the young people describe how they negotiate spaces and mediate identities. They talk about a sense of 'double conciousness' (Du Bois, 1996 [1903]), or knowing how to "split" their lives in two and "adapt" to different contexts accordingly. For example, Pete and Steve, who are both white, remark on how their middle-class friends from work are reluctant to visit them in Moss Side, and, consequently, they have to spend time with their friends in what they describe as more 'neutral' spaces, such as the city centre.

Simon is mixed race. He had worked for a time in a youth centre in Moss Side and other parts of Manchester. He was telling me how he was made angry by middle class white people turning up at youth centres thinking they understood what was going on and assuming superior knowledge, because of their education, rather than life experience. He described middle-class white workers as "righteous" "do-gooders". He was particularly annoyed by a former colleague who had put one young person at risk by taking them to an area where rival gang members

82 *Anticipating race*

were known to be present and mocked other workers who had been caught out by young people's pranks. Hamid too complained that white middle class people he met at work would come to Moss Side and make assumptions, and so he stopped inviting them over to his house. He made an exception of one friend who he said:

> [He] didn't act like another middle class kid, he wasn't apprehensive, he did ask the odd questions, like the odd questions the idiot, like, "Is it dangerous around here?" Well it's dangerous anywhere you go. "What happens if this happens, or?" Which I understood, he's new, he's heard stories, at least he's asking instead of making assumptions, so I explained to him this and that, it's a load of bollocks. He comes round on his own now. He's probably one of the only . . . well there's two other white people that walk in here [the café] freely.

Hamid was telling me this whilst we were sitting in the café that he describes only 'two other white people' go into. Here, he describes how he has split his 'life in two':

Bethan: Would you ever invite the lot that don't live round here back here [to the café], or go round to yours?

Hamid: There's one or two [friends from work] that do, that would have an open mind and wouldn't be intimidated and would not be really afraid. You see I have brought friends from out the way, like from Sale and all they talk about is Moss Side, gun shots, gun shots, but that never happens here, it's over exaggerated and if you do hear about it, it's gangs. No one shoots no one for nothing. The shooter's got to be very precise. It's a life or death matter here so it's not going to happen to you. But they're very, "What's he doing?" they're very . . . on edge. So I don't really bring them round but the ones I have brought round that I think are alright. With friends like that I kind of test the water. I bring a few round I tell them to come over or I tell 'em to come round and chill with us for a night and blaze up and see how it runs with them. If he's very quiet and very intimidated, watching his step, watching what he's saying and that then I wouldn't bring him round again. Plus I have got one or two friends from around here that are just like me. Kind of open and westernised and then I'll take them to meet them first to break the ice so at least if I do bring them round there'll be someone they know apart from me.

Hamid's story not only reflects the way in which Moss Side is pathologised, but gives us a sense of how the young adults negotiate their relationships and identities within different spaces of the city. Like Hamid, many of the young adults frame their narratives in ways that rely on our understanding of those different spaces of the city. Markers of class and race, articulated together, are implied through the locations from which he draws. We are left to assume that friends from white

Anticipating race 83

middle class neighbourhoods are themselves white and middle class, whilst his friends from his own neighbourhoods, who are 'westernised', we assume are black. It is notable that they are always constructed within a gendered context of mixing with people who are produced as racially or ethnically different. Gender is, however, rarely, made explicit. Again it is the shared location, which gives us an indication towards class and race that is employed as a safe lens through which to emphasise similarity (within this cohort) and breach imagined racialised boundaries.

In Chapter 2, I highlighted the way that similarity between inner city neighbourhoods is emphasised, and this is reflected here in the way that people from these areas are mostly described as sharing similar levels of competency when interacting with difference. However, when attention is paid to how the young adults describe experiences of these places and give examples of interactions, they present contradictions. The quote above from Hamid describes his role in bringing together his white friends, ostensibly from middle class areas, and his black friends from Moss Side. But, it is only his white friends who do not reproduce racialised stereotypes and his black friends who are "westernised" that are described by Hamid as competent. Elsewhere, Hamid suggests that in order to be competent it is necessary to become "westernised":

> A few guys I know are westernised and some stay to their old traditional roots which is . . . I can understand but, when in Rome, do as the Romans [laughs].

Hamid is constructing an identity that conflicts with representations of what it is to be Somali in Moss Side. As an antidote to these fixed identifications both he and Ian claim to hold an interim position, which they construct as classless and raceless. A 'classless' position is also claimed by Zoe:

Zoe: It's dead hard to understand what class is, isn't it? . . . I wouldn't say that I was particularly in either classes now. I'm not saying I'm classless or anything but I don't know, I think there is . . . there must be a wave of people that are hard to categorise, there must be . . . So my dad's . . . I've been brought up like middle and working class because I was born into a working class family, no a middle class family but my mum and dad were about 17 when they met each other, so we moved to London and we moved to Gorton and um, so I was brought up not particularly privileged cos they were so young and then when my mum and dad split up my mum started going out with some proper scallies, like real pisshead scallies, so I've been exposed to that other culture as well.

Bethan: Is that why you think you have that range of experience then?

Zoe: Probably yeah, cos I've never looked down on anyone, I've always hung around with different types of people.

A connection is made by Zoe between the ability to transcend both class and racialised difference, although again this relies on very particular understandings

84 *Anticipating race*

of class and race. These various negotiations of place thus intersect with the ways in which identities are formed, claimed and negotiated. Maz, for example, explains how he does not invite his white friends from college or work to Longsight, because the way he identifies with them "would not work in that context". But, similarly, he says he does not meet up with friends from Longsight in what he describes as "cosmopolitan" spaces, which can be read as white and middle class. Maz is working with certain ambiguities here. He directly draws the link between the way in which place and identity can be closely intertwined beyond the crudely defined neighbourhood ascriptions, but also points to how this relationship is shaped by a complex range of other factors which are not easy to disentangle. The effect of this ambiguity in how people are positioned and how they want to be identified becomes the focus of attention in the chapter that follows.

Conclusion

This chapter has explored how the young adults anticipate difference in their encounters. It began by emphasising how race does not only shape the discursive repertoires of place, but also how people can relate to and engage with their material environment. This required paying attention to the more than representational (Lorimer, 2005), including the affective qualities race possesses. Many of the white young people expressed considerable anxiety about their encounters. Their discomfort was evident in the way they anticipated race in their everyday lives and again in their narratives. To deal with race they often resorted to awkward silences, or protracted descriptions of physical structures to disavow the presence of racialised bodies and to avoid confronting their discomfort about relationships between bodies and their proximities to each other. These silences became more audible because difference was embraced so emphatically in white working-class neighbourhoods, where it was acceptable to speak openly and disparagingly about the local population, and in commercialised 'ethnic' spaces, where young people could easily access repertoires of liberal consumption. For the black young people, who are conscious of being produced as 'different', there are different issues at stake. They described learning how to encounter the city in multifaceted ways. They reflected on how they had to negotiate their relationships in different spaces to avoid being produced as 'different' and in doing so expressed nuanced and complex understandings of how the city works.

This chapter is presented in juxtaposition to the way in which the young people elsewhere emphasise commonalities across their 'generation'. In placing these discussions next to each other, the contradictions that underpin the notion of a post-racial generation come to the fore. It is in looking through encounters that I suggest that we can see how difference is produced, but also how we might confront the risks inherent in over-simplifying how people live multiculture as much of the policy recommendations on mixed neighbourhoods is prone to do.

Note

1 There is of course also a vivid cultural scene that disrupts and challenges colonial discourses and fetishized representations of difference.

References

Ahmed, S. (2000). *Strange encounters: Embodied others in post-coloniality*. London: Routledge.

Ahmed, S. (2014). *The cultural politics of emotion* (2nd Edition). Edinburgh: Edinburgh University Press.

Alexander, C. (2011). Making bengali brick lane: Claiming and contesting space in East London. *British Journal of Sociology*, 62(2), 201–220.

Amin, A. (2012). *Land of strangers*. Cambridge: Polity Press.

Amin, A. (2013). Land of strangers. *Identities: Global Studies in Culture and Power*, 20(1), 1–8.

Back, L. (1996). *New ethnicities and urban multiculture: Racisms and multiculture in young lives*. London: UCL Press.

Back, L. & Keith, M. (1999). 'Rights and wrongs': Youth, community and narratives of racial violence. *In:* Cohen, P. (ed.) *New ethnicities, old racisms*. London: Zed Books.

Bailey, N., Haworth, A., Tony Manzi, T., Paranagamage, P. & Roberts, M. (2006). *Creating and sustaining mixed income communities: A good practice guide*. York and Coventry: Joseph Rowntree Foundation and Chartered Institute for Housing.

Becares, L., Nazroo, J. & Stafford, M. (2009). The buffering effects of ethnic density on experienced racism and health. *Health & Place*, 15(3), 700–708.

Blokland, T. (2003). Ethnic complexity: Routes to discriminatory repertoires in an inner-city neighbourhood. *Ethnic and Racial Studies*, 26(1), 1–24.

Cantle, T. (2001). *Community cohesion: A report of the independent review*. London: Home Office.

Carter, B. & Virdee, S. (2008). Racism and the sociological imagination. *British Journal of Sociology*, 59(4), 661–679.

Casey, L. (2016). *The Casey review: A review into opportunity and integration*. London: Department for Communities and Local Government.

Castells, M. (1996). *The rise of network society*. Cambridge, MA: Blackwell.

Commission on Integration and Cohesion. (2007). *Our shared future*. London: Commission on Integration and Cohesion.

De Certeau, M. (2011 [1984]). *The practice of everyday life* (Vol. 3rd Edition). Berkeley: University of California Press.

Douglas, M. (1984 [1966]). *Purity and danger: An analysis of the concepts of pollution and taboo*. London: Routledge.

Du Bois, W. E. B. (1996 [1903]). *The souls of black folk*. Harmondsworth: Penguin.

Fanon, F. (1986). *Black skin, white masks*. London: Pluto Press.

Finney, N. & Simpson, L. (2009). *Sleepwalking to segregation? Challenging myths about race and migration*. Bristol: Policy Press.

Gilroy, P. (2004). *After empire: Melancholia or convivial culture?* Abingdon: Routledge.

Hage, G. (1998). *White nation: Fantasies of white supremacy in a multicultural society*. London: Pluto.

Hall, S. (1992). New ethnicities. *In:* Donald, J. & Rattansi, A. (eds.) *'Race', culture and difference*. London: Sage.

86 *Anticipating race*

Harries, B., Byrne, B., Rhodes, J. & Wallace, S. (forthcoming). Diversity in place: narratives of diversity in an ethnically mixed, urban area. *Journal of Ethnic and Migration Studies*.

Hartigan Jr., J. (1999). *Racial situations: Class predicaments of whiteness in Detroit*. Princeton, NJ: Princeton University Press.

Haylett, C. (2001). Illegitimate subjects? Abject whites, neoliberal modernisation and middle class multiculturalism. *Environment and Planning D: Society and Space*, 19(3), 351–370.

hooks, b. (1992). *Black looks: Race and representation*. Boston: South End Press.

Isin, E. (2012). Citizens without nations. *Environment and Planning D: Society and Space*, 30(3), 450–467.

Keith, M. (2005). *After the cosmopolitan: Multicultural cities and the future of racism*. London: Routledge.

Keith, M. & Pile, S. (1993). Introduction: The place of politics. *In:* Keith, M. & Pile, S. (eds.) *Place and the politics of identity*. London: Routledge.

Knowles, C. (2013). Nigerian London: Re-mapping space and ethnicity in superdiverse cities. *Ethnic and Racial Studies*, 36(4), 651–669.

Lawler, S. (2002). Narrative in social research. *In:* May, T. (ed.) *Qualitative research in action*. London: Sage.

Lefebvre, H. (1996). Space and politics. *In:* Kofman, E. & Lebas, E. (eds.) *Writings on cities*. Cambridge, MA: Blackwell.

Lewis, G. (1985). From deepest Kilburn. *In:* Heron, L. (ed.) *Truth, dare, promise: Girls growing up in the fifties*. London: Virago.

Lipsitz, G. (2011). *How racism takes place*. Philadelphia: Temple University Press.

Lorimer, H. (2005). Cultural geography: The busyness of being more-than-representational. *Progress in Human Geography*, 29(1), 83–94.

Massey, D. (1994). *Space, place and gender*. Cambridge: Polity Press.

Massey, D. (2005). *For space*. London: Sage.

Melamed, J. (2006). The spirit of neoliberalism: From racial liberalism to neoliberal multiculturalism. *Social Text*, 24(4), 1–24.

Nayak, A. (2009). Beyond the pale: Chavs, youth and social class. *In:* Sveinsson, K. (ed.) *Perspectives: Who cares about the white working class?* London: Runnymede Trust.

Nayak, A. (2011). Geography, race and emotions: Social and cultural intersections. *Social and Cultural Geography*, 12(6), 548–562.

Park, R. E. (1925) The City: suggestions for investigation of human behavior in the urban environment. *In* R.E. Park an E.W. Burgess with R.D. McKenzie and L.Wirth, *The City: suggestions for investigation of human behavior in the urban environment*. Chicago: Chicago University Press.

Pile, S. (2005). *Real cities: Modernity, space and the phantasmagorias of city life*. London: Sage.

Puwar, N. (2004). *Space invaders: Race, gender and bodies out of place*. New York: Berg.

Reay, D. (2002). Shaun's story: Troubling discourses of white working-class masculinities. *Gender and Education*, 14(3), 221–234.

Reay, D., Hollingworth, D., Williams, K., Crozier, G., Jamieson, F., James, D. & Beedeell, P. (2007). A darker shade of pale? Whiteness, the middle classes and multi-ethnic inner city schooling. *Sociology*, 41(6), 1041–1060.

Rhodes, J. (2011). Stigmatization, space and boundaries in de-industrial Burnley. *Ethnic and Racial Studies,* 35(4), 684–703.

Rose, G. (1993). *Feminism and geography*. Minneapolis: University of Minnesota Press.

Ruddick, S. (1996). Constructing difference in public spaces: Race, class, and gender as interlocking systems. *Urban Geography*, 17(2), 132–151.

Skeggs, B. (1997). *Formations of class and gender*. London: Sage.

Swanton, D. (2010). Sorting bodies: Race, affect, and everyday multiculture in a mill town in northern England. *Environment and Planning A*, 42(10), 2332–2350.

Tizard, B. & Phoenix, A. (1993). *Black, white or mixed race? Race and racism in the lives of young people of mixed parentage*. London: Routledge.

Valluvan, S. (2016). Conviviality and multiculture: A post-integration sociology of multi-ethnic interaction. *Young*, 24(3), 204–221.

Watt, P. (2006). Respectability, roughness and 'race': Neighbourhood place images and the making of working-class social distinctions in London. *International Journal of Urban and Regional Research*, 30(4), 776–797.

Wilson, H. F. (2016). On geography and encounter: Bodies, borders, and difference. *Progress in Human Geography*, First published date: 13 May 2016, 1–21.

5 Going against the grain

Resistance to identifications and the claim for multiple subjectivities

This chapter addresses questions of identity by engaging with the young people's routine experiences of being positioned as 'different', but it is ultimately concerned with how the young people manipulate and resist processes of identification and (mis)recognition. This discussion thus shifts attention from exploring the contextual backdrop introduced in previous chapters, including the collective identities narrated about the city and generation, to concentrate on the ways that the young people describe how they are positioned and construct their identities within this context. The contextual work done to set the scene in earlier chapters therefore remains pertinent in that it provides us with a point from which to understand how identities are constructed, performed and lived.

So far the discussion has raised a series of important questions that relate to the terms of recognition. In particular, questions have been raised about what and who is recognised as part of the city's fabric, and what kinds of difference are recognised in the young people's encounters. I have explored how much of the narratives of the young people often attempted to smooth out forms of differentiation (including race) to suggest that 'we are all the same'. And, whilst this sense of universalism had an air of optimism, it nevertheless often adhered to debates on integration and thus spoke directly to, rather than against, modes of exclusion. This chapter takes up this contradiction and considers how, within this context, young people counter and negotiate processes of racialisation and identifications that position them as different. In doing so, I explore how the young adults understand themselves to be positioned in relation to a set of codes, or 'norms' (Butler, 2005), but also how lived identities are shaped, negotiated and resisted.

Within race studies there is now a general sense that identity can be interpreted as a 'continuous process of becoming' (Hall, 1997), rather than some sort of static entity that risks associations with innate characteristics. However, understanding identity as a continuous process is not always easy to convey, because the language of identity is so often steeped in categories that relay a sense of fixedness. Consequently, there remains a risk in overlooking dynamic and shifting interactions and positionings (Gunaratnam, 2003) by remaining 'group-oriented' (Wacquant, 1997), with the consequence of reinforcing ethnoracial divisions and connoting 'groups' with fixed subjectivities (Majumdar, 2007). Such a risk has particular salience for young ethnic minorities. When ethnic identity is conveyed as fixed, as

90　*Going against the grain*

it often is in popular representations, it is also represented as if having character-istics that are 'transmitted from generation to generation' (Hall, 2000: 223). Hence, ethnic minorities born in the UK are enduringly represented as if they are migrants. The tendency to categorise individuals by the number of steps away from migrant ancestors, as second-, third-, fourth- generation, reinforces this link. Succeeding generations of minorities thus become caught up in a position of what Gilroy refers to as the 'perpetual outsider'(Gilroy, 1993). This has specific consequences for young people growing up in the UK when racial or ethnic categories come to be perceived as absolute and associated with notions of community separated by impenetrable boundaries (Gilroy, 1993; Back, 2002). British born children of migrants are often represented as being 'caught between two cultures' (Baumann, 1996; Solomos and Back, 1996), or torn between the 'host' culture and that of their parents/grandparents. But the idea that British youth are 'torn' implicitly suggests that young people are themselves 'culture-less' or lost between two immovable 'objects' crudely and usually uncritically labelled as cultures (Kalra et al., 2005). It is significant too that much of these ways of seeing emerge in a broader political climate that emphasises integration and the crisis of British identity. Young Mus-lims, for example, are often represented as epitomising a crisis of identity, as they work out modes of community and national belonging – two imagined positions that are nevertheless impossible to reconcile not least because Muslims are con-structed as a threat to British identity (Rashid, 2016). Indeed, it is this impossible position that might be more accurately redolent of a crisis facing young people. There is certainly a need, as others have argued, to move away from thinking about abstracted notions of identity, and 'threats' to it, to focus instead on lived identities (Harris, 2009; Nayak, 2003; Solomos, 2003) in order to get beyond crude inter-pretations of people's lives.

To start, this chapter draws on individual stories to illustrate how young people are often expected to reproduce very fixed representations of what it means to *be* 'ethnic' and to *be* 'white-working-class'. The first section illustrates how stories of the self invariably start from a point of misrecognition. I want to stress here, however, that this is not solely a matter of misrecognition. For the black young people there is also the relentless *anticipation* of being positioned as different, and in many ways it is this anticipation and the emotional registers that this invokes that marks the distinction between their experiences and those of their contempo-raries positioned as white-working-class. Important to note too is that moments of misrecognition are only starting points and act only as partial glimpses for under-standing the multi-faceted nature of lived identities (Back, 1996). As such, the rest of the chapter moves on to examine the ways the young adults deal with processes of misrecognition and includes a discussion on how the young adults reflect on categories of identity and attempt to manipulate conflicting forms of identification. Overall, the chapter argues that there is an expectation to speak to discourses of race, class and gender, and this includes an expectation to be accountable to dis-courses of integration and inclusion. I suggest that by focusing on the ways in which the young people play with and manipulate different potential identities we can grasp how race can be undermined.

Starting from the point of misrecognition

I want to start by reflecting on how our understandings of others often begin in our interactions from a point of misrecognition. Here I take the early conversations and beginning extracts from interviews with the young people in order to illustrate how they begin to tell their story and how we might begin to understand them. It will perhaps come as no surprise that much of these early conversations are marked by the recalling of a series of well-worn tropes through which the young adults and I present ourselves and read each other in ways that attempt to make some sense. These starting points thus serve as an important part of the social context and reference point from which we can then speak against or resist certain forms of identification. They speak to the ideologies and discourses of race, class, gender and culture in which individuals are placed as well as to the social interaction itself (Back, 1996).

Each interview began in much the same way. The respondents were asked to talk through their photo diaries or, when there was not one, to talk about places they spend time in and with whom. The purpose was to elicit stories about everyday lives, including their mundane interactions with people and places. A brief look at the first page of many of the transcripts reveals that, within the first moments of interviews with young people who identified as black, ethnic or cultural references were drawn upon as a means to begin their story. Much the same can be said of how my initial conversations were directed by the young people in our first encounters, before the interview. This was the case even when they later dismissed them as irrelevant. My position as a white woman interviewer partly produced this, but it also reflects a broader expectation on black people to produce an ethnicised account of themselves in everyday practice, when black bodies are always considered to be 'bounded by their race' (Puwar, 2004: 65). It is also indicative of the expectation to explain oneself in relation to whiteness (Fanon, 1986 c1952) and Englishness or Britishness (Gilroy, 2002). The young people are well aware of such expectations. Indeed, Tony draws direct attention to it when he explains later in the interview, 'I am always asked where I come from *because* I'm black.' In contrast, the young adults read as white British do not introduce themselves in racial, ethnic, national or cultural terms. That is not to say, as I will go on to discuss, that they do not face other expectations particularly in relation to the way class and gender work in different spaces. However, these are not starting points for their narratives. This perhaps simple point draws attention to the different demands that are placed upon some and the privileges afforded to others, according to how they are read and positioned accordingly. The expectation to produce a narrative of oneself might be a universal experience (Stanley, 2000; Steedman, 2000), but it is not received or experienced in a universal manner.

The young people, who are identified as 'Asian' and 'black', are also positioned as typical of the spaces in which they live or are perceived to primarily inhabit. Black and Asian residents, or those assumed to be residents of Moss Side and Longsight, are expected to account for both their appearance and the postcode location in which they are assumed to belong, both of which also have clear class

92 *Going against the grain*

and gendered associations that are mutually imbricated with race in place. The coupling of people to place is therefore experienced as problematic in multiple ways as the meanings ascribed to young people are entwined with these places. For example, Mina is positioned both as an 'Asian' *and* implicitly as an Asian working class woman-in-an-Asian-neighbourhood. In the first place, the significance of these different markers of identification functions as a means to match people to place according to how their physical appearance is interpreted. As Carina says:

> I do it myself, you categorise that area by the people that live there. So obviously with Rusholme it's predominantly Asian, Moss Side's predominantly black, here [Didsbury] it's predominantly white.

But, the consequences of this kind of matching are far greater than merely knowing that physical appearance works to reiterate place and vice versa. And, as I go on to explore, these identification processes intensify the emotional registers that are associated with being misrecognised and having to struggle against them.

Inner city neighbourhoods, or 'ghettoes of the mind' (Simpson, 2007), act as important sites of reference for critics of multiculturalism in the policy realm who link its failure to the 'non-British' practices of black people and the refusal of people who do not pass as white British to integrate. Policies of multiculturalism and community cohesion imply a demand that ethnic minorities reflect on the way in which they relate to different communities and choose allegiances to one group over another. Physical descriptions of self-segregation are employed as visual metaphors to represent a lack of assimilation to 'British' culture. These are important issues to consider because they not only shape discourses of place but also shape the physical and psychic boundaries of place and feed into the allocation of social resources. That they are so deeply embedded also means that they are important to bear in mind when reading how young people begin to give an account of themselves.

The following exchange took place shortly after Mina and I first met. We were standing in a queue together in a shop in Rusholme. In this introduction to herself, Mina uses elements of a shared history and a dominant narrative of the 'British-Asian-woman' that speaks to discourses and ideologies of race, class, gender and culture. In telling her story, she locates herself by drawing on a series of typical representations of Asian women in the UK. She does this even though, at the same time, she explains how she does not meet this representation.

Mina: I have to prepare for [my friend's] mehndi night. You know like what you lot would call a hen night. It's for the girls to get together and do our mehndi. Have you ever been to an Asian wedding?

Bethan: No, but I've been to a mehndi night.

M: For Asian weddings there's loads to organise. Are you married?

B: No.

Going against the grain 93

M:	No? Do you live with your parents?
B:	No.
M:	Who do you live with then?
B:	I live on my own.
M:	Really? Where are your family?
B:	All over.
M:	Are they not in Manchester?
B:	Some of my mum's family are.
M:	How long have you been in Manchester?
B:	About three years.
M:	Where are your parents?
B:	Mid-Wales.
M:	That's miles away, are you not lonely? Have you got brothers and sisters?
B:	Yeah, I've got two brothers. How about you?
M:	I've got a brother and two sisters. Where are your brothers?
B:	One's in London and one's in Prague.
M:	What's he doing there?
B:	He's lived there for years, that's where his family are.
M:	That's funny cos in Asian families the woman goes to live with the man. So did he go live with her?
B:	That's where they met [. . .]. Do you live with your family?
M:	No [laughs] actually I live on my own, just round the corner.
B:	Where are your sisters?
M:	I don't get on with them, well one of them I do, but not the eldest.
B:	Are you the youngest?
M:	Youngest daughter yeah.
B:	Is there a big gap?
M:	[Laughs] Asians don't have gaps, they just keep coming [laughs]. Every two years, there is another one. Well not me. I've only got her and I'm not having more now.

Throughout the beginning of our conversation, Mina marks our difference by contrasting our experiences, but, significantly, this is very much linked to common perceptions of what constitutes a British Asian women's identity, which so often stresses the role of family ties and marital status. Coupled with this expectation, the location in which the research took place and how this relates to the national also bears relevance. Here, after all, we are situated in neighbourhoods with strong identities that resonate beyond Manchester's city limits, and the young people's own subjectivities are caught up with these representations. As such, her narrative entails speaking to a series of tropes that are embedded in nationally and locally constituted narratives about 'Asians' and ideas about community that are articulated through gender, heteronormativity and class. For example, for Mina to be read as an Asian-woman-in-an-Asian-neighbourhood means that she must also account for herself against the pre-meditated understandings of what that means.

94 *Going against the grain*

This likely includes an expectation to account for herself against the notion of community and all of the baggage about integration and self-segregation that entails, as well as related discourses about marriage and family ties, and so on. Mina, who is constructed as culturally different, 'can display [her] difference, but only in such a way that it supplements *what is already assumed to be the coherence of culture itself* (Ahmed, 2000: 105, italics in original). This is amplified because of the way in which she is located in a geographically defined 'ethnic neighbour-hood', and especially an Asian neighbourhood that is typically articulated with collective community identities (Keith, 2004).

The young adults have to make, and anticipate making, persistent efforts to carve out their identities against these discursive backdrops in their everyday encounters. Indeed Mina, like many of the other young adults, must routinely confront these discourses even though she does not identify with a 'community' beyond her friendship group, nor does she have close family ties and has not had what might be described by others as a 'traditional' relationship. She is, in her own words, somewhat lonely, but this has little to do with her 'ethnic' identity. Her story points to the difficulty and the emotional intensities invoked in locating oneself without reproducing those very groupist ascriptions that she goes on to speak against, because they relentlessly shape her experiences and interactions. By directing our initial encounter around common tropes through which Asian women are seen (through marriage, attachment to her partner's family, etc.) she narrates herself as performing 'Asianness' in a way that reflects how she is often positioned. However, as Appiah notes, 'it does not follow from the fact that identification shapes action, shapes life plans, that the identification itself must be thought of as voluntary' (Appiah, 2000: 609). Assumed membership of a 'community' is always part of a much more complex multi-faceted identity that is not fixed in place, even whilst it is often assumed to be. What I hope to convey is the layers of frustration and emotional concentrations that can be involved when asked to produce a nar-rative of oneself.

White working class identities

One weekend when I was in Gorton I went along to the market. There was an event on celebrating 100 years since Gorton became part of Manchester or, as the locals joked, 100 years since Manchester became part of Gorton. Inside the market were a number of stalls and bands playing alternately. I got chatting to a couple of young men who were part of a drumming group that were playing intermittently outside the entrance to the market. We chatted for some time about music, the market, Gorton and life in general. They invited me to come down and meet the rest of their group at a rehearsal later in the week, and we swapped numbers in case I would get lost trying to find their rehearsal space. I went along later that week. The church they were meeting in was, as they had suggested, not so easy to find and was nestled between some dilapidated industrial warehouses. It was not an old church and was brick built. Like its surroundings it was not in prime condition. The paint on the walls was peeling away, the ceiling was heavily cracked and the grass outside was overgrown. I walked in that day to find a group of young people standing around chatting with drums scattered around them. Beyond was the nave separated by a thin glass wall partition through which I could see a group of teenage girls laughing and dancing around. I looked around but could not see the two men that had invited me along, and as I was thinking about whether to text them another man walked up to me and asked if I was looking for someone. I explained the situation and he told me they were always late for rehearsal, but I could wait. He then walked away and grabbed a large surdo and brought it over and began strapping it around my waist. With a cheeky and kindly face he told me that, 'No one *just* waits.' Before I knew it I was standing in a circle playing, or attempting to play along. When Paul and Andrew arrived half an hour later they spotted me there and laughed good naturedly. That night marked my first of many rehearsals with the group. I also joined them in gigs, sometimes playing at community festivals or with a dubstep sound system in Manchester clubs. The way in which I accidentally joined this band and was welcomed in to "the family", as some referred to us, was a perfect illustration of the group's overall dynamic of being open and unquestioning.

In the other room the group of teenage girls practiced to the booming sounds of Beyoncé and Rihanna. Often we found ourselves competing for levels of noise. Other times they would join us and work out routines to our music. They joined us too at community festivals and would put on routines for public display. They made themselves matching outfits for these occasions. Someone stitched together shiny red and green flared skirts, and the girls each put their own design on a white t-shirt with fabric pens. Shortly before I first arrived the group had gone along to a big drumming festival to play alongside numerous other bands from the Greater Manchester area. The young girls were looking forward to putting on their practiced routines, but before they could do so they were approached by the organisers and told they could not perform. Their outfits were not suitable. The other dancing groups had stylised outfits that looked professional. The look of the festival could not incorporate the creative and improvised look of the girls. It was after I had joined the group that one of the women, Flora, who had been helping the girls with their routines, told me this story. It had decimated their already wavering confidence and shattered their dreams of re-enacting X-Factor style fame on the fields of their own city. Flora told me she had been struggling to boost the girls' confidence. It seemed to her, and to me as we watched, that their head and shoulders were collapsing into their chests as they danced and their confidence retreated.

Previous research points to the stigmatisation of white bodies when they are located within areas of deprivation (Nayak, 2009; Rhodes, 2011). The construction of an 'underclass' white or 'chav' culture, for instance, is largely dependent on the matching of people to such spaces of deprivation. And, as such, the manner in which white working class areas like Gorton are stigmatised emerge in different ways to those labelled as 'ethnic' (Rhodes, 2011). The white young people resident in Gorton were typically positioned against an underclass, or chav culture, but, when white bodies were not located in these places, other signifiers of

96 *Going against the grain*

identification such as dress and speech were drawn upon to position them in such a way. Class did, however, become a central concern when young people read as white-working-class explained how they were interpreted in specified spaces. The 'single mother' and the 'scally' or the 'scruffy male' have been singled out as epitomising an underclass culture (Rhodes, 2011), and it is to precisely such examples that I now turn.

The term 'chav' has become a means to distinguish the rough from the respectable white working class (see for example Nayak, 2009; Skeggs, 2005; Nayak, 2006b; Jones, 2011), but it is mostly associated with young people in post-industrial cities (Nayak, 2006b). Reference to chavs in this study primarily emerged in descriptions of Gorton. Here I focus on the way that some of the young men described being positioned as 'chavs', because of their age, appearance and location, and how they attempt to shake off this identity. Both Steve, Ian and Damien, for example, were keen to disidentify with the chav label through an emphasis on respectability by attending to, or 'looking after', their appearance and dressing in 'respectable' and 'elegant' clothes, much like the means through which the women in Skeggs' study (1997) disidentified with a 'rough' identity.

Damien explains how, although he is mixed race, he is typically read as white and as "a chav". Here, he explains that he understands this through his age, but also details the lengths he goes to in order to be seen as respectable:

> When I'm walking about I want to, sometimes I just wear my suits because I want people to think that I'm not the average 20 year old and I'm more than just a chav, I'm more than just a 20 year old and whatever they think, so I try and wear a suit and I try and dress smartly so that they see past being young and stuff like that and also, when I'm talking to people like I say, "Have a good day" and stuff like that, so people see past the age and people don't see me as a chav or whatever . . . I want to be seen more than just an average teenager, I tell people that I'm trying to set up my own business, I tell people that I'm hard-working and I do try and make them see me as more than just a 20 year old and more than just a chav and stuff. . . . I don't dress like that to be noticed, I dress like that so when I'm on a bus and I do sit next to an old lady they don't, "Oh crap I'm being marked, he's got the seat". I want to be seen as a respectable person. Yeah come and sit next to me any day type if you get me.

In a similar way, Steve explains how he has grown a beard in order to look more 'mature', and Ian describes muting his accent and dressing more smartly. The process of disidentifying thus suggests the need for access to money, education and the ability to talk right. It is not a simple process, and there is always the risk of being found out. Damien, for example, explains how he was asked if he was "stoned" in a shop whilst wearing his suit, "because of the way I speak". Having access to money and a suit is therefore not always sufficient to allow him to pass as 'respectable'. And whilst there are greater opportunities for ambiguity here, which allows them to construct more multi-faceted identities from the outset, these

Going against the grain 97

encounters are nevertheless experienced as embarrassing and are incredibly frustrating to deal with.

Caroline is 29, but she explains she is usually read as a woman in her early twenties. She has three children. She describes herself as middle class, but talks about how she is conscious of being read as "another young mum" when in white middle class spaces. She used to attend a mother and toddler group in a white middle class area close to where she lives. However, she explains how she has stopped going because she was conscious of the way she was identified in contrast to the other white middle class mothers in attendance:

Caroline: I think because I had my kids quite young, it just feels a bit different going in to Chorlton 'cos some of the mothers are like, a bit older, which is fine, I just didn't feel as welcome there or maybe like . . . there was some preconceptions of the type of mother I was because I was a young mother sort of thing and I didn't feel well . . . it didn't seem as friendly or as welcoming when I went. It might have been just the ones I went to but, erm . . . yeah I didn't feel as like anyone can be there whereas the ones I go to in Fallowfield . . . there's more of a mix in Fallowfield so it just feels a bit more . . .

Bethan: In terms of ages you mean mixed?

Caroline: In terms of ages, in terms of racial mix, in terms of like . . . all sorts of ways really, different backgrounds.

Bethan: So how do you feel they typed you as a young mum?

Caroline: [Laughs] probably just like a bit chaotic, a bit, like I had . . . this is probably totally unfair, but I just felt that sometimes people would look at you and be like, oh there's another young mum and all the kids have got different dads and you know . . . kind of . . . and no one wanted to chat to me cos they had their own friends or whatever already and you know I'm probably like that at groups . . . not on purpose, but I'm sure I could be perceived as that by other people, it's just not very nice being at the receiving end of it . . . I think sometimes people just see you with the buggy and three kids and you look really young and I don't know, they're like, oh you've got a handful, or you've got this you know, and you just, I don't know, you just feel like they're making judgements about you that, I don't know, it's like your life choice isn't it? We wanted to have a family and to have them close together so they got on, I don't know, it's weird. So yes I guess that's the thing I'm most sensitive about.

Place is central to the way in which Caroline is positioned. The way she is positioned shifts in different spaces, but it is also dependent on whether her children accompany her. Without her children she can pass unnoticed in white middle class areas. But, of particular interest here is the way she goes on to explain that she can also evade the stereotyped positioning of the 'young mum' when she occupies, what she describes as, "mixed" spaces. Mix for Caroline is not a class

98 *Going against the grain*

mix, but rather is found in neighbourhoods that are ethnically diverse – people of "different backgrounds", as she says. As such, we are reminded of the way in which 'ethnic' or 'migrant' neighbourhoods are associated with deprivation and other class indicators, but are nevertheless read primarily through the way they are racialised. For Caroline, who is white, this then means that 'mixed' spaces offer her an ambiguous location in which she can take up a more privileged position, because she is no longer over-determined by class and by her status as a 'young mum'.

What I want to convey here then is not that the way in which white working-class identities are not important and are not problematic – indeed in the current climate there is somewhat a need to adopt a broader critical lens to counter some of the simplified correlations between racism and working classness (see, for example, Haylett, 2001; Lawler, 2005). The point I want to stress here is that white identifications have a more malleable texture because whiteness is not conceived as a collective identity held accountable for its mode of inclusion, nor is whiteness always over-determined by class. And, as such, the terms of how we might understand how class affects how people are positioned is quite different to the way in which race works. Each social category has a different ontological basis (Yuval-Davis, 2006). The white working class young people are positioned in relation to economic and cultural processes, whilst for the black young people who are also working class they are additionally positioned in relation to racist structures and groupist discourses for which they are expected to be accountable. In short, a white working class identity is not visibly marked or marked as a coherent 'community' in the way that 'ethnic communities' are, and the young people can therefore escape being interpellated in such a way. The lack of association with a fixed group offers a more malleable identification and permits the possibilities of ambiguity when people are positioned as white. Black and Asian respondents explained how they were naturally associated with inner-city areas of deprivation because the possibility of being read as being from a middle-class neighbourhood eluded them. In contrast, white respondents were only read as such outside of these areas if they dressed, spoke or behaved in a certain way. It is because of this potential ambiguity, along with other privileges afforded white bodies, that class positionings do not typically emerge as starting points for the young people in their conversations in the way that ethnicity did. Put simply, there is less at stake here because white people are not expected to account for structures that fall outside their immediate experience when creating an account of themselves. That said, the feeling of humiliation experienced in these encounters and the frustration of being read and understood only in very limited ways is shared.

Being 'different' and undermining identities of difference

> "It is a peculiar sensation, this double-consciousness, this sense of always looking at one's self through the eyes of others, of measuring one's soul by the tape of a world that looks on in amused contempt and pity. One ever feels this two-ness

Going against the grain 99

– an American, a Negro; two souls, two thoughts, two unreconciled strivings; two warring ideals in one dark body, whose dogged strength alone keeps from being torn asunder."

(Du Bois, 1996 [1903]: 5)

The above starting points in our conversations are produced in such a way partly because they are encounters between strangers 'composed of a mixture of both the familiar (rather than natural) and unfamiliar (especially to the respondent)', and, as a consequence, 'shared social meanings (whether we agree with them or not) are drawn on by interviewer and interviewee alike to produce an imagined familiarity in an unfamiliar context' (Harries, 2016: 53). However, they are only starting points. In speaking to the identity of 'an Asian' or 'a black person' by way of introduction does not mean that the young people cannot and do not make sense of themselves in other ways. Indeed, the extract from the interview with Mina above did not show her straightforwardly narrating herself. She was mixing her talk with humour whilst leading our conversation from one trope to another. Indeed, when she joked about keeping babies coming every two years, she was being facetious in a manner akin to the young men in Claire Alexander's study (1996) as they talk about what it means to *be* black. The differences that the young people mark are intended to make sense in the context in which we are talking and one through which they are probably commonly positioned by white middle class people. However, it would be wrong to assume that by speaking directly to a series of stereotypes the young people are not demonstrating power to direct their own subjectivities. Therefore, important as these starting points are it is nevertheless equally, if not more, important to reiterate that identities do not end (or even really begin) here. These starting points in the young people's narratives only tell us about some of the social forces at work. They do not tell us how identities are lived, negotiated or resisted, but only alert us to part of the context in which that is done.

What I want to do in this section is to explore more closely how the young people challenged and manipulated certain forms of identification to undermine identities of difference. Questions about British identity – perhaps better characterised as being about English identity (Harries, 2015) – rooted in Britain's melancholy for empire (Gilroy, 2004) found vehement expression from the 1990s onwards. Norman Tebbit, the Conservative MP for Epping and Chingford, kicked off the decade by questioning the allegiance of south Asians and Caribbeans resident in the UK to Britain when they were supporting 'home' cricket teams rather than England. But the cricket test, which it came to be known as, was only the thin end of the wedge. An almost compulsive fascination with Britishness and British values has ignited calls for a national celebration of St George's Day and fuelled political debate, newspaper columns and TV slots with relentless questions about what is Britishness (if Britain is multicultural). There have also been increasing mainstream cultural outputs that glorify a sense of British purity and wholesomeness (jus soli!). For example, we have witnessed an increasing number of documentaries on heritage and nature ('Countryfile', 'Coast', 'The Nature of Britain',

100 *Going against the grain*

'Heritage! The Battle for Britain's Past' and so on), whilst the number of critical political documentaries appears somewhat lacking (Valluvan, 2017; Harries, 2015). These cultural outputs have intensified in the context of the urban unrests in northern mill towns in the early 2000s, 9/11, 7/7, the migrant crisis, devolution and Brexit; all events that have been hijacked by a broader spectrum of political bodies than is often acknowledged. Liberals, conservatives along with the 'far right' have all drawn on these events to provoke concerns about numbers of migrants from Asia, the global south and Eastern Europe and articulated these concerns as if they are logical responses to economic crises, war and terror. And so, whilst the question of British identity has been, and still is, typically framed as a cultural question, rather than one of political citizenship, it nevertheless confirms the way in which British national identity is broadly conceived of as white but is also inscribed by a 'value' laden ideology that implies that a sense of moral (middle class) worth is fundamental to being properly British.

Since many of these debates have been set within the paradigm of integration, 'who really belongs/deserves to belong?' I would suggest that a somewhat unfortunate response has been to tackle questions of British/English identity on their exclusionary nature by attempting to define alternative 'integrated' identities. For example, in the 1990s and 2000s there were considerable attempts to challenge the fixedness of popular notions of Britishness by emphasising *mixed* cultural identities, *mixed* neighbourhoods and *mixed* experience. The power of these discourses was illustrated in Chapter 3 when the young people drew on them to assert a progressive liberal city and generational identity. To a degree, many of these approaches were initially concerned with the language of exclusion that the *categories* of ethnicity and nationality inferred, i.e. the sorts of categories that are used to classify the population. Thus, they emerged within a context of reimagining some sort of 'British' label that could incorporate marginalised identities. Michael Banton, for example, advocated for the possibility of identifying with more than one ethnic group. He suggested that an individual could be ascribed both a primary ethnicity that would denote the ethnic origin identified with at the state level and a secondary ethnicity at the sub-state level (Banton, 2008). However, this did not address the meanings that these categories inferred and risked subordinating one ethnic, or national identity to another. Following a similar binary structure, Modood et al. (1994) suggested the introduction of hyphenated or 'bi-cultural' identities. However, this would allow for different nationalities and faiths to be subsumed under one label, e.g. 'Asian' and would denote an inferior and superior identity in the case of British Asian (Brah, 1996; Solomos and Back, 1996). Since then there have also been calls for a new model of classification that allows people to demonstrate 'allegiances' to multiple groups (Aspinall, 2009) to get away from a binary identity. But, paradoxically, these kinds of attempts at promoting inclusion and disturbing fixedness reinscribed a black/white paradigm, or non-white/white in the case of Aspinall's suggestion, and fail to recognise the meanings that the labels inferred and how identities are in fact far more multiply inflected. So, although intended as part of a struggle against racist nationalism, hyphenated identifications or mixed identities did not

Going against the grain 101

adequately address issues of racial justice, but instead risked reinforcing national identification because they were always hyphenated to 'British'. Furthermore, although they were framed as responses to questions about belonging, they effectively asked ethnic minorities to choose their adherence to certain identifications and in doing so, they emulated the state's demand to choose between assimilation and marginalisation (Kalra et al., 2005).

In everyday life people do not have a strong sense of where black-white boundaries lie and are resistant to the idea of choosing a singular position (Tizard and Phoenix, 1993; Ali, 2003). Understanding blackness and whiteness, for example, as discrete categories that can be hyphenated, or mixed, masks their malleable nature and ignores the multi- faceted positionings that individuals occupy (Ali, 2003; Ifekwunigwe, 1999). Consequently, overly simplistic notions of identity, even when they are conceived as *mixed*, also entail 'ascribing symbolic and frequently oppositional meanings to perceived or real (i.e. physical) difference' (Ifekwunigwe, 1999: 188). There has often, therefore, only been 'a *presumption* that intellectual focus has shifted from homogeneous grafting of races to a heterogeneous fusion of cultures' (Ifekwunigwe, 1999: 9, my emphasis). Primarily, this is because notions of 'cultural' mixedness can often be 'founded on the metaphor of purity' (Friedman, 1997: 82), because they assume a mix of *things* that are themselves essentialised (Young, 1995). Although, it is important to note that these critiques can only really apply to readings of crude understandings of mixedness, which do indeed pervade popular misreadings of multiculturalism. They do not apply well, however, to more complex ways of seeing hybridity or cultural syncretism often brought to life through ethnographic encounters, as I will go on to discuss. It is worth reiterating here nonetheless that additive versions of mixing (the unlived multiculture, if you like) that we continue to hear so much about do little to erode the hegemonic status of race and its relation to nation (Solomos and Back, 1996).

More recently we have witnessed a turn to the concept of diversity to challenge static understandings of both national and local identities and the urban landscapes in which they are produced. It is suggested that by capturing the increased ethnic, national, linguistic and status differences that make up the populations of European cities we can disrupt otherwise homogeneous understandings of 'communities' or city neighbourhoods (see, for example, Sandercock, 2000; Keith, 2005; Vertovec, 2007; Berg and Sigona, 2013; Gidley, 2013). However, because the concept is often applied to bounded places it can fail to capture the ways lives are lived across local and national borders. The knowledge that a place is diverse therefore does little to shift embedded conceptions of place, or give us a sense of how the local, national and global collide to produce these places. To illustrate this one need only think about how, to say, Manchester is diverse has a different resonance than saying Longsight or Moss Side is diverse (see Chapter 2 for a fuller description of these locations). Instead, much (not all) of the work on diversity tends to hone in on the local. In some instances academics collaborate with policy-makers and journalists to identify the most diverse areas of Britain – a self-defeating exercise when the definition of diversity needs to retain a sense of fluidity in order to avoid

102 *Going against the grain*

an ontological flatness. Nevertheless, areas that are identified in such a way can then become the focus for political concerns about integration and migration, distracting us from the lived experience of diversity and over-emphasising certain characteristics (such as race and class) over others (Knowles, 2013).

Whilst the correlation between the notions of mixed identities and the work on diversity might not be immediately obvious, they are both important to this discussion because they have both shaped the spaces the young people occupy and how they go on to manipulate forms of identification. In the rest of this section I explore how the expressions of the young people towards processes of racialisation and identification illustrate the weaknesses of focusing on any kind of mixedness. In doing so, I therefore heed the caution raised in Valluvan's (2016) work on conviviality in which he importantly guards against exploring the politics of recognition through the expression of multiple identities when it risks underpinning the logic of minority inclusion. As he notes, it is in taking such an approach that the emphasis can fall all too readily on the need for accommodation of identities of difference 'vis-à-vis the white majority'. Indeed, a similar concern was highlighted in Chapter 4 through the way in which mixed relationships (just as identities here) can be claimed as if the property of integrationists as a solution to difference. Hence, whilst this chapter has started from the ways in which the young people are misrecognised through these very logics, the focus remains on the ways such identities are manipulated and resisted, rather than accommodated.

I have divided the following discussion into three sections though the intention is not to present some kind of typology on how identities can be negotiated. The three sections merely offer different themes that emerged in the research, but there is of course overlap in the ways these work.

De-categorising identities

One of the key concerns that many of the young people expressed was about how their lives may be reduced to a series of limited racialised or ethnic social categories. These concerns were strongly articulated in response to the equality monitoring form used in the research and the role of categories therein. In Chapter 6 I will return to think about how the usage of such forms is understood in relation to race equality and institutional racism. Here I want to focus on how categories of identity are understood by the young people as a site through which to mark their resistance to the ways race is reproduced and to the ways in which they are positioned more broadly. In this discussion I reflect on the challenges faced by the young people who must make claims to and demand recognition for, a multi-faceted identity, as opposed to a normatively prescribed one that is steeped in crude stereotypes. This includes some reflections on the use of categories of identity and specifically the ethnic categories found on equality monitoring forms that the young people are regularly and increasingly exposed to when applying for jobs, courses or signing up to health, leisure and other public services.

When reflecting on the categories of ethnicity, Tony, like other black and Asian respondents, explains how he must continuously work against the notion of the

Going against the grain 103

'typical' black young man in Longsight, even within his friendship groups. He says he is "*always*" asked to answer to his blackness and the way this is articulated with the inner city, when he is asked where he is from. He explains how he has been told that he could not be both black *and* English. The denied access to Englishness is reiterated in his view on football when he explains how he thinks Rio Ferdinand will never be permanently made captain of the England team, because he is black (this conversation took place shortly before Rio Ferdinand's exclusion from the Euro 2012 squad). He says his white friends expect him to support the West Indies at cricket because his parents are Jamaican, even though he does not describe himself as Jamaican. Tony thus draws attention to the way in which ethnicity and nation are articulated together. He is required to answer both to his blackness and to explain his 'origins'. Born in England and yet denied access to Englishness, he describes how white people expect him to perform in "a black way".

Tony's story also highlights the way in which geographies of race work to reinforce this overly simplistic way of understanding identity. Living in Longsight, part of the expectation is that he is also involved in criminal and gang activity and is, to quote Tony, "a failure" at education and work. As he explains, his neighbourhood is always invoked as "ethnic" and working class, and he is always assumed to be from there or "somewhere similar", because he is black. The meanings and values ascribed to his blackness shift according to the spaces he occupies, as well as when and how he occupies them. Tony thus draws attention to the way in which he, as a black 20-something living in Longsight, makes it difficult to claim recognition in any other way. But more than that, he goes on to explain how this crude way of being read extends to an understanding that he is "just like" anyone of a similar skin colour:

> I was walking with my brother and some woman said, "Oh I've got a mixed race son just like you", excuse me. . . . "A mixed race grandson just like you" and my brother was like, "I'm not mixed race", but he was stood under a light so his skin was slightly lighter, so she thought he was mixed race. I don't know, it just gets a bit complicated for me.

Tony is exasperated with the way that he is crudely positioned. He talks about how, despite having a respected job, dressing smartly and interacting with 'high profile' people, he is still interpreted as black and from a rough area:

> I've been to Westminster for instance and met really high police officers and stuff like that. I might change the way I dress, but from what most people go off if it was myself, "Oh you're black", Oh you're from a rough area", they're still gonna see that I'm black.

Here we can see how 'complete ontological complicity' cannot always be obtained in white dominant spaces by those who are racialised, even when people otherwise conform to normative codes and behaviours (Puwar, 2004: 129). Particularly problematic for Tony is the way in which he is simultaneously positioned as black and

104 *Going against the grain*

working class, reflecting their mutual significance; 'race is as important in class formation structuration, as class is in race structuration' (Anthias and Yuval-Davis, 1992: 71). Rollock et al. (2011) have suggested that black people who transition from working class to middle class are able to make use of the assets they have accrued in their encounters with white middle class spaces in order to better navigate the 'WhiteWorld'. Tony is only just beginning to access such spaces through his work and, like the other respondents, would not describe himself as middle class. Nevertheless, the expansion of the kinds of spaces that are accessed by the young adults, in particular through work and further and higher education, does make them aware of how they are racialised and positioned in these multiple spaces in different ways. This knowledge will become salient in the discussion below in relation to the way the young people use this awareness to navigate their way across different parts of the city and play off their different identities.

Tony responds to these kinds of experiences and crude processes of racialisation by rejecting forms of categorisation. Put simply his response is a set of refusals. For example, he explains how he refuses to describe himself as British or designate himself an ethnic label when he is confronted with Census and equality monitoring forms, most typically when applying for jobs. He understands the term ethnic and the ensuing categories as a means of pathologising groups, but struggles to find the words to explain this in relation to race and racism. The following quote suggests that he sees this as a problem affecting a growing number of people as the focus of stigmatisation shifts from one group to another according to patterns of migration, which creates what he calls 'confusion':

Tony: Ethnic [pointing at the form] kind of bothers me a little bit, um . . .
Bethan: You mean the word ethnic?
Tony: Yeah, what is it? [laughs] That's what I'm saying, what is it? It seems to be like, first it was black people, then Asians got involved, now the Polish are involved, now this is involved and I'm thinking, it kind of give me the idea that you're nothing, if I'm going to be nothing then I'm not gonna answer any of these questions and I don't know what I want to be, do you know what I mean, why make it confusing, I'm just me innit.

The challenges involved in talking about racism become the focus of Chapter 6. Here it is worth noting that what emerges from this discussion is that Tony says he is expected to "*be*" black and to "*be*" Jamaican, but does not want to identify with these labels because they have no meaning for him. At the same time, he explains how he is denied access to a British label, leaving him with "nothing". We should interpret these statements with caution. Tony is frustrated. He is angry that he has to struggle to be recognised in a multi-faceted way with which he identifies. It is the labels he cites that have lost any practicable meaning for him, rather than a disavowal of more complex identities that incorporate blackness or Britishness and so on. In his response Tony constructs himself as unique, category-less even, but not because he does not understand how his blackness and Britishness shapes his life or how he identifies with other black and British people, but rather because he does not fit and yet often cannot evade what he calls a

Going against the grain 105

'typical' representation of a black man in Longsight. In other words, whilst Tony does not choose to be identified as black in the way it is signified in this context, being black and knowing how he is read does nevertheless shape his actions and interactions (Du Bois, 1996 [1903]). Again we are reminded of the importance of understanding these narratives and these modes of resistance within the context in which they are produced.

Tony was certainly not alone in his feelings about ethnic categories. It is telling that when I brought out the equality monitoring form at the end of the interview with the intention of discussing these very issues, the immediate reaction of many of the young people was disappointment and irritation. The disappointment they had in me was palpable. I had got to know some of these people over fairly long periods, we had shared personal stories, and, whilst I would not go as far as to say we had become friends, we had developed certain expectations from the relationship. The form was not one of these expectations. For many of the young people the appearance of the form was experienced as a betrayal. I had not anticipated this. This part of the interview was intended for thinking more deeply about how the young people perceive they are represented by others and to identify problems associated with using these markers of identification as analytic categories.

The process of categorisation featured in the equality monitoring form and replicated on Census forms etc. thus became a key site in which the young people expressed their frustration with the way in which they are positioned. For many, the individual categories are not only meaningless, but are also representative of a broader system of oppression that does not recognise them in multiply-inflected ways. Many describe the way in which they resist these categories and their symbolic meaning by corrupting the forms by ticking all the categories, scratching them all out, ignoring them completely or by writing 'HUMAN' in capital letters across the form and over the text. Again we see the suggestion that difference does not/should not matter – a common narrative for this group of young adults (see Chapter 3). It also illustrates the adherence to a collective identity of youth, rather than other kinds of shared experience when the young people explain away these categories as belonging to another time. This emerges too when Tony disregards the relevance of labels to his peer group when he describes the diversity of his friends:

> I've got a set of white friends and I've got a set of black friends, or mixed race or whatever, but to us it's not a thing if that makes sense, but to other people, a lot of people have said, hang on a minute.

In terms of the quality of their relationship the salience of these labels is almost certainly irrelevant. Nevertheless these kinds of intrusions on their friendships mean that difference has significance in that it must be accounted for, dealt with or explained. More broadly, it also points to the way categories map onto people's bodies and are experienced as relational and mutually constitutive (Nayak, 2006a). Tony explains his own response to this through his feelings towards "labels" and categories rather than by addressing the intrusion itself, and instead he attempts to carve out an alternative label – one that is more neutral and cannot be categorised. He, like many of the other black and Asian young people, insists

106 *Going against the grain*

that he is category-less. He argues that he is "*just* Tony" as others argue that they are "just HUMAN". That is not to say that when Tony says he is "*just*" Tony, he is asserting an individualistic sense of self, but rather that he is trying to rid himself of a well-worn trope that is stuck to him in the context of a neoliberal discursive shift away from collective mobilisation. It is possible to think of a 'group' in different and contradictory ways, both as imagined and always changing and one that is located within a political struggle. However, the reluctance to engage in any other way with these labels and to disengage from them entirely perhaps speaks to the shift in discourse in Britain in which the label 'black' has been reduced to recognising racialised groups, rather than related to a political, historical or cultural category (Alexander, 2002). Alongside this, the persistent use of group-oriented approaches also illustrates how society continues to *believe* in race and ethnicity as a means of explaining behaviour. This is often visible in policy-oriented research that seeks to *explain* events and practices as a product of an ethnically defined group, rather than understanding them as mutually constitutive of each other. Ethnic categories are after all deeply embedded in the social and are taken for granted and the language used to talk about identity is itself steeped in labels and categories that are linked to all sorts of culturalist stereotypes. Tony is well aware of this.

Before moving on to consider other ways young people manipulate and resist categorisation, it is worth briefly reflecting on the difference in the way the white young adults responded to these forms of categorisation. One of the reasons I had decided to introduce the form was to encourage white respondents who talk in coded references about race, class and gender, to confront these, where necessary by using the categories on the form to externalise their expressions. The first thing to note is that when I got out a copy of the form with the white interviewees nearly all immediately reached for it and began ticking the box marked white British without being asked to do so and without questioning its application. Not all did this. Indeed, Tony's childhood friend Ian was perhaps the most visibly angered by the form, knowing how frustrating the categories are for his friend. However, most of the white young people said they were "not fussed", or "don't mind" filling in equality monitoring forms and did so without being prompted, by reaching out to take the form, looking for a pen and beginning to fill it in. When prompted to reflect on this process, they remarked on how easy it is for them to fit themselves into a category. In doing so, they explained it made them feel "boring" and "normal", because they are in "the majority one" – answers that by themselves point towards the embedded nature of race and difference making. This simple contrast in the way people use and respond to these kinds of forms is indicative of the ubiquitous nature of whiteness as a privileged marker of identification. Put simply, whiteness itself is often imagined as if 'neutral', because it is rarely problematised or challenged but embodied in the normative as if it is neutral (hooks, 1992) This is well covered in the literature on whiteness (see, for example, Byrne, 2006; Bonnett, 2000; Frankenberg, 1993). When asked questions specifically about the use of each of the categories, the difficulties respondents identified were directed solely at those categories listed as 'non-white'. And, whilst this indicates a certain willingness to engage with some of the problems and complexities entailed in the application of categories when prompted to, it also indicates the way in which whiteness is not seen as an ethnicity and the failure to understand processes of racialisation in relation to whiteness.

Reworking the label: claiming a multi-faceted identity

Within the research process, power is often understood to be held by the researcher, and yet research participants, just as in other encounters, direct power in a number of ways to subvert the researcher's intrusions, by protecting certain parts of their lives from scrutiny, by questioning the role and motives of the researcher and by withholding information (Gunaratnam, 2003: 89). The young people positioned me and made judgements about me as much as I did them, and our understandings of each other were continually made and remade throughout our interactions. The young people were also well aware of how they are read and often pre-empted how I might make assumptions about them during our initial conversations, or from the photo diaries I received before meeting them at any length. For example, I wrongly assumed that Laurence was Somali because he is black and wears a skull-cap, when actually he describes himself as the son of Jamaican Rastafarian parents and had recently converted to Islam. He pre-empted this and told me a lot of people get him wrong. I also wrongly interpreted Nasreens's photo as of her praying, because I knew she is Muslim. She is actually doing pilates. And, when Nasreen and I met to talk through these photos she pre-empted my assumption by laughing and asking directly: 'It looks like I'm praying doesn't it?'

Figure 5.1

108　*Going against the grain*

What I want to emphasise here then is that whilst the young people often speak to the set of prescribed identities that they are associated with, they are nonetheless very aware of how they and others are positioned and what this means. As Alexander (1996) notes, it is not a case, as suggested elsewhere (see, for example, Waters, 1990), that black people cannot manipulate symbolic forms of representation and resist prescribed identities. Indeed, there has been a great deal of recent work that illustrates this through research of lived practice (see, for example, James, 2015; Bramwell, 2015; Kim, 2014). Studying the lived experience of race can help avoid the kind of 'meta-theoretical reification' that Back (1996) cautions against, by attending to the way race intersects with other transforming social processes and is 'done' in different spaces.

The examples above demonstrate the way in which the young people are expected to locate themselves in response to how they are positioned as 'Asian' and 'black' and are associated with particular spaces. This section extends this discussion to argue that any other identification must subsequently be claimed. These claims are interpreted here as demands to be read in a multi-faceted, non-homogeneous way, rather than claims to some form of mixed identity made up of separate axes of identification. Claiming an identity beyond the way in which one is positioned is complicated, since it requires challenging the 'regime of truth' and risks questioning how one's 'being' and 'ontological status, is allocated' (Butler, 2005: 22–23). It is nevertheless important to make such claims because they speak to how one constructs a sense of self and can be an expression of rights to citizenship, rights which are often otherwise precluded at the local and national level, but also the global if we consider the way border controls are enforced to target ethnic and religious minorities, irrespective of nationality.

This section makes use of Nasreen's story to demonstrate how, whilst aspects of her identity as an 'Asian-Muslim-woman', are often interpellated in crude ways that make little sense to her, Nasreen *does* make use of these labels. She is not making a claim for them, but rather she is reworking them to make a claim against the rudimentary and essentialised representations of what being an Asian-Muslim-woman means in the spaces she occupies. In doing so, her experience demonstrates how she must actively rework these categories and claim other identifications, like Britishness, because they are never otherwise assumed. Nasreen explains how she is assumed to be from Longsight, which positions her as working class and in an area strongly associated with Asianness:

> If I speak to white people, they might assume, "Oh yeah, she's Longsight, a lot of Asians there".

Nasreen grew up in Chorlton, a middle class white neighbourhood, but this identity is denied to her. Nasreen's association with Longsight is more than certainly exacerbated because she wears a hijab. Her scarf compliments the image of the 'traditional' Asian woman living in the 'traditional' Asian neighbourhood (Dwyer, 1999). In this way, Nasreen represents the 'quintessential Other' (Brah, 1996: 135). To resist this identification, she relies on a representation that exemplifies not only

Going against the grain 109

her everyday life as a woman constructed as 'Asian' in Manchester, but also as a Muslim and as British. She uses her photo diary to construct a narrative by including people, practices and objects to illustrate this multi-faceted identity. For example, Nasreen emphasises the importance of her faith as a central component to her life by including photographs of herself teaching children how to read the Qu'ran and working as a volunteer for a Muslim charity. The following photographs and text show her husband at home doing things they "normally" do:

Figure 5.2

Figure 5.3

110   *Going against the grain*

Nasreen: That's another thing that we normally play especially when the family comes together. Just simple, football on the PlayStation 3 and the Scrabble and that's enough to get the whole family together. And the shisha as well, that's a big part of it. . . .

Bethan: And the Irn Bru next to it. . . .

Nasreen: [Laughs] my husband calls Irn Bru water. He's from Glasgow so . . . Irn Bru is a very Scottish drink so it's like the Irn Bru . . . he was very like yes, make sure you get the Irn Bru in [the photo] kind of thing [laughs] like we *have* to have Irn Bru in the house, it's just one of those things.

Bethan: That's his main staple is it?

Nasreen: It is yeah, he's very Scottish and proud my husband.

Nasreen uses the photographs to draw attention to the everyday things that might be considered typical of a British family, such as the Scrabble and PlayStation. She is also keen to draw attention to the "pride" of her husband in being Scottish through the purposeful inclusion of the Irn Bru bottle. These objects are not only 'things', but are carriers of meaning which resonate with 'broader public narratives and symbolic systems' (Lawler, 2002: 252–253). They work because both she and I inhabit the same cultural space where these meanings are produced.

In other parts of the interview, Nasreen talks about the way she met her husband through friends, in what she describes as a "non-traditional" manner. She explains that they are "non-traditional" because theirs is a "mixed' marriage" – she is Bangladeshi, he is Pakistani. This reflects how she understands her marriage to be mixed, which might often go unnoticed on the streets of Manchester, which tends instead to prioritise mixedness as white+other. These formulations thus also rely on our shared knowledge of how Asianness is typically constructed within a UK context, as some 'thing' that is static. Nasreen talks against these representations as a means to both disrupt stereotypes and to carve out her own position. By emphasising a multi-faceted identity through her "non-traditional" or non-essentialised Asianness and her Britishness, Nasreen is also acting to legitimate her account. Like Tony, who explained how he was told he could not be both black and British, Nasreen also explains how she is never assumed to be British. Her 'origins' or her 'background' are always under suspicion, but she nevertheless rightly demands to be recognised as British not least, as she emphatically states, "Cos I've got a British passport".

"I am not who I am supposed to be"

In this section I explore the ways in which the young adults 'play' with their potential for misrecognition as part of their own everyday practice. To an extent, the way the young adults play with their identities reflects the way in which many of them refused to categorise themselves using a form. However, here, a deeper expression of refusal is apparent when this practice is embedded in their day-to-day interactions. Unlike in Song's (2003) work on ethnic identity, I am concerned not with

Going against the grain 111

how ethnic minorities *choose* identities, or indeed are constrained from choosing, but rather in how the young people work with their multiple subjectivities, their understandings of misrecognition and the broader contexts in which they are situated to resist being read in particular ways and at particular moments. Identity is produced through struggles over its multiple and conflicting forms, meanings and possibilities, and I hope to illustrate how the process of negotiating identities is complex and is constituted in and by the transforming social contexts in which they are at play. The rapidly changing demographics of our city neighbourhoods are salient. Increased diversity opens up a range of subject positions and complicates the way blackness is understood. Hence, when Laurence is misidentified as Somali, as noted above, this points to the increased recognition of multiple forms of blackness, and, although these different forms are susceptible to similar forms of characterisation, they are signified in different ways and have different meanings. I want to suggest here that the young people are able to play with the possibilities of different forms of blackness and Asianness, and, although this is not without problems, in doing so they can manipulate and undermine processes of racialisation and racialised identities.

Research on the lived experience of race focuses on and draws out the complicated and fluid interactions and negotiations that make up everyday life. In doing so, this body of research has directly and indirectly challenged static notions of identity which have dominated more popular understandings of racialised everydayness that remain oriented around dichotomous questions of segregation/mixing, in-group/out-group, belonging/not belonging and so on. Instead, research on lived identities, presents us with more nuanced understandings of identity and social relations and the interactions between them to consider how all forms of culture are related to each other (Rutherford, 1990). What emerges through these enquiries is an understanding of race as something that is 'unruly' (Gilroy, 2004). Thinking about race from such a position makes a good deal of sense since the meanings of race are always shifting and the ways in which they are negotiated, as a consequence, are complicated and messy. Of particular salience here is the way in which thinking through such a lens also gives us space to consider how rules and norms are resisted, corrupted, negotiated and renegotiated through this messiness.

The young people were conscious of the ways they are positioned in different places and in different moments. What I want to illustrate here is how they use their knowledge of how they are read to "play" with these identifications. Of particular interest is the way in which the young people play with the way in which they are read in different parts of the city and when they adapt the way they dress, speak and so on. Identities are mediated according to where and when they are interpreted (Hylton and Law, 2009), and practices of representation are inextricably linked to spatialisation (Massey, 2005), but place also affects the way we *do* race. Hence, whilst broad generalisations are made about specific places the young people can negotiate their encounters in these multiple spaces in different ways. One common means of doing this, which has been touched on briefly above, is the way in which the young people can change the way they act,

112   *Going against the grain*

dress and speak according to how they want to work with different elements of their identity.

Nadia is never who she is supposed to be. She grew up and now works in Moss Side, she was born in Tanzania to parents from Burundi, she tells people she is East African, or from Moss Side or both. She is multilingual, a Christian, well-educated and a big fan of basketball. However, this spectrum of skills and global resources are nevertheless reduced to a few simple gestures in her everyday encounters. She starts by explaining how she is typically assumed to be "Caribbean". She drives a Mercedes, which, she says, reinforces assumptions about her blackness when in Moss Side, not least because of the moral panic that forms an association between black people, or more specifically "Caribbean people", Mercedes cars and drug selling (Swanton, 2008):

> They don't expect me to work and it's weird, because when you're in Moss Side, like for instance, I drive a Mercedes and people think, "OK what do you do?" And cos you're in that environment, cos you're from Moss Side, people think you're selling drugs so . . . you go "Well I work" and they just go kind of like "Oh, OK" . . . people from outside probably think, "Oh well she's from Moss Side, she probably sells drugs, or she has sold drugs" [laughs] and I don't know what else.

When she corrects people and tells them that she was born in East Africa, that assumption changes to a different, but equally crude, meaning entirely:

Nadia: You know the weird thing is, even being black kind of that happens, because [laughs] this is thing about us black people, we kind of like think . . . I think this kind of like what I've learnt, there's kind of like Caribbean and African, anyone who's well-presented and well-dressed, they're Caribbean and anyone who's wearing traditional clothing they're African. If you're not wearing traditional clothes then they kind of like get confused, they're like, "Are you African?" "You don't look African". So many times I've heard that, "You don't look African". How am I supposed to look? [Laughs] How am I supposed to look? What am I supposed to have? Am I supposed to be walking with trees stuck in my hair! [Laughs] cos that's the only way . . . but that happens quite a lot.
Bethan: So do people assume you're Caribbean?
Nadia: Yeah, straight away. And first I think when I was 15 when I came back from Africa, it was like you walk down Moss Side and someone would shout, "African girl" like that, just . . . which there's no need really. It's just like, I'm just a female, you don't need to shout African girl, but . . . [trails off].

The way in which Nadia is read and understands how she is read is bound up with the way she is visibly interpreted (Ali, 2005) and inextricably linked to the space in which she is situated. This is exacerbated by other symbols, including the car

Going against the grain 113

that she drives and the clothes that she wears. But what Nadia goes on to explain is that she negotiates her relationships by playing on different aspects of her misreadings and confuses people by acting in alternate ways than she is 'supposed to'. Her choice of car is just one element of that confusion. Her close friends are south Asian; they are Muslim and Hindu. Like many of the other participants, she talks about how people approach their relationship from a lack of comprehension and explains how she and her friends take some enjoyment from their bewilderment. She argues that to them it is simply not important, because much of their differences are manufactured in ways that they do not relate to anyway. Arguably these intrusions nevertheless do impact on their lives, but she indicates how she plays into that confusion to challenge people's fixed ideas.

Nadia may not be immediately recognised as African – she is told she does not "*look* African" – because she does not wear the right clothes, drive the right car or live in the right neighbourhood. But those ways of understanding 'African' are as spurious as the symbols of the neighbourhood and Caribbeanness. Nadia goes on to explain that she plays to some of these different facile understandings in different places. In Moss Side she can be more Moss Side, at parties in the Tanzanian community she can be more African, by which she means that she changes the way she speaks and presents herself. Whilst at work she explains she has gone to some lengths to change her speech to sound more professional:

> Like I came from Moss Side, I used to hang around Moss Side a lot and my language was quite ghetto, a lot more . . . and at times I was so conscious [at work], I don't think they could understand what I mean and I really did try at that time, and I came out of there and I was really like. I did get rid of a lot of ghetto terminology by the time I finished.

One thing she has not changed though is the way she dresses and with a keen taste for fashion she is reluctant to do so, but is pondering whether this is something that she might have to do for work. She explains, 'I don't have any different looks, I look the same, maybe that's something I need to look at if I need to change.' Her duplicity threatens to 'undermine the stability of racial categorisation'(Young, 1996: 85). And, even though when playing into certain tropes she risks supporting 'the enunciative power of those who are telling the difference' (Ahmed, 2000: 125), the passing through one identity to another implies a power to subvert that gaze. The point I want to emphasise is that it is the combination of these multiple subjectivities that undermines any one of the ways she might be represented. She is not so much attempting to pass as some *thing* else but rather her identities become blurred and confused for the onlooker, and she understands how this acts as a form of resistance.

Place is always key to the way in which the young people manipulate identities. Maz describes his own frustration with being relentlessly positioned in a particular way and, reflecting on this experience, says that he is never who he is "*supposed to be*". In addition to a number of changes he says he makes in order to appear more and less respectable in different moments, he explains how he also keeps his

114   *Going against the grain*

friends separate in order to strategically work with his multiple subjectivities. For example, he does not invite his friends from college or his job, who tend to live in what he describes as 'cosmopolitan' neighbourhoods, to Longsight because the way he identifies with them would not work in the Longsight context.

> I chill out, with friends I've know for a long time from Longsight, I've got a certain type of relationship and bond with them . . . I do have one unique personality, but my behaviour perhaps might not change drastically where it's a complete personality change, but it's not a bad thing either, it just shows you're able to adapt and you know relate to these people and in terms of my like dress sense . . . or whatever and the way I talk, yeah obviously if I'm speaking to someone who knows how to hold a conversation I'm going to change, but somebody who doesn't know how to hold a conversation, I'm not going to try and speak like as if I know, I'll probably drop it down, put a few slang in there, you know, so yeah, so maybe my talk and my tone of voice changes as well but I'm the same person. I just want to be known as the same guy actually.

These kinds of adaptations that Maz and others make are always constructed in relation to (racialised, classed and gendered) space, as well as the positions that people are typically understood to occupy. They represent attempts to escape marginalised positionings by taking care not to resemble the 'real' thing (Bev Skeggs (1997). However, they arguably do more than that. Here Hamid describes manipulating his identity in conjunction with the way he occupies different places in complex ways. Hamid is a young British Somali living in Moss Side. He explains how he works with different aspects of his identity and the ways he is positioned in order to fit in. In our conversations, he often describes himself as classless and raceless, and yet he recognises that he is nevertheless always at risk of being read simply as black and from Moss Side. Responding perhaps to the discourses around mixing more generally, he places a great deal of emphasis in his interview on how he mixes with people from a range of backgrounds and describes himself as comfortable in areas ranging from those associated with white working classness, to those like Alderley Edge, home to a wealthy population signified by large houses and famed for Man United players' residences. He describes himself as classless and conscious of various codes that he has picked up from living in different parts of Manchester and mixing with people from different racialised, class and religious backgrounds. He explains, however, that he has to keep these groups separate in order to maintain an effective blurring. In other words, in order to pass effectively in each space, like Maz, he must change the way in which he interacts with it, for example, by meeting some in certain spaces but not others. He has learned how to fit in by reproducing dominant representations.

"When in Rome, do as the Romans", he jokes.

Hamid is assumed to be "Caribbean" and from Moss Side because he is black and walks with the so-called 'Moss Side limp'. This assumption is made based on

Going against the grain   115

where he lives and how he acts, but in spite of the fact that he has a Muslim name. Hamid finds this amusing. Indeed, his passing is so successful that when fasting during Ramadan, people think he is joking. He says:

> If I walk with a limp it's cos I'm from Moss Side [laughs], if I talk with a bit of slang it's cos I'm from Manchester . . . my name's Hamid, you can't get more of a Muslim name than that, but 90% of the people at work didn't think I was Muslim . . . which in a way was a good thing because certain barriers were automatically down then and I weren't treated like an outsider . . . I was treated equal . . . The major thing that's changed now is that it's not more of a black thing it's more of a religious thing. So, the emphasis has been taken away from the black people onto the Asians, from one brown to a lighter brown. So people are not so interested in the gangbangers, they're looking for more religious terrorists, so that kind of helps you out.

Hamid explains how he understands this misrecognition to emerge because he is black and walks and talks in a certain way. He also recognises an advantage to being associated with a Caribbean identity "these days". He is well aware that, in light of the intensification of Western discourses about Islam, passing as "Caribbean" has advantages and allows him to evade Islamophobic gestures and pathologising stereotypes through which young Somali men are connoted with high levels of violence as if an inevitable outcome of having lived through civil war, or are associated with terrorism. At a more mundane level, for Hamid, passing as "Caribbean" also means that he is included in social activities that he would be otherwise excluded from due to a growing fear and prejudice of Muslims. This seems at odds with the way in which black, and especially those read as 'Caribbean', Moss Siders are typically pathologised. It points to a transforming hierarchy in which Hamid adopts an ambiguous location. This allows him to, if not go unnoticed, gain access to spaces he otherwise would not be able to, although this requires him to both disavow certain identifications and be complicit in the reproduction of fixed ideas about black 'Caribbeanness'.

By paying attention to the way people live their identities in multi-faceted ways we are able to get at a way of seeing how '*all* forms of culture are continually in a process of hybridity' (Bhabha, 1994: 37). Hybridity in the sense that Bhabha refers to here is not the crude sense of mixedness for which the term hybridity can sometimes be used (as in Friedman, 1997, for example, as noted above), but a means through which to render understanding of cultural purity obsolete and to instead call attention to cultural syncretism (Back, 1996). What we see emerge in these depictions by the young people above is the opening up of what Bhabha refers to as the 'third space', a space that manifests as a site of ambivalence. It is a space that does not permit identifications to take on fixed meanings, but allows for the articulation of cultural meanings and multiple subjectivities. Such a location thus blurs dichotomous or oversimplified understandings of identity and renders them insubstantial. In this way, hybridity need not be conceptualised as additive, but rather as a 'metamorphosis' (Ali, 2003).

116   *Going against the grain*

Importantly too, the way in which the young people find ways of calling attention to these multiple subjectivities undermines alternative ways of seeing. Bringing attention to their experiences helps isolate and destabilise cruder writings of identity. That is not to say that they are experienced unproblematically, nor as noted above that we need to disregard who is 'telling the difference' as Ahmed puts it. Indeed with this in mind, in the next chapter I will turn to think about how, although 'multiply inflected forms of social identity are being expressed within cities', these are as Back notes 'equally being met by multiply accented forms of popular racism that sometimes operate inside urban multiculture and at other times prey on these fragile forms of dialogue from outside' (Back, 1996: 7).

Conclusion

This chapter has engaged with the different ways young people negotiate how they are positioned as different in their everyday lives. It began by illustrating how their early encounters serve as useful reminders of the way in which black people are overdetermined by race and must often narrate themselves from a point of misrecognition. In doing so it also highlighted the different expectations that people are under to create an account of themselves. Of importance too was the way in which the young people demonstrated power to direct these conversations in the social contexts in which they are produced and draw attention to multiple subjectivities. The narratives presented here illustrate how the lived experiences of young adults can disrupt the notion of essentialised subjects by reflecting multi-faceted lived experiences and challenge dominant ascriptions of what it means to be black or be British. In the process of refusing identifications the young people alert us to the way in which the body is entwined with categories and the struggles the young people confront when resisting these processes.

The young people alert us to the far more complex ways in which identities are lived, despite our relentless drive to categorise. Taking these narratives into account, the idea of multiple or mixed identities appear superficial at best, marking nothing more than an attempt at hyphenated identifiers which do not reflect how people live and experience race, class and gender. Indeed, understandings that stem from such simplicity are indicative of the kind of multiculturalism that 'tolerates' and 'bestows rights' on the Other, but does nothing to demythologise the Other (Amin, 2010). What is going on here is more complicated than the interplay of multiple identities. The young adults are not merely working with different so-called intersections, but are negotiating and playing with the very ways in which they are identified or read and positioned in order to be heard in spaces from which they may otherwise be excluded. This is done as a form of resistance to fixed representations that they are associated with, but also emerges as part of claims to occupy a more nuanced and complex position.

References

Ahmed, S. (2000). *Strange encounters: Embodied others in post-coloniality*. London: Routledge.

Alexander, C. (1996). *The art of being black*. Oxford: Oxford University Press.

Alexander, C. (2002). Beyond black: Rethinking the colour/culture divide. *Ethnic and Racial Studies*, 25(4), 552–571.

Ali, S. (2003). *Mixed-race, post-race: Gender, new ethnicities and cultural practices*. Oxford: Berg.

Ali, S. (2005). Uses of the exotic: Body, narrative, mixedness. *In:* Alexander, C. & Knowles, C. (eds.) *Making race matter: Bodies, space and identity*. Basingstoke: Palgrave Macmillan.

Amin, A. (2010). The remainders of race. *Theory, Culture and Society*, 27(1), 1–23.

Anthias, F. & Yuval-Davis, N. (1992). *Racialized boundaries: Race, nation, gender, colour and class and the anti-racist struggle*. London: Routledge.

Appiah, K. A. (2000). Racial identity and racial identification. *In:* Back, L. & Solomos, J. (eds.) *Theories of race and racism*. London: Routledge.

Aspinall, P. (2009). The future of ethnicity classification. *Journal of Ethnic and Migration Studies*, 35(9), 1417–1435.

Back, L. (1996). *New ethnicities and urban multiculture: Racisms and multiculture in young lives*. London: UCL Press.

Back, L. (2002). The fact of hybridity: Youth, ethnicity and racism. *In:* Goldberg, D. T. & Solomos, J. (eds.) *A companion to racial and ethnic studies*. Malden, MA and Oxford: Blackwell.

Banton, M. (2008). The sociology of ethnic relations. *Ethnic and Racial Studies*, 31(7), 1267–1285.

Baumann, G. (1996). *Contesting culture*. Cambridge: Cambridge University Press.

Berg, M. L. & Sigona, N. (2013). Ethnography, diversity and urban space. *Identities: Global Studies in Culture and Power*, 20(4), 347–360.

Bhabha, H. (1994). *The location of culture*. Abingdon: Routledge.

Bonnett, A. (2000). *White identities: Historical and international perspectives*. Harlow: Prentice Hall.

Brah, A. (1996). *Cartographies of diaspora: Contesting identities*. London: Routledge.

Bramwell, R. (2015). *UK hip-hop, grime and the city: The aesthetics and ethics of London's rap scenes*. London: Routledge.

Butler, J. (2005). *Giving an account of oneself*. New York: Fordham University Press.

Byrne, B. (2006). *White lives: The interplay of 'race', class and gender in everyday life*. London and New York: Routledge.

Du Bois, W. E. B. (1996 [1903]). *The souls of black folk*. Harmondsworth: Penguin.

Dwyer, C. (1999). Veiled meanings: Young British Muslim women and the negotiation of differences. *Gender, Place and Culture*, 6(1), 5–26.

Fanon, F. (1986 c1952). *The fact of blackness: Black skin white masks*. London: Pluto.

Frankenberg, R. (1993). *White women, race matters: The social construction of whiteness*. Minneapolis: University of Minnesota Press.

Friedman, J. (1997). Gobal crises, the struggle for cultural identity and intellectual porkbarreling – cosmopolitans versus locals, ethnics and nationals in an era of de-hegemonization. *In:* Werbner, P. & Modood, T. (eds.) *Debating cultural hybridity: Multi-cultural identities and the politics of anti-racism*. London: Zed Books.

118 *Going against the grain*

Gidley, B. (2013). Landscapes of belonging, portraits of life: Researching everyday multi-culture in an inner city estate. *Identities: Global Studies in Culture and Power*, 20(4), 361–376.

Gilroy, P. (1993). *The black Atlantic*. London and New York: Verso.

Gilroy, P. (2002). *There ain't no black in the Union Jack* (2nd Edition). Abingdon, Oxfordshire: Routledge.

Gilroy, P. (2004). *After empire: Melancholia or convivial culture?* Abingdon: Routledge.

Gunaratnam, Y. (2003). *Researching 'race' and ethnicity: Methods, knowledge and power.* London: Sage.

Hall, S. (1997). The work of representation. *In:* Hall, S. (ed.) *Representation: Cultural representations and signifying practices*. London: Sage.

Hall, S. (2000). The multicultural question. *In:* Hesse, B. (ed.) *Un/settled multiculturalisms*. London: Zed Books.

Harries, B. (2015). Yma o Hyd? Gwyn o Hyd? (Still here? Still white?). Race, Identity and Nationalism in Post-Devolution Wales. *Racism and Nationalism after the Scottish Referendum and 2015 General Election*. Birkbeck Institute for Social Research, University of London, 13 November 2015, London, UK.

Harries, B. (2016). What's sex got to do with it? When a woman asks questions. *Women's Studies International Forum*, 59(1), 48–57.

Harris, A. (2009). Shifting the boundaries of cultural spaces: Young people and everyday multiculturalism. *Social Identities*, 15(2), 187–205.

Haylett, C. (2001). Illegitimate subjects? Abject whites, neoliberal modernisation and middle class multiculturalism. *Environment and Planning D: Society and Space*, 19(3), 351–370.

hooks, b. (1992). *Black looks: Race and representation*. Boston: South End Press.

Hylton, K. & Law, I. (2009). 'Race', sport and the media. *In:* Hylton, K. (ed.) *'Race' and sport: Critical race theory*. Abingdon, OX: Routledge.

Ifekwunigwe, J. O. (1999). *Scattered belongings: Cultural paradoxes of 'race', nation and gender*. London: Routledge.

James, M. (2015). *Urban multiculture: Youth, politics and cultural transformation in a global city*. Basingstoke: Palgrave Macmillan.

Jones, O. (2011). *Chavs: The demonization of the working class*. London: Verso.

Kalra, V., Kaur, R. & Hutnyk, J. (2005). *Diaspora and hybridity*. London: Sage.

Keith, M. (2004). Racialization and public spaces. *In:* Murji, K. & Solomos, J. (eds.) *Racialization: Studies in theory and practice*. Oxford: Oxford University Press.

Keith, M. (2005). *After the cosmopolitan: Multicultural cities and the future of racism*. London: Routledge.

Kim, H. (2014). *Making diaspora in a global city: South Asian youth cultures in London*. London: Routledge.

Knowles, C. (2013). Nigerian London: Re-mapping space and ethnicity in superdiverse cities. *Ethnic and Racial Studies*, 36(4), 651–669.

Lawler, S. (2002). Narrative in social research. *In:* May, T. (ed.) *Qualitative research in action*. London: Sage.

Lawler, S. (2005). Disgusted subjects: The making of middle-class identities. *The Sociological Review*, 53(3), 429–446.

Majumdar, A. (2007). Researching south Asian women's experiences of marriage: Resisting stereotypes through an exploration of 'space' and 'embodiment'. *Feminism & Psychology*, 17(3), 316–322.

Massey, D. (2005). *For space*. London: Sage.

Going against the grain 119

Modood, T., Beishon, S. & Virdee, S. (1994). *Changing ethnic identities*. London: Policy Studies Institute.

Nayak, A. (2003). *Race, place and globalisation: Youth cultures in a changing world*. Oxford and New York: Berg.

Nayak, A. (2006a). After race: Ethnography, race and post-race theory. *Ethnic and Racial Studies*, 29(3), 411–430.

Nayak, A. (2006b). Displaced masculinities: Chavs, youth and class in the post-industrial city. *Sociology*, 40(5), 813–831.

Nayak, A. (2009). Beyond the pale: Chavs, youth and social class. *In:* Sveinsson, K. (ed.) *Perspectives: Who cares about the white working class?* London: Runnymede Trust.

Puwar, N. (2004). *Space invaders: Race, gender and bodies out of place*. New York: Berg.

Rashid, N. (2016). *Veiled threats: Representing the Muslim woman in public policy discourses*. Bristol: Polity Press.

Rhodes, J. (2011). Stigmatization, space and boundaries in de-industrial Burnley. *Ethnic and Racial Studies*, 35(4), 684–703.

Rollock, N., Gillborn, D., Vincent, C. & Ball, S. (2011). The public identities of the black middle classes: Managing race in public spaces. *Sociology*, 45(6), 1078–1093.

Rutherford, J. (1990). The third space: Interview with Homi Bhabha. *In:* Rutherford, J. (ed.) *Identity: Community, culture*. London: Lawrence and Wishart.

Sandercock, L. (2000). Cities of (in)difference and the challenge for planning. *disP-The Planning Review*, 36(140), 7–15.

Simpson, L. (2007). Ghettoes of the mind: The empirical behaviour of indices of segregation and diversity. *Journal of the Royal Statistical Society: Series A (Statistics in Society)*, 170(2), 405–424.

Skeggs, B. (1997). *Formations of class and gender*. London: Sage.

Skeggs, B. (2005). The making of class through visualising moral subject formation. *Sociology*, 39(5), 965–982.

Solomos, J. (2003). *Race and racism in Britain* (3rd Edition). Basingstoke: Palgrave Macmillan.

Solomos, J. & Back, L. (1996). *Racism and society: Sociology for a changing world*. London: Palgrave Macmillan.

Song, M. (2003). *Choosing ethnic identity*. Cambridge: Polity Press.

Stanley, L. (2000). From 'self-made woman' to 'women's made selves'? Audit selves, simulation and surveillance in the rise of public woman. *In:* Cosslett, T., Lury, C. & Summerfield, P. (eds.) *Feminism and autobiography: Texts, theories, methods*. London and New York: Routledge.

Steedman, C. (2000). Enforced narratives: Stories of another self. *In:* Cosslett, T., Lury, C. & Summerfield, P. (eds.) *Feminism and autobiography: Texts, theories, methods*. London and New York: Routledge.

Swanton, D. (2008). Everyday multiculture and the emergence of race. *In:* Dwyer, C. & Bressey, C. (eds.) *New geographies of race and racism*. Aldershot: Ashgate.

Tizard, B. & Phoenix, A. (1993). *Black, white or mixed race? Race and racism in the lives of young people of mixed parentage*. London: Routledge.

Valluvan, S. (2016). Conviviality and multiculture: A post-integration sociology of multi-ethnic interaction. *Young*, 24(3), 204–221.

Valluvan, S. (2017). New nationalism and old ideologies. Institute for Policy Research, University of Bath. Available from: http://blogs.bath.ac.uk/iprblog/2017/04/07/new-nationalism-and-old-ideologies/[Online].

120 *Going against the grain*

Vertovec, S. (2007). Super-diversity and its implications. *Ethnic and Racial Studies*, 30(6), 1024–1054.

Wacquant, L. (1997). For an analytic of racial domination. *Political Power and Social Theory*, 11, 221–234.

Waters, M. C. (1990). *Ethnic options: Choosing identities in America.* Berkely, Los Angeles and Oxford: University of California Press.

Young, L. (1996). *Fear of the dark: 'Race', gender and sexuality in the cinema.* London: Routledge.

Young, R. (1995). *Colonial desire: Hybridity in theory, culture and race.* London: Routledge.

Yuval-Davis, N. (2006). Intersectionality and feminist politics. *European Journal of Women's Studies*, 13(3), 193–209.

6 When is racism?

In this chapter I examine how racism is defined and recognised as a feature that structures the young people's everyday lives. I begin by reflecting on some of the ways that definitions of racism have become undone to assume a status that marks it as a historical phenomenon and yet one which is abstracted from its historical roots. To do this I consider some of the growing literature that critically engages with post-racial imaginaries and place this in the context of some of the key debates that shape the way that the young people talk about the city and the neighbourhoods in which they live.

This chapter illustrates how there is popular currency in the notion that racism is a phenomenon of the past and yet not grounded in history. Indeed, it suggests that the young people find this idea alluring in a way similar to that which drew them to the idea that Manchester (like many other European cities) is a future-facing global city and one that espouses liberal values of diversity (see Chapter 2). I am interested in how, in light of such an influential context, the young people can then also talk about their own experiences of racism. In doing so, I draw on the experiences of the young people to think through how they must negotiate a series of contradictory logics that shape how the racism they experience can be understood and conveyed.

The problem of racism

In one of my conversations with Mina the topic turned to how she had come to live where she did. We were sat in a local Afghan café drinking tea and sharing a snack with her daughter. She had been telling me how, whilst growing up, she and her family had moved around quite a bit and lived in several different neighbourhoods. She recalled how, in each of these spaces, she and her siblings were repeatedly the targets of racism from neighbours. When I asked how she had ended up living in the Moss Side/Rusholme border – an area in which she had not previously lived – she explained how these earlier experiences have continued to affect the way she uses spaces *even though*, as she was keen to emphasise, they had happened in the past. Consequently, she explains that she now elects to live and socialise in areas where there is a more visible ethnic mix and in particular a more visible Asian population. She says of the area she currently lives, 'It feels safe because there's

122 *When is racism?*

a lot of Asians round here.' But, it is in this telling that she becomes concerned that she might be interpreted as racist:

> Please don't think I'm racist, I'm not racist. It's just what I've experienced when I was younger. . . . You're going to think that I'm racist. Honest to God, please don't think I'm racist, I'm not racist.

In this conversation Mina is keen to put her own experiences of racism in the past and keen not to be perceived as racist. Her anxiety about the latter is palpable. To name racism, she worries, could itself be interpreted as racism. But, how we have come to such a point? Using this anecdote I want to introduce some of the ways in which the literature on contemporary modes of race and racism can help us untangle how Mina has come to assume this position. In the first place, it is worth reflecting on how Mina has come to express such a concern by taking account of the context in which she is situated. Second, it is also worth returning to some of the post-racial debates that were introduced in Chapter 3 as a means to explore the way in which the young adults constructed themselves as a generation, often in relation to post-racial narratives. These two lines of enquiry, while listed separately, are in fact mutually constitutive. The discursive and structural arrangements of the city are, after all, based on similar neoliberal foundations from which post-racialities stem. What the chapter illustrates is that Mina and the other young adults are reflecting back the way in which racism is both imagined as belonging to the past and outside any structure, so that its definition can be simplified and its meaning and effects lost or blurred.

In Chapter 5 I considered how both local and national policies, narratives and conditions influenced the way in which Mina and the other young adults gave an account of themselves. I illustrated how the young people often began to construct a self-identity in relation to discourses of segregation and community, which resonate at the local and national level and can be formed in response to global events. In the conversation with Mina detailed above we again get a sense of how those same discourses influence the way in which she articulates her decisions about where to live and how to talk about past experiences of racism. It is, for example, worth reflecting on where Mina's concern arose, and this requires thinking about the specifics of our conversation and how she chooses to direct it. I did not ask Mina to *justify* her choice to live in an area often described locally as an 'Asian' neighbourhood. There are things, however, that we can draw from her decision to direct the conversation in this particular way. The way in which she does so suggests that Mina is concerned with defending this decision, which is perhaps particularly important for her to do in light of the discourses of self-segregation that in the UK often focus on communities of Asian Muslims. These have gathered pace since 9/11, the riots in 2001 and emerge with greater vehemence with each new global terror alert and each set of policy guidance on integration – all of which are used to bring into question her citizenship. It is in this context that we have to understand her concern about being read as racist. Her anxiety emerges in a context where the onus for integration and being a responsible citizen, as dictated by

When is racism? 123

neoliberal governance projects, lies with her and not with her white former neighbours, not even with those responsible for threatening her and her siblings. But it also emerges within the context of a city that claims an absence of racism – a claim that is produced in relation to other scales as Manchester seeks to position itself as a global city and as the UK's second city and leader of the Northern Powerhouse.

Policies on integration, community cohesion and their equivalents illustrate how ethnic minority housing choice is understood as self-segregation – as Mina fears her choice will be interpreted. These policies ask that ethnic minorities reflect on the way in which they relate to different communities and choose allegiances to one group over another (Solomos and Back, 1996). They also reproduce a form of racial historicism (Goldberg, 2001) through the way that 'ethnic communities' (typically inner city neighbourhoods with a proportionately high ethnic minority population) are represented as 'backwards' and out of step with the liberal ideals, or values of nation, even whilst the meaning of British values remains ever elusive. Such policy approaches have a long history but were encouraged under New Labour's community cohesion agenda and taken up by the coalition government via its Big Society initiative. They have again been entrenched in the recent Casey Review (2016). Indeed the latter has undoubtedly been influenced by critics of multiculturalism that complained that too much diversity had allowed for *some* ethnic minorities to be *too* different, by encouraging people to adopt values that are not part of a 'common' national identity (see, for example, Goodhart, 2004; Goodhart, 2013). It is also worth drawing attention to the spatialisation of these policies, and the material and discursive effects that they generate. These have been well documented elsewhere (see, for example, Simpson, 2007; Phillips, 2006), but worth noting here because they centre around the very kinds of neighbourhoods in which the young adults live.

The range of policy approaches that have emerged over the years serve the purpose of providing an 'acceptable' means of exclusion and marginalisation to be further developed (Fortier, 2008). It should be noted that they have also helped to generate a wide range of related popular cultural responses (see for example Make Bradford British, Channel Four, 2012, or Muslims Like us, BBC, 2016). But in this discussion I am interested in how they have an impact on the way in which racism is recognised or not. I would suggest that what these policy foci on integration represent is a piece of a larger picture that attempts to replace race with terms of ambiguity. This is also notable in the ways that the parameters of debates about living with diversity can be framed through 'benign' or 'de-racialised' discourses that tap into culturalist paradigms, rather than a means to address modes of inequality. Indeed, so much of what we see across a broad spectrum of political and cultural domains about diversity is often bent on negating racism and obscuring the relations of power.

Locally, research in Manchester illustrates how Muslim residents in the city express disappointment in the way that the local authority emphasises diversity and integration but fails to address their concerns about increased racism/Islamophobia by issuing any kind of statement that directly supports Muslim citizens

124 *When is racism?*

(Harries et al., forthcoming). Instead, the local authority prefers to persist with a liberal discourse of togetherness under such slogans as '#We Stand Together' that engages largely with already amenable civic organisations, rather than broader civil society, and resembles the kind of holistic messaging that has become common across Europe. This is akin to the way in which the neoliberal city appropriates the hard won gains of LGBT and anti-racist social movements to produce a representation of a place that is intended as tolerant and progressive (see Chapter 2). Hence, whilst slogans of togetherness might emphasise the coming together of cultural difference, the difference that typically remains overlooked is that which marks our differentiated experiences and orientations. Cultural difference is emphasised or exaggerated as a point of departure for these campaigns, but the terms on which "we" are defending against racism are not universal. A similar mistake is often made in social research that fixates on cultural mixing as if this is meaningful evidence of non-racism that can be claimed for 'our' (i.e. white) collective local and/or national narratives. But, such an emphasis has little to do with racism or anti-racism and fails to adequately capture the cultural work that is going on in relationships that cross imagined boundaries. This has particular significance for the young people when, as I go on to discuss below, they are often keen to emphasise crude and often staged forms of 'mixing' across essentialised boundaries as evidence that both they and the city they live in are not racist, rather than rely on their convivial relations to do that kind of work.

The absence of the terms race and racism in policy-making has become increasingly conspicuous and of increasing concern (Kapoor, 2011). Race equality has been subsumed under a more generic and suitably vague heading to encompass all 'protected characteristics' (principally age, gender, disability, race and religion). And whilst there has been a reported increase in reports of racism and Islamophobia (see, for example, Allen, 2010), these experiences are typically overlooked as points of concern at institutional levels. The way in which race is overlooked and expunged from the political arena is examined in the growing literature on the post-racial; although notably this body of work is not exclusive in doing so, and this line of critique predates claims to the post-racial (Hesse, 2011). What the literature on the post-racial does effectively is directly address the political and social climate that 'claims that racism has finally been transcended and that the "illusion" of race has finally been eliminated' (Winant, 2004: 214). In particular, recent work has paid attention to neoliberal political machineries that seek to manage difference by deferring the responsibility of racism away from structural arrangements and outside of any proximate relationship to other prevailing conceptions of normative belonging, including the nation (see, for example, Amin, 2012; Lentin and Titley, 2011; Goldberg, 2009; Winant, 2006). The charge made within this body of work is that a post-racial society is imagined as a means to conceal and legitimise racism and protect white privilege. Hence, Goldberg (2015) argues that the post-racial is not limited to disavowing or silencing racism, but is itself a racist expression because it is organised and reproduces structures of domination (Titley, 2016). It is, as he explains, 'racism without racism'.

It is also worth reflecting on what happens to definitions of racism under these conditions. Put simply, racism, from a hegemonic perspective, becomes detached from structures of domination and is thus oversimplified. Hence, more often than not, indictments of racism centre only on intensely individualised instances, such as physical violence and right wing propagandists. Indeed, so readily are these incidents labelled as racist that rarely do we see attempts to try to understand how they are racist (Song, 2014). Hence, whilst overt instances of racism are typically only a symptom of a much broader picture and broader structures of domination (Omi and Winant, 1994), more often than not they are reduced to mere name-calling. This then has an accumulative effect, because the more that we assume that the problem of racism is limited to these outliers, 'the less we understand that racial domination is a collective process' (Bonilla-Silva, 2014: xv). This means that the majority, and significantly those in positions of power, can be let off the hook. Hence, as Bonilla-Silva notes, 'the main problem nowadays is not the folks with the hoods, but the folks dressed in suits' because structures of domination are reproduced at a higher level – structures that are so deeply embedded that they are taken for granted. In the UK, perhaps the most important review into institutional racism to date was certainly not helpful in this regard. Beyond its consideration for institutional racism, the Macpherson report that came out of the inquiry into the Metropolitan Police's investigation of the murder of Stephen Lawrence redefined racism more broadly by concluding that, 'A racist incident is any incident which is perceived to be racist by the victim or other person' (Macpherson, 1999 reprinted in Song, 2014). It seems quite clear that such a definition has no practicable application because it implies racism can be considered as a set of individual incidents and is an entirely subjective phenomenon.

Miri Song (2014) draws on Macpherson's definition of racism as one example amongst many to illustrate how the loosening of definitions of racism has allowed for the emergence of a culture of racial equivalence. By imagining racism as an individualised and subjective phenomenon, abstracted from its historical basis and power, means that the term can be applied to almost anyone or to any scenario (Song, 2014). A similar discussion confronting such a culture of equivalence is common in debates that scrutinise claims to reverse racism. And so it is that one of the most pernicious ways that post-racial racism has gathered momentum is one that works with narrowed definitions of racism to argue for racial self-interest. In short, it is argued that racism is not racism at all, but is instead an expression of 'justifiable concerns' about the loss of identity, access to resources and protection of claims to sovereignty. Such arguments are not new but do nevertheless appear to be increasingly mainstreamed and legitimate, across the political spectrum. It is argued that it is reasonable, natural even, to prioritise the needs of one's own 'racial group', and that this should not be mistaken for racism (Kaufmann, 2017; Goodhart, 2017). It is precisely such logics that can allow for racism to be treated as if a psychological disorder (Ambikaipaker, 2015) or imagined as if existing only at the extreme edges of society. In a recent report published by the think-tank, Policy Exchange, the author

126 *When is racism?*

maintains that 'racial self- interest' is justifiable because it represents a natural and reasonable expectation rather than an expression of any kind of prejudice (Kaufmann, 2017).[1] Further, this report attempts to pre-empt its critics by also asserting that calling 'racial self-interest' racism prevents the possibility for having discussions about immigration that foster debate rather than division. In doing so it pre-emptively names the aggressors as both the 'snowflake' liberals and anti-racists (who are perversely discredited within this logic by virtue of their aims). The report does not represent an isolated moment, but is indicative of a narrative that is emitted across a broad political spectrum in which we are asked to be more understanding of white people who have 'legitimate' concerns about what is happening to 'their' country. Indeed, we are asked to appreciate the legitimate concerns that white people express about being labelled as racist when challenging immigration. Although, inevitably, these challenges to immigration for which we are to understand people have 'natural' apprehensions only tend to centre on concerns over certain types of migrants and migration flows (as well as racialised citizens who can be read as such). These are concerns that are often couched in culturalist terms to make them more legitimate. Casey (2016), for example, expresses concern that white people should not have to fear challenging sexist, misogynistic and patriarchal behaviour at the risk of being labelled as racist. Much of the basis of these arguments thus regurgitates cultural racisms whilst taking on new justifications. Indeed, every time we hear the iteration, 'We need to have an honest debate about immigration or integration' one can almost hear the segue into a denunciation of so-called culturally defected communities, which value-laden Britain must seek to redress.

The dominant narrative has therefore not only developed rationalisations about the status of other racialised groups in order to defend its collective interests (Bonilla Silva), but also inverted the direction of hostility inherent in racism. No longer is it racists that are condemnable, but, perversely, it is those who call out racism that are considered hostile. No wonder Mina is anxious about expressing her own experiences. So invasive is this discourse that the once publicly condemned Rivers of Blood speech from Enoch Powell has taken on a renewed life. Powell is no longer the sock puppet of the far right, but is drawn on from across the political spectrum as a medium through which 'to enact [. . .] anxieties about swamping, security, failed multiculture, social cohesion and home-grown terrorism' (Gilroy, 2008). Such rhetoric has momentum because it takes on common sensical logics. However, it also somewhat conveniently assuages the haunting guilt of racism without requiring any effort to undo it (Goldberg, 2015: 162). That these iterations of justifiable concerns are in fact deeply exclusionary and abstracted from the colonial history from which they stem becomes increasingly difficult to point out because to do so risks being silenced as the aggressor, the killjoy (to use Sara Ahmed's, 2010 term) and one who is not willing to fall in step with this so-called progressive way of moving on from the past and dealing with the 'real' and contemporary issue of immigration. If we take these shifts and the ways they impact at different scales into consideration and then reflect on the extract from Mina above, we can start to understand the processes against which she must struggle. In the rest of the chapter I turn to explore more fully how the young people talk about racism.

Talking racism

The above discussion has illustrated how a political and social climate has developed in which it is difficult to name racism both because definitions of racism have narrowed and because naming racism has itself come to be treated as a mode of aggression and division in certain domains. However, in spite of the fervour around the significance of the silencing of race and post-racial logics, little has been done to explore the everyday effects of living with these processes, including how they might be resisted (Harries, 2014). This is important to address since the notion that race is being silenced does not only point to a public disavowal of race, but also to the potential to silence resistance to racism. In the following I therefore consider some of the issues raised by the above discussion in the context of the young people's everyday lives. I am particularly interested in the challenges the young people face when they attempt to convey their understandings and experiences of racism, in light of the discursive shifts that historicise and weaken definitions of racism.

Racism and the weight of categorisation

One of the concerns that emerges in relation to how definitions of racism have narrowed relates to the way in which racism is increasingly interpreted as essentialism and categorisation and thus does not always incorporate an understanding of hierarchies and power in the construction of difference (Song, 2014). This has been considered within the lens of the post-racial because categorising can become an alibi for more pernicious, structured and implicit forms of racism – hence the overemphasis on name-calling, rather than on the embedded structural features of race. The emphasis on categorising and essentialising shifts attention away from the 'weight' of racism in which the categories are rooted (see, for example, Goldberg, 2009; Winant, 2001; Ahmed, 2004; Lentin and Titley, 2011). This problem is also hinted at in the tension between the way in which race is under scrutiny within the academy when research that comes from an epistemological starting point of seeing race as a social construction, nevertheless collapses and sorts bodies into categories as if their status exists in isolation (Gunaratnam, 2003; Nayak, 2006).

In this section I reflect on how the young people understand categorisation as a form of racism, and how that sits with their notions of post-racialism. I draw especially from the part of the interviews in which I used the ethnic monitoring form to provoke a discussion about ethnicity and its relationship to identity. The young people were most familiar with the forms from job applications since many were working in a casualised labour market and were therefore applying for jobs and completing these forms on a regular basis. There was a general sense that the

128   *When is racism?*

categories on the form did not adequately capture diversity but instead risked reinforcing differences that many of them considered irrelevant in the contemporary city. Subsequently, most of the young people rejected the use of ethnic labels and suggested they no longer matter, as if they once did. In light of this initial emphasis on the practice of labelling rather than the meanings behind them, it might seem at first glance that it is the process of essentialising that is understood to be the most important distinguishing feature of race making, rather than racism, but this would be a simplified interpretation. And, of course their experiences of filling them in varied significantly, and there is thus a case for considering how the white young adults, and the young adults who are racialised, reflected on them separately.

In Chapter 5 I explained how the equality monitoring form was rarely problematised by the white young people unless they were directly asked about specific ethnic categories and their usage. On reflection, and after being asked, they typically expressed an understanding that the use of ethnic categories risked reawakening old divisions and old racisms. But, the meaning and effects behind the labels were rarely fully recognised as still being salient. Instead, the categories were treated at a surface level and were conceived as a means to ensure representation in today's job market. On reflecting on the use of categories on the equality monitoring form Zoe, for example, says:

> They've got a duty to be, they've got a duty because they've persecuted blacks for years, I think they've got such a guilt that they have to represent all these racial groups so this is their way of doing it and proving that they are now, not racist and democratic or whatever.

Zoe describes the form as a "superficial method" to atone for "white man's guilt", but she does so by apportioning the origin of these categories and the potential to discriminate to a "they" who are fixed in a previous moment. In doing so, she therefore also implies that discrimination is not relevant in the same way today. She explains how she understands the categories on the form as a means to ensure representation for "all of these racial groups". Zoe is quite sarcastic in her tone, which indicates that she is sceptical of the sincerity of these intentions. However, somewhere the actual problem of discrimination has nonetheless become lost as a contemporary phenomenon and the emphasis instead remains on this old practice of categorising.

Amongst the black young people equality monitoring forms were certainly not thought of as an effective anti-discrimination device in job recruitment, as one might assume is their intention. And, parallels were drawn with the way neighbourhoods are pathologised and discriminated against. Laurence explains this here:

> I feel like [the form] could be used in a . . . a discriminatory way because if you apply for something and you tick that you're from one box it might rule you out, just like if you put your postcode on some things it rules you out.

When is racism? 129

Damien goes further by critically challenging the hierarchies that the categories on the form represent. Damien describes himself as mixed race. He is casually employed within the market trade, working largely for cash and trade-offs for temporary accommodation. During the time we met he had been making repeated attempts to get more formalised employment and had previously attempted to set up his own business. But he repeatedly had poor experiences of getting through application processes and felt that he was consistently knocked back in interviews – a problem exacerbated by the vicious circle of his lack of experience. Each time he says he finds the application process increasingly demoralising. In one of our later conversations, Damien explained his understanding of how the forms work as a discrimination device using a currency structured around white privilege:

Damien: I reckon they see occupation, "OK, nice job, but he's this religion, oh no, but he's this ethnic group" and then they'll look at the age. I think that's how people will look at it.

Bethan: In terms of importance you mean?

Damien: Yeah, yeah I think people will look, "OK, good occupation, but he's this type of religion, forget that for a game of soldiers".

Bethan: So he passes on the occupation and fails on religion?

Damien: "OK, he's a doctor, but he's this [Muslim] forget it". "He's unemployed, but he's like Christian, oh OK". "Unemployed, but he's Muslim, oh what a typical type". I think that's how they do it [laughs]. So "Unemployed, Christian, oh, but he's white, OK that's OK". "Unemployed, but he's Sikh, typical guy". That's how they look at it I do genuinely think that. If it said, "He works in a shop, but he's Sikh, OK, but he's white-Asian, but he's Asian". I think that's how they look at it. I think so yeah. I do genuinely think that's how they look at it, yeah.

He also goes on to explain how he and a friend conducted their own mini research by switching names on applications for the same jobs to find that the Muslim name was not selected – a finding redolent to those of formal research studies (see, for example, Esmail and Everington, 1993).

The general concern that these forms were being used as a means to discriminate are understandable. We know that disparities in employment are persistent, both in relation to employment rates (Nazroo and Kapadia, 2013b) and positions in the labour market (Nazroo and Kapadia, 2013a). Hence, potential targets of racism 'are concerned less with and about the category than with the conditions, the artifice and fabrication, of their restriction and exclusion, their humiliation and degradation' (Goldberg, 2009: 22). However, persistent inequalities in employment typically go unrecognised or are poorly explained through culturalist discourses that centre on certain behaviours that are incompatible with employment. Therefore, when looking for a job it is hard to draw attention to the possibilities of being discriminated against at risk of falling foul to a culturalist narrative, or having ones concerns misrecognised as one solely of essentialised misrepresentation. Hence

130   *When is racism?*

Tony explains how he wants to be considered for his ability rather than his ethnicity even whilst he knows that:

> It's not a perfect world, but I know that people don't employ people because of one thing or another, female, gender, sex, race, ability or disability, so yeah when I look at it. I just think what's that for? . . . It's like having an establishment going, oh we need to recruit a few ethnic minorities, now that's gonna work for me innit, but I want to know if I'm better for the job, or is the white guy or the white girl better, do you understand what I'm saying? That's the only thing I have with it.

Though the practice of categorising does not of course fully address the complexities behind race and how it works, it does alert us to the need to differentiate between racism and racialisation, even when it is not always clear-cut. We must, for example, be careful to distinguish between when the young people are criticising *labels* without thinking through the conditions that surround them and when they are criticising the way that labels and the practice of categorisation represent something bigger. The latter distinction is a particularly important one in light of the regularity that they are used in the UK; a repetitive practice that, like some policing tactics, can be frustrating and humiliating. Indeed, I would suggest that it is the frequency that they are used and the way in which they pervade all aspects of social life that stimulated such enthused discussion about the practice of categorising, or 'labelling' as it was more commonly referred. So pervasive were the forms deemed to be that they were perceived to represent an incursion. Angela, for example, expressed a great deal of frustration about the secretary in her doctor's surgery who called her back to correct her form because she had described herself as mixed race when the secretary felt that she was "too black" to be able to tick that box. It is significant that Angela's stance on this means that she risks being put in the position of aggressor. She is at risk of being perceived as making trouble – it is only a label after all! And yet if it were *just* a label then we would have to also wonder why the receptionist cares to correct her. Categories therefore have a symbolic effect. They produce anxiety not just because people struggle to fit into one box or another, but because the practice of categorisation represents one of the most mundane ways in which race is structured into our lives in incoherent ways, in ways that appear common sensical. And whilst there is a broad understanding that the categories do not make sense (including among the white young people), what is often lacking is the means to draw attention to their broader effects.

Social mixing – an inadequate counter to racism

In this section I focus on the role of social mixing as a counter to racism. This subject has come up at different stages of the book, where it has been argued that an emphasis on *mixedness*, rather than multiculture or hybridity (using Bhabha's, 1994, definition), risks oversimplifying identities and relationships and rendering them insubstantial by ignoring the complicated and fluid interactions and negotiations that make up everyday life. Here I look at how the idea of social mixing (notably distinct from the more nuanced aspects of lived multiculture) can obscure the way racism is (mis)understood, or perhaps more precisely, how it is misunderstood as representing 'non-racism'.

I met Carina in Gorton at a social event. She is black and lives in a predominantly white middle class neighbourhood. Carina, like many of the other young people, was keen to convey a sense that her 'generation' is moving beyond race because they are more socially mixed (see also Chapter 3). In the following quote she explains one means that she has of making sense of racism:

> [My friend] was saying that her gran was quite racist, but it's not intentional racism, it's just because it's what she knows and the generation she's come from and the experiences she's had with different cultures and so we started talking about you know how privileged we are and how open-minded we are, but at the same time we're as close-minded as the next person who doesn't like black people because they've had a different experience to us, so you know, ok it would be better if they accepted you know people for who they were not because of the colour of their skin or whatever, but if we can't accept that they find it challenging to think openly then we're not giving them credit in a sense.

In her narrative, Carina invokes the idea of racial equivalence by reversing potential hostility. She is eager to explain away racism by implying that it is a natural consequence of a set of unnamed experiences and argues that failure to understand why someone is racist signifies closed mindedness. Here then we see the effect of the power of post-racial logics that historicise and simplify how racism is understood. In addition, as with many of the other young people, Carina infers that racism is the dominion of older generations. This is made possible because she explains racism as though it is an attitude, i.e. she explains this not through a grounded account or a history of racism, but rather through a natural and inevitable consequence of the "experiences" her friend's grandmother's generation has had with "different cultures". Indeed this also infers that it is the responsibility of these 'other' cultures to affect attitudes more positively. This quote needs to be read too within the broader context of Carina's interview, which is discussed elsewhere, in which she disregards the significance of race and ethnicity in her own encounters, echoing the tendency to emphasise instead a notion of tolerance and mixing (rather than multiculture). It seems reasonable to assume, therefore, that she means to say that her friend's grandmother has had a more limited set of encounters with different cultures than Carina and her friends. And as such, her example reflects the way in which inter-ethnic contact has come to be understood as crucial in overcoming racism over and above understanding the roots of racism. Or, that prejudice can be redressed through 'contact' (see, for example, Allport, 1979 [1954]) without giving adequate consideration to inequalities and relations of power that shape the effects of encounters (Wilson, 2016). The way

132   *When is racism?*

that these contradictory logics are at work in Carina's narrative are worth bearing in mind as I turn to think about two further examples.

Hamid is someone who, as I have previously introduced, has a somewhat ambiguous identity. He is often misread as a black 'Caribbean' youth rather than Muslim with a Somali background (see Chapter 5 for a fuller account of this). In many ways Hamid also claims to epitomise the very notion of conviviality. But frequently, he describes friendships and interactions that cross acute dichotomies of ethnicity and class, rather than drawing on more mundane and unremarkable relationships in a way that would allow us to consider them for their convivial appeal. For example, he typically draws only on relationships that appear as if at opposite ends of a spectrum – with a white middle class elite or poor white traveller community. These are relationships that he explains he has cultivated at different stages of his life, but are often people he has met at work and since leaving school. Through these narratives he then emphasises his ability to transcend social structures through his different life experiences, from growing up in east Manchester close to an Irish traveller community to Longsight and now living in Moss Side. He explains how he now also has friends in affluent white suburban neighbourhoods that are also home to wealthy footballers from Manchester United. He talks often about how he is able to talk to anyone and describes himself as "classless" to explain how he can fit in to any space. It is evident that he wants to convey a particular identity that allows him to express his openness to difference and his right to the city. However, notably, many of these relationships become oversimplified in the process and his descriptions of his relationships are often reduced to emphases on cultural mixing across polarised boundaries that, in many ways, detract from the potential qualities of his friendships. They also push to the background the way that some (not all) of these relationships rely on him taking on a different identity and principally on not being recognised as Muslim. In this respect these examples stand in stark contrast to more nuanced understandings of multiculture. They are nevertheless important for him to express in this way, as Carina did, because crude social mixing has become the principle means to understand living with difference. But it is certainly worth noting that his white middle class friendships are not uncomplicated. For example, he explains that some of these people will not come round to his house because they are wary of the local black community. This is a common experience for many of the young adults who have to negotiate their encounters and friendships in relation to the geographical boundaries of race and class.

Paradoxically then, whilst 'mixing' is invoked to legitimate the meaninglessness of interactions with racialised difference, respondents' narratives adversely draw attention to the significance of processes of racialisation in everyday lives and everyday spaces. But what I want to emphasise here is that such an approach to multiculture – an approach which is overly simplified – gives no space to talk about racism. Indeed, these oversimplifications make racism difficult to name. This problem is facilitated because definitions of racism are vague and are not understood by his white peers as a structuring feature of society. Hence Steve, who is white and lives nearby in Moss Side, was able to claim that he did not think being black

When is racism?   133

"would make a difference" and that "there is obviously no racism in this area, because the people who beat you up are from every race".

Nasreen lives in Longsight. She describes herself as British, Muslim and Bangladeshi. Her difficulty in naming racism is evident in the following two extracts. Both of which come as a response to the question:

Bethan: Do you think some people hold these kinds of things [categories on the equality monitoring form] as more important than others?

In the first extract, Nasreen equates a "strong" Muslim and Caribbean community with an unwillingness to mix with people of different ethnicities and is quite disparaging of this kind of attitude. Again, like Carina above, she puts the responsibility for integration onto these marginalised groups. In the second, she talks about a TV documentary about and called 'BNP Wives', in which a woman refuses treatment from a black midwife. Here, whilst she says she cannot understand the attitude, she says she recognises that it is something important to the woman in question:

Nasreen: I know people who hold their ideas of being Muslim very strong and they don't want to mix and things and I don't agree with that. I am aware of that and I know with the Caribbean community, one of my friends, she's Caribbean and she put some henna on her hand and her dad was like, "You're not Somalian, what are you putting that on for?" So it must be in that kind of community as well kind of thing.

Nasreen: You've got the people like the BNP's as well. They're very much white English aren't they? With their identity being white and that probably affects who they interact with and their opinion of things, yeah, cos I was watching this programme about BNP wives and she was saying that in her birth plan that she wrote down that she wanted a white lady to deliver her baby and when it came to labour, a black woman went and she was very very angry about it and I didn't see what . . . to me it doesn't make sense, what difference does it make? But that clearly is something that mattered to her, why I don't know, but I suppose it's just something that's important to her.

Nasreen is conscious of the problem of engaging in a discussion about whiteness and racism. Certainly there is a lot at stake here. And, in both extracts, she responds in a way that might be interpreted from a hegemonic perspective as inconsistent with how she is positioned as a headscarf wearing, Asian-Muslim-woman. When talking about the subjects in the TV show she infers that women in the show are expressing racial self-interest (not racism), and, although she cannot understand their decisions, like Carina above, she does not think their decision should be judged because this itself would show a lack of tolerance. Shrugging these incidents off can be a means of dealing with them. Indeed, Nasreen's attempt to explain racism and understand prejudiced views can, therefore, also be interpreted as a

134   *When is racism?*

form of resistance to the way she is positioned. But it is notable that in doing so she also makes comments about Muslims, Caribbeans and Somalis that speak to generalised culturalist discourses because these are part of an acceptable way of speaking and allows her to get heard within the dominant discourse. She, like the other young people, meets limitations in what is acceptable when describing racism because the language necessary to talk about these encounters is arguably more difficult to access.

Naming racism, naming racists

On one occasion when I met up with Nasreen I suggested that we meet up in a café in the early evening, not far from where she would be finishing work in Moss Side. When we arrived the café was empty. We ordered tea and quite soon the place started to fill up. We found ourselves surrounded by groups of men sitting around us, some of whom were paying us a lot of undue attention. We joked about this incident when we met up a week or so later, making fun of the men's crass behaviour. I asked her if she thought that people ever made assumptions about her based on what she looks like. She thought about this and then proceeded to tell me this story about an interview she had had for a job in a shop:

Nasreen: They looked at me, Asian, wearing a scarf, I must be very traditional, or I must have, or must be what they think is a stereotypical girl that's just going to get married and I was like, I can't say to you, I don't know, I'm not looking, I'm not getting married right now, so how does that matter. And I came out thinking, that's so weird, but I didn't know so much about my rights then as well, that they shouldn't have really have asked me that. Would they have asked that if someone went who was a white woman, would they have asked her about whether she was getting married, assuming that she's going to go away? What is that assumption that I'm going to leave my job and move kind of thing, so that's something, I have had that, so perhaps looking at me they assumed that.
Bethan: And they were Asian, the people making the assumptions did you say?
Nasreen: They were Asian yeah, um I can't think of anything that's . . . I can't think of any racist experience that I've had, maybe from white or black people.

In explaining this story, she refers to the behaviour of the Asian shopkeepers as racist because of the way they have made a certain set of assumptions about her. Of particular interest here is that she adds to this account that she cannot recall any racist experience from white or black people. And yet this latter statement contradicts part of our earlier conversation when she recalls two separate incidents of racism. In the first, she talks about visiting a friend in east Manchester and describes white people throwing stones at her car and shouting 'Paki'. In the second, she talks about house hunting with her husband. After visiting one property on her own she found the front door graffitied with the words, 'No Pakis'. She explained how she returned the next day with her husband to meet the white estate agent to discover the agent had removed the graffiti and did not inform them about it. However, Nasreen does not talk about these incidents as examples of racism in the way that she does about the job interview with the Asian shopkeeper. Instead, she downplays these moments. She adds to the story about having stones thrown at her that, 'I suppose a couple of times over what, six years is not really . . . like when I started going there a lot, I suppose is not that bad.' It may be that, like Mina, she struggles to talk about racism amongst white people because she is talking to someone who is white. If it is, it certainly makes the matter no less significant. Nasreen's account draws attention to the difficulty of articulating racism, but also to a disparity in the way that the racism of white people can be articulated. It is, for example, notable that Nasreen does not struggle to identify the Asian shopkeeper as racist. But it is also worth bearing in mind the conditions in which Nasreen has to work. We can, for example, conclude that there is less at stake for her in talking about her job interview (not necessarily at an individual level, but at a structural level) in part because what she is describing can fall within a common trope of how Asian men are depicted in the UK and does not incriminate her as a disruptive minority woman as she is reserving culpability for other members of her own assigned ethnicity.

The difficulty in naming racism and identifying individuals as racist also comes up in one of my conversations with Hamid. In one of our conversations I asked him if there are any parts of Manchester that he avoids. He responded by explaining that he avoids Salford because of his experience of racism there. Although he is also compelled to reiterate that he *could* go there but chooses not to:

> [I avoid] certain parts of Salford, but that's because it's pure and utter racist. It's not that I'm afraid of certain people; it's just that you just don't want to be the one to go there; it's not worth the hassle.

There are multiple claims at play here which somewhat rub up against each other. On the one hand he wants to defend his right to the city, but this is a challenge because of the way that he recognises he is positioned as 'other' and encounters racism in some areas. Tony, who is black and lives in Longsight, echoes this sentiment:

> You'll get some people who think they can't go some places, but as far as I'm concerned there's no place that I can't go, I was born in this country, do you know what I mean?

Later in the interview, Tony also appears to contradict this statement because, it emerges, there are places that he says he would not go. Like Hamid, he explains how he would not go to Salford because "they are nuts and beat black people up" there. The point that Tony and Hamid are making, therefore, is an important one but it is that they have the *right* to go anywhere, even though this is not always made possible. Returning to my conversation with Hamid what becomes

136 *When is racism?*

interesting is that once he has raised the subject of racism unprompted he then begins a retreat. Following from his initial description of Salford above, I asked him if he has had similar experiences in other parts of Manchester. He begins by downplaying racism when he says the following in a jocular manner:

> It's not as blatant and as predominant [in Gorton] as it is Salford in that part of . . . you'd get one or two gangs that'll give you dirty looks or shout out, "You black bastard", but it won't be like, they won't chase you down the street like in Salford. It is not as predominant and it's not as blatant and in your face.

But then he continues and appears to change his mind about racism altogether:

> I think most people who say they're racist ain't racist. Especially in Salford, I don't think Salford's a racist area.

The emphasis on disavowing racism in Salford, in light of what he has said above, gives extra stress to his negation. When I then asked him why some people describe themselves as racist, he tells me that people are just "confused". Like Carina above, he suggests that it's not really their fault and proffers an explanation of why some people in Salford act the way they do:

> There might be one or two people that are . . . that they're afraid of or look up to that are out and out racist and just to be in their good people's good books, they act racist.

This statement again carries a telling contradiction since he acknowledges that being racist carries some kind of value and respect, whilst at the same time suggesting it is not really credible. Within this shift in his narrative, he is particularly keen to convey that when racism 'appears' to emerge he is not subjected to it anyway because of his ability to pass as "normal":

> The fact is, they'll be racist to you but if you're from the area, or you know someone that they know then they won't see you as a black person but just as a friend, or someone they know. It's when they don't know you, is when the racism comes into it. I know a friend he's got racist family members but cos I'm friends with him, they treat me like they must be colour-blind and like I'm just normal, another one of his white friends, but when I'm not with him and they see another black person in the street, you see the racism in them, they're hating him and that proves they're not being racist. It's just a thingy for them innit.

The way that Hamid explains racism here is significant. In this example he assumes the logic that 'real' racism is something innate which precludes it from being an organised expression of power that structures society. Hence Hamid can conclude that because the people to whom he refers enact racist behaviour as part of a machoistic means to assert control and get into other white people's "good books", this is not really racism. Hamid develops a location within his narrative as someone who can explain how racism works locally and someone who is not subjected to racism because he is local and is perceived as "normal". But his narrative also reflects the discomfort that acknowledging racism entails, and I would suggest it is compounded because in the example described above he is always alone and he risks being perceived as undermining aspects of his masculinity. These can therefore be more easily conceived as exceptional moments that might be more readily dismissed by others or overlooked as questions around his masculinity and his ability to deal with these situations.

Hamid speaks with far greater ease about recognised institutional racisms in which he is of course notably not alone in experiencing. Policing practices and racial profiling in particular were highlighted when he explains how the police raid his local Somali-run café on an almost weekly basis. He also talks about how stop and search is a shared experience and regular topic of conversation among his peers through which they also advise younger boys in the area on how to avoid being taken into custody under suspicion of not meeting immigration criteria. This is obviously a different experience for Hamid to talk about, both because it is not an individualised occurrence, but also because it is an institutionalised phenomenon. This is perhaps helped because racism within the police is a better-known problem. Indeed the only report into institutional racism in the UK did focus on the police and the issue was given brief attention when David Cameron admitted during Prime Minister's questions in January 2016 that the fact that black people are more likely to be sentenced to custody than white people required investigation. Research in Manchester illustrate how there has been a long history of repressive policing in the city; complaints about which have often centred on public order policing in multi-ethnic neighbourhoods (Jeffery et al., 2015). In Moss Side, where Hamid lives, policing is widely seen as a significant problem, and Moss Side is often unfairly the subject of media reports on what are Manchester-wide crime-related issues (see, for example, Minott and Chowdhury, 2017). The Northern Monitoring Project was set up in 2012 at a meeting in Moss Side to offer legal assistance and 'provide a genuine challenge to the official narrative on crime and policing' (Gilmore and Tufail, 2013) and continues to actively work in the area. All of the young people were familiar with this issue, and it was notable that when they were talking about the representations of different areas Moss Side was said to be depicted as the area of Manchester that is "ahead" in terms of crime.

Simon, who grew up in the Moss Side area, explains that he and his friends are regularly stopped by the police because they are black and mixed race. He also notes how the neighbourhood is subject to regular police patrols that, he says, act as a form of negative "conditioning" for people who live there. He describes these patrols as disproportionate and at odds with the policing of other areas and explains how this relates to racist practices within the police and their profiling of black people:

> It is a conditioning, cos you don't get. You don't see certain patrols going in to other areas all the time, you just don't see it, and they go, "Oh well there's

138 *When is racism?*

not a need for it". Well there is, there is a need for it, cos you know, there is stuff that goes on in these areas. . . . Like you were saying, they stopped the Somali people, they'll just say, "Oh well we'll stop them cos they're black" and you know what, that is the truth. Do you know what I mean? The police in the area, I don't know, I haven't got any great examples to give you in a way, but I can feel it from just the vibes. It might sound weird, you know how you can get vibes off people, just being around them, it's a very negative thing.

Policing also comes up in some of the narratives of the white young people. Caroline, who lives in a predominantly white middle class area, for example, explains how a police officer suggested to her that criminal behaviour is most likely to be associated with 'ethnic minority groups':

Neighbourhood Watch that came up like with the police guy that came round saying like a lot of crime's this, and it's like, "No it isn't, cos all the guys who've jumped over our fence have been white", so [laughs] I mean that's anecdotal, but it's kind of do you know . . . I think there are still perceptions that go with some ethnic minority groups that are not true, but then that affects how people view areas because of the people who live there and what they've seen.

Leading on from this example, Caroline also highlights a contradiction in the way that UK society is portrayed as "non-racist" and at the same time keeps criminalising young black men.

I would say like Moss Side is perceived a certain way partly because of the way our society still, despite being a "non-racist" society views like young black males

(Air quotes around non-racist gestured by Caroline).

Discussions of institutionalised racism in the police thus create a space that appears to allow for an 'escape' from post-racial logics that appear to have stronger purchase in more mundane and individualised encounters in the city. Indeed, it is often only on the topic of policing that many of the young people, who in other moments reproduce the narrative of the tolerant city, begin to question its relevance. This might be because institutional racism in the police force has been one of the only avenues through which racism has been addressed (no matter how inadequately) at a political level (see Macpherson, 1999). It might also be because among young people and people living in dense urban areas, it is acceptable to construct the police as the enemy within (Scaglion and Condon, 1980; Wacquant, 2008). Certainly this is worth bearing in mind in terms of how we might begin to work on sites of recognition and think about how we might expand on these to open out those conversations to highlight how other processes link in – rather than allow policing to be treated as another case of exception, or as a stand-alone issue.

Conclusion

One of the common themes running through this book is the tentative way in which the young adults often talk about race and infer that it is something that belongs to the past. So in answer to the question, 'when is racism?', the answer is almost always in reference to something that has happened and indeed does usually refer to specific events in the past. In the above discussion I noted how isolated events and individuals can act as convenient moments in which to account for racism without dragging the rest of society into a relationship with them. And as such, they represent the ways in which definitions of racism have been narrowed to produce a space in which racism can go unquestioned and remain part of the past, or abstracted from social and political structures. And so, as well as claiming that racism belongs to the past, it is also considered, when indeed admitted into the contemporary, to be highly peripheral to mainstream society.

The young people were understandably drawn to such post-racial imaginaries since they can assume the guise of progress and optimism that have rhetorical appeal beyond their limits. Indeed, the young people also drew on notions of future to imply a process of improvement and maturation, primarily grounded in the increased diversity of their social relations (see also Chapter 3). Hence, this research often very much reflected the way in which racism is historicised and retained as the domain of extreme right-wing groups, older generations and/or existing in places they described as 'backwards'. However, there was also a strong awareness that race, articulated with class, shaped the representations of their neighbourhoods and how they were commonly positioned. This presents a somewhat contradictory dilemma for the young people.

What the research presented in this chapter illustrates is the way in which naming racism is challenging in a context in which racism has been expunged from the popular public imagination. It is also difficult in a city that bases much of its attraction on suggesting that it is a progressive and tolerant (non-racist) space. The challenge however is not solely that these contexts make it harder to be heard, but the discourses through which they manifest are deeply embedded and have a common-sensical appeal, so as to be attractive. The pernicious successes of arguments that make use of post-racial logics, or logics of natural self-interest, rely on the principle that they are common sensical in their simplicity, even whilst they are incoherent and contradictory (Hall and O'Shea, 2013). Hence, it is on reflecting on the pervasiveness of the post-racial that Goldberg argues that we are all 'postracial structurally by being drawn into the generalised and now unavoidable social logic of postraciality' (Valluvan and Kapoor, 2016: 113). It is not so much then that the young people do not recognise their encounters with racism, nor that they do not consider them to be problematic. However, they struggle to reconcile multiple and often contradictory levels of experience and situate these within the broader social and political contexts that shape their everyday lives. This dilemma sets us quite particular challenges. However, if we want to confront racism in the

140 *When is racism?*

everyday, one can reasonably conclude that confronting the perception that racism is an anomaly and is both historicised and ahistorical would be a good place to start.

Note

1 Thank you to a blog by Rimi Saini (2017), published on Media Diversified, for bringing my attention to this report. See Saini, R. (2017). *'Racial self-interest' is not racism: Populist correctness gone mad?* https://mediadiversified.org/2017/03/23/racial-self-interest-is-not-racism-populist-correctness-gone-mad/[Online].

References

Ahmed, S. (2004). Declarations of whiteness: The non-performativity of anti-racism. *Borderlands ejournal*, 3(2). www.borderlands.net.au/vol3no2_2004/ahmed_declarations.htm

Ahmed, S. (2010). *The promise of happiness*. Durham and London: Duke University Press.

Allen, C. (2010). *Islamophobia*. London: Routledge.

Allport, G. W. (1979 [1954]). *The nature of prejudice*. Reading, MA: Addison-Wesley.

Ambikaipaker, M. (2015). Liberal exceptions: Violent racism and routine anti-racist failure in Britain. *Ethnic and Racial Studies*, 38(12), 2055–2070.

Amin, A. (2012). *Land of strangers*. Cambridge: Polity.

Gilroy, P. (2008). A land of tea drinking, hokey cokey and rivers of blood. *The Guardian*, 18 April 2008. www.theguardian.com/commentisfree/2008/apr/18/britishidentity.race

Minott, A., Chowdhury, T. & Williams, P. (2017). Unfair criminalisation of Moss Side residents. *The Guardian*, 27 February 2017. www.theguardian.com/uk-news/2017/feb/27/unfair-criminalisation-of-moss-side-residents

Goodhart, D. (2017). White self-interest is not the same thing as racism. *Financial Times*, 2 March 2017. www.ft.com/content/220090e0-efc1-11e6-ba01-119a44939bb6

Bhabha, H. (1994). *The location of culture*. Abingdon: Routledge.

Bonilla-Silva, E. (2014). *Racism without racists: Color-blind racism and the persistence of racial inequality in America* (4th Edition). Plymouth: Rowman & Leftfield.

Casey, L. (2016). *The Casey review: A review into opportunity and integration*. London: Department for Communities and Local Government.

Esmail, A. & Everington, S. (1993). Racial discrimination against doctors from ethnic minorities. *British Medical Journal*, 306(6879), 691–692.

Fortier, A. (2008). *Multicultural horizons: Diversity and the limits of the civil nation*. London: Routledge.

Gilmore, J. & Tufail, W. (2013). Police corruption and community resistance. *Criminal Justice Matters*, 94(1), 8–9.

Goldberg, D. T. (2001). *The racial state*. Malden, MA: Blackwell.

Goldberg, D. T. (2009). *The threat of race: Reflections on racial neoliberalism*. Malden, MA: Wiley-Blackwell.

Goldberg, D. T. (2015). *Are we all postracial yet?* Cambridge and Malden, MA: Polity Press.

Goodhart, D. (2004). *Too diverse? Prospect Magazine*.

Goodhart, D. (2013). *The British dream: Successes and failures of post-war immigration*. London: Atlantic Books.

Gunaratnam, Y. (2003). *Researching 'race' and ethnicity: Methods, knowledge and power.* London: Sage.

Hall, S. & O'Shea, A. (2013). Common-sense neoliberalism. *Soundings: A Journal of Politics and Culture*, 55, Winter, 8–24.

Harries, B. (2014). We need to talk about race. *Sociology*, 48(6), 1107–1122.

Harries, B., Byrne, B., Rhodes, J. & Wallace, S. (forthcoming). Diversity in place: narrations of diversity in an ethnically mixed, urban area. *Journal of Ethnic and Migration Studies.*

Hesse, B. (2011). Self-fulfilling prophecy: The postracial horizon. *The South Atlantic Quarterly*, 110(1), 155–178.

Jeffery, B., Tufail, W. & Jackson, W. (2015). Policing and the reproduction of local social order: A case study of Greater Manchester. *Journal on European History of Law*, 6(1), 118–128.

Kapoor, N. (2011). The advancement of racial neoliberalism in Britain. *Ethnic and Racial Studies*, 1, 1–19.

Kaufmann, E. (2017). *'Racial self-interest' is not racism: Ethno-demographic interests and the immigration debate.* London: Policy Exchange.

Lentin, A. & Titley, G. (2011). *The crises of multiculturalism: Racism in a neoliberal age.* London: Zed Books.

Macpherson, W. (1999). *The Stephen Lawrence inquiry: Report of an inquiry by Sir William Macpherson of Cluny.* London: Home Office.

Nayak, A. (2006). After race: Ethnography, race and post-race theory. *Ethnic and Racial Studies*, 29(3), 411–430.

Nazroo, J. & Kapadia, D. (2013a). Ethnic inequalities in labour market participation? *Dynamics of diversity: Evidence from the 2011 Census.* University of Manchester: Centre on Dynamics of Ethnicity, Manchester, UK.

Nazroo, J. & Kapadia, D. (2013b). Have ethnic inequalities in employment persisted between 1991 and 2011? *Dynamics of diversity: Evidence from teh 2011 Census.* University of Manchester: Centre on Dynamics of Ethnicity, Manchester, UK.

Omi, M. & Winant, H. (1994). *Racial formation in the United States: From the 1960s to the 1990s.* New York and London: Routledge.

Phillips, D. (2006). Parallel lives? Challenging discourses of British Muslim self-segregation. *Environment and Planning D: Society and Space*, 24(1), 25–40.

Saini, R. (2017). 'Racial self-interest' is not racism: Populist correctness gone mad? Available from: https://mediadiversified.org/2017/03/23/racial-self-interest-is-not-racism-populist-correctness-gone-mad/[Online].

Scaglion, R. & Condon, R. (1980). Determinants of attitudes toward city police. *Criminology*, 17(4), 485–494.

Simpson, L. (2007). Ghettoes of the mind: The empirical behaviour of indices of segregation and diversity. *Journal of the Royal Statistical Society: Series A (Statistics in Society)*, 170(2), 405–424.

Solomos, J. & Back, L. (1996). *Racism and society: Sociology for a changing world.* London: Palgrave Macmillan.

Song, M. (2014). Challenging a culture of racial equivalence. *The British Journal of Sociology*, 65(1), 107–129.

Titley, G. (2016). On are we all post racial yet? *Ethnic and Racial Studies*, 39(13), 2269–2277.

Valluvan, S. & Kapoor, N. (2016). Notes on theorizing racism and other things. *Ethnic and Racial Studies*, 39(3), 375–382.

142 *When is racism?*

Wacquant, L. (2008). *Urban outcasts: A comparative sociology of advanced marginality*. Cambridge: Polity Press.

Wilson, H. F. (2016). On geography and encounter: Bodies, borders, and difference. *Progress in Human Geography*, First published date: 13 May 2016, 1–21.

Winant, H. (2001). *The world is a ghetto: Race and democracy since World War II*. Oxford: Basic Books.

Winant, H. (2004). *The new politics of race: Globalism, difference, justice*. Minneapolis: University of Minnesota Press.

Winant, H. (2006). Race and racism: Towards a global future. *Ethnic and Racial Studies*, 29(5), 986–1003.

7   Conclusion

Very early on in the research I met Amal on the main street running through Moss Side. Amal was on his break from work, the weather was nice and we stood together for a while chatting. He told me he was about to sit some exams and then go traveling and was asking me what university was like when his interest turned to my research. In reply, he said to me with earnest:

Amal: Actually, I see what you're doing. It's interesting, but you know what you'll find?
Bethan: What's that?
Amal: The world's a much bigger place than what people think. Like people talk about Moss Side like it's this small world on its own, as if it's different to everywhere else, but do you know what, you'll find that everyone's the same wherever you go.

I only met Amal on this one occasion, but this statement was set to become a central motif throughout the research. I did not know it at the time, but claims to sameness would arise in multiple forms. In some ways the book marks an engagement with these claims as it seeks to unravel the multiply inflected ways that race takes form. Indeed, one of the central concerns has been to address the tension implied in claims to sameness, in spite of difference. This is a tension that shares some of the characteristics of wanting to move beyond race but needing to recognise the multiple ways racism manifests. In doing so, the book tells a story of the different ways that race is recognised, reproduced and managed in everyday life. It has brought together multiple layers of representation and explored how they shape and are shaped by the social and material relations that make up the lived experience of young adults in Manchester.

In situating this work, I was alert to the increasing attention paid in the scholarly literature to processes that silence race from the national imagination. This has largely been interrogated through a critical analysis of neoliberal political machineries that seek to manage difference by referring the responsibility of racism to bounded structural and institutional arrangements and to the margins of society (see, for example, Goldberg, 2009; Lentin and Titley, 2011). But, the effects of the silencing inferred are not new. The denial of responsibility for racism has, for

144 *Conclusion*

example, long been charted as part of the UK's way of dealing (or not dealing) with the legacies of colonialism (Young, 1995; Gilroy, 2004; Hall, 2000). This book has contributed a unique perspective to these discussions, by exploring the reproduction and effects of discursive processes of denial and silencing in young people's everyday lives in terms of how they construct their identity and recognise and talk about racism. This work is also situated in the broader context in which national identity is treated as if in crisis and in which policy remains focused on integration. The book therefore also importantly draws attention to how black young people are positioned, marginalised and held accountable in different ways to their white peers. It has been particularly important to address these issues with young adults because the young have been imagined as the potential future of multiculture and have become a key focus in current policy guidance on integration. Focusing on people in their twenties has allowed for an examination of how race is experienced across a range of thresholds as they expand their lifespace and leave school and home and become increasingly mobile as they look for work and housing. And, as they live out their social and cultural lives with new friends from different parts of the city. This work has therefore complimented previous research with young people that has often centred on the peer group or specific location, such as the youth club, school or neighbourhood, but opens up the discussion to think about how young adults navigate the wider city.

Manchester as a city was represented in multiple, and often contradictory, ways, as explored in Chapter 2. Primarily, I was concerned with how meanings given to difference varied in different parts of Manchester, which, I argued, was necessary in order to understand how the young adults made sense of their lives and could situate their own subjectivities and experiences. One of the ways seemingly contradictory processes of racialisation manifests is through cartographies of race that are constructed in distinct ways. The discussion centred on a comparison between the ways in which difference was articulated in the city centre and the neighbourhoods where the research was located. For example, spaces of the city were differentially constructed as 'accessible' and 'pathological' sites of ethnic or racialised difference. This revealed just how fixed, static and limited the spaces of a city can be made to appear, but also drew attention to a set of boundaries that could be manipulated as a means of exclusion.

In the first place, the chapter explored how the city of Manchester depicts itself as a forward facing global city, which partly relied on constructing itself as a site of tolerance and celebration of cultural diversity. Old narratives of Manchester as a radical city that had roots to its connection to various social movements were resuscitated and reinterpellated within a neoliberal paradigm to contemporary liberal concerns. However, I argued that such a portrayal of Manchester paid little attention to the meaning or value of multiculture beyond its commercial value and did not resemble progressive, or indeed 'radical', thinking on the politics of race or inequality. To exemplify this, it was noted that migrants were portrayed as lucky to be part of Manchester rather than the reverse, and that ethnic minorities were depicted as being 'accommodated' rather than recognised as active contributors and makers of the city.

Conclusion 145

Second, the neighbourhoods where the young adults in the research lived were constructed in opposition. These areas, usually referred to as the inner city, are more ethnically diverse but were not articulated in sympathetic ways. Instead, in line with research elsewhere, the inner city was where difference (not diversity) became the key focus and its population was produced as if alien or 'other'. These areas were imagined as if dislocated from the boundaries of the city's commercial cultural centre that they bordered, as well as more specifically from its economic prowess and imagined moral worth. Indeed, whilst the city was conceived as part of the future, the inner city was deemed to be backwards and out of step.

I argued that if we want to understand the emergence of social identities, politics and organisation we need to pay attention to the different ways race is articulated across the city. The city is thus a key site through which to analyse processes of racialisation and the relationship between people and place. It is also an important means through which to reflect on other scales of analysis. Principally, this involved reflecting on how national and global forces formed Manchester and shaped local identities. I argued, for example, that racialised difference took on specific meanings when they were trapped in national immigration debates or were removed from their global dimensions and conceived as if produced from nowhere but in the local (Sassen, 1996). The chapter thus formed an important basis from which to explore potential boundaries of exclusion and a context in which the young adults could construct their own identities and navigate the spatial configurations of the city in which they lived.

Chapter 3 was the first of two chapters to address questions of identity with the young adults. This discussion centred on the way that they found appeal in the liberal notions of tolerance and future thinking that epitomised the neoliberal brand of Manchester. I explored how they took up parts of this message to construct an identity that worked with the notion of being a 'generation'. This generational narrative, produced in close articulation with the city, was used to mark a break between themselves and their parents' and grandparents' generation in terms of tolerance to difference and attitudes to racism. It was also employed as a means to distinguish themselves from people located elsewhere in the UK, but principally smaller towns in the northwest that have been the centre of debates on integration and community cohesion, and which have been constructed as 'backwards' in the local and national imagination.

This discussion engaged with some of the literature on the post-racial to contextualise some of its features, arguing that logics of the post-racial held a certain allure for the young adults. I suggested that a framing of the post-racial was drawn upon to reproduce a myth of sameness (such as that alluded to by Amal) and the illusion of non-racism through somewhat naïve calls to universalism. What was significant was the way that narratives of tolerance and open-mindedness were constructed as inherent to the present moment. And, in particular, to people who have learned competencies of dealing with difference as a result of growing up in, and always knowing, a multicultural city. Processes of racialisation were evident in the representations of place produced by the young adults, but were then largely imagined as the legacy of a past generation. This did not leave space for the

146 *Conclusion*

recognition of the contemporary relevance of structural hierarchies nor an understanding of the way in which racism is rooted in a longer history. The chapter paid particular attention to the silence around white privilege in narratives and the contradictions that arise when this is placed alongside demands for a humanistic approach to the categorising of 'non-white' bodies. Hence, I argue that the way young adults talk race resonates with national discourses of multiculture that imagine liberal ideals of multiculturalism but do not recognise inequalities and exclusion.

The chapter also addressed the ways in which young people have been imagined as symbols of the future of multiculturalism (Amin, 2010) and have become the specific targets of simplistic calls to integrate. I suggested that the way in which the young people talked about their relationships was shaped by rhetoric of integration that relies on crude groupisms and notions of mixing, and which overshadowed the complexities of lived multiculture. This had special significance in light of recent policy guidance from the government that targets young people and their need to 'mix' socially (Casey, 2016). I argued that, against such a context, the young adults were encouraged to overemphasise difference in their encounters. At the same time, relationships that possessed a convivial quality and unsettled imagined boundaries struggled to be considered for their everydayness because they do not fit into the paradigm of integration. This work therefore highlighted a troubling paradox that arose when, instead of relying on mundane forms of multiculture, the young people drew on crude and often staged forms of mixing that spoke to integrationist and post-racial logics, thus reproducing culturalist tropes rather than moving beyond race as we might hope was their intention.

What was conspicuously absent from the narratives detailed in Chapters 2 and 3, was any recognition that people experience the city in different ways. The emphasis on sameness suggested that there is no inherent difference between people who are read as Asian, black and white, for example. What was missing was the acknowledgement that being read and positioned as black or Asian represents a different experience to being read and positioned as white. Chapters 4, 5 and 6 addressed these omissions by building on the representational narratives presented in the first part of the book to think about how they shape and are shaped by social and material conditions and lived experience.

In Chapter 4 I paid close attention to the ways that the young adults talked about their engagements with difference including, where relevant, their avoidance of such encounters. This included a discussion of how black and Asian young people, who were often constructed as different through a hegemonic lens, made sense of their own encounters and reflected on the experience of *being* encountered. This required paying attention to the affective qualities that race possesses. Principally, I was concerned with the affect that the anticipation of race had on encounters. The young people developed their own sense of how to navigate the spatial configurations of the city through their expectations of the local social and cultural context. But it was also the relationship between bodies and their proximity to each other that was important for understanding the function of race and how it is made (Ahmed, 2014). The position of whiteness comes to the fore here. Many of the white young people anxiously anticipated race, so much so that they often ignored all forms of difference, even disavowing the presence of black bodies, including in the racially diverse areas of Moss Side and Longsight. These avoidances were made all the more audible when the young people talked about white working class areas instead. Here they demonstrated little regard for how the associations they made between a particular kind of working classness and immorality and lack of values might be perceived. And, whilst black bodies were disavowed in neighbourhoods like Moss Side and Longsight, white working class areas like Gorton emerged as if over-populated and chaotic. These encounters did not only tell us about the acceptability of derogations of 'chavs', but also hinted at the silences and carefully constructed metaphors contained within their stories about black and Asian spaces, which appeared uninhabited. Notable exceptions to this emerged when the white young people talked about notions of community by imbuing 'ethnic neighbourhoods' with culturalist tropes. But, these encounters were typically borne not so much from the everyday, but through engagements with commercialised areas and were mediated by the relationship of consumer and service provider. If we place these failures to recognise difference in experience alongside the neutralised descriptions of everyday Manchester, those descriptions become even less convincing as depictions of everyday life. Instead, they read like carefully nuanced descriptions of an everyday that is selective and exclusionary in its scope.

In contrast, the black and Asian young people were aware of being interpellated as different, despite their joint calls for a universal generational identity. Consequently, within their stories the young people expressed a more nuanced and complex understanding of how the city works. They described a sense of 'double consciousness' and learning how to anticipate different expectations, according to where they were located and who they were with. For example, a common strategy for the young adults was to develop their relationships in specific places, by only inviting certain friends back to their neighbourhoods or choosing to meet in more neutral locations in the city centre. These negotiations brought to life the complexities of living in the city that are imagined in conflicting ways. They also stimulated questions about how the young people negotiated their identities according to where they were located, which became the central focus of the following chapter.

Chapter 5 engaged with the young people's routine experiences of being positioned as different, but was primarily concerned with how ascribed identifications were manipulated, negotiated and resisted. The chapter began by exploring how many of our encounters start from a point of misrecognition. It dealt separately with the ways in which the black and white young people were positioned and argued that, although feelings of frustration and humiliation were shared when they were positioned in derogatory ways, there were different issues and different intensities at stake. Black and Asian young people were 'naturally' associated with the inner city and with deprivation wherever they went, whilst the white young people were only read as such outside these areas if they dressed, spoke or behaved in a particular way. White identifications have a more malleable texture, which

148   *Conclusion*

also means there was less at stake for the white young people. They were not always over-determined by class but importantly, they were also not conceived as if representatives of a collective, or coherent community for which they are liable. Hence, whilst the whole group of young people might share a position in relation to economic processes, the black young people were additionally positioned in relation to racist structures and groupist discourses, for which they were expected to be accountable.

In the second half of the chapter I focused on how the black and Asian young people challenged and manipulated certain forms of identification. I drew out three key ways in which they did this. The first largely focused on the role of category formation and allocation. The young people expressed a great deal of frustration with prescribed identity categories, both because they are allocated by institutions and because they limit claims to a multi-faceted identity. The young people preferred to abandon categories altogether to claim instead a unique, category-less identity for themselves. But these, I argued, should not be read as claims to individualism, but rather were resistances to well-worn tropes that become stuck to bodies. This move is framed by the context of a neoliberal shift away from collective mobilisation, in which the label 'black' has been redirected to identify a racialised group, rather than a political, historical or cultural category (Alexander, 2002). Second, another means of claiming a multifaceted identity was by actively reworking the categories to make a claim against rudimentary interpretations and to demand to be recognised in a multi-faceted or non-homogeneous way. This was also important when claiming rights to citizenship – the identity of British being one that must be actively claimed because it is never assumed. Finally, the chapter explored some of the ways in which the young people manipulated or 'played' with their potential to be misrecognised. Black young people, for example, were alternately associated with 'African', 'Caribbean', 'Muslim' or 'Christian' identities. In the process of refusing certain identification and playing with others the young people alerted us to the way in which the body is entwined with categories that must be confronted. By playing with the different possibilities of recognition, this strategy emerged as part of a claim to occupy a more nuanced and complex position and presented an opportunity to undermine and destabilise more simplistic ways of seeing.

Finally, in Chapter 6 I examined how racism is recognised and defined as something that structures young lives. I was interested in how, in light of the contextual features of Manchester and their own generational narrative, the young adults were then able to talk about their own experiences of racism. As such, the chapter returned to some of the debates that critically engaged with the notion of the post-racial that were introduced in Chapter 3. This was built on to incorporate a closer engagement with a literature that analyses the shifting way that racism is being interpreted through an increasingly narrowed lens. I was particularly interested in the ways that definitions of racism have been constricted to produce a space in which racism can go unquestioned and be seen as only a historical phenomenon, abstracted from social and political structures. I also returned to some of the questions about social mixing that were raised earlier in the book. I noted that, whilst

Conclusion   149

mixing was invoked as a way to convey the meaninglessness of interactions with racialised difference, they adversely drew attention to the significance of race. Furthermore, social mixing was claimed to be emblematic of non-racism, emulating policy and academic work that emphasises 'contact' without acknowledging the roots of racism, or giving adequate consideration to inequalities and relations of power. This then blocked off a space to talk about racism and overshadowed the work of anti-racism. In light of these contextual features, the young adults had to negotiate a series of contradictory logics when trying to convey their own experiences of racism and, at times, were reluctant to do so.

It became clear that, for some black young people, to articulate racism was difficult because it risked being read as racist themselves. This reflected a concerning shift in a dominant narrative that has not only developed rationalisations about the status of other racialised groups to protect white collective interests (Bonilla-Silva, 2014), but also the way in which the direction of hostility inherent in racism has been reversed. Arguments have been put forward across Europe and the US that seek to legitimise 'reverse racism' or 'racial self-interest' by arguing that it is justifiable and natural even to express concerns about the loss of identity, access to resources and protection of claims to sovereignty. The effects of this are clearly felt when the young people were unable to articulate even the crudest forms of overt racism that they have repeatedly experienced without feeling anxious about the way they will then be perceived. It is surely relevant to this concern that their white peers did not classify racism as a contemporary concern and failed to recognise the significance of race as a structural feature of society.

Finally, I examined the challenges faced by the young adults to get their voices heard. Several examples were drawn upon to highlight the difficulties in voicing experiences of racism. One area provided an exception to this, however. Experience of racism from the police opened up a space that allowed for an escape from post-racial logics. Institutional racism within the police has been one of the only avenues through which racism has been addressed at a political level (albeit somewhat inadequately). At the same time, amongst the young and people living in dense urban areas it is acceptable to construct the police as the enemy within. I suggested that this small gap was important and might enable work on other sites of recognition and help expand these conversations to think about how other processes link in rather than treating police as some sort of exception to the rule.

Final comments

In the UK we live in an apparent paradox. Racism persists, but a post-racial imaginary has developed to suggest that we are in a moment in which racial discrimination and inequalities are largely overcome. A rise in popularity of the far-right in Europe and the US has done little to challenge the imagined notion of the post-racial within mainstream politics and social life. Indeed, we are instead seeing a deepening of post-racial racism through the legitimation of arguments that suggest that prioritising one's own 'racial self-interest' is a natural and reasonable

150   *Conclusion*

expectation, rather than an expression of any kind of prejudice (see, for example, Kaufmann, 2017). These changes reflect the shifting nature of racism and alert us to the difficulties involved in addressing something that is constantly under transformation. In this book I have drawn out some of the inherent tensions and contradictions that surface when young adults try to make sense of their own city and their own lives within it, and the broader social and political context that shapes it. To cite Back here, 'the impact of racist discourses on young lives is partial and complex' (Back, 1996: 238). Certain aspects of the post-racial have an evident allure for the young people. For some, there was a clear sense of optimism about a future without racism, even whilst there was a certain level of naivety to their claims for universalism. Consequently, race was presented as something that we are moving away from, but without acknowledgement of the complexities and historical foundations that such a move entails. Instead, attitudes to difference were constructed within a chronological narrative that reflected notions of a civilising process and suggested a process of maturation (Brown, 2006). However, this closed off the possibility of talking and acknowledging the relevance of race to structures and meanings in the present. In addition, there was little reflection on how these factors nevertheless shape and are shaped by contemporary factors. Their narratives were constructed as if to tell the story of the 'here' and 'now', but really illustrate how constructions of past, present and future work together to tell a particular tale. Everyday practice was often presented and performed in such a way as to simultaneously emphasise (racialised) difference and (humanistic) sameness. Hence the emphasis fell on aspects of non-racism, rather than anti-racism. The young people wanted to construct themselves as people who do not see racialised difference, but this was often defined as living alongside difference, as if it were not seen. Furthermore, it was motivated by an implied understanding that living with difference is in itself an act of anti-racism. This understanding has partly been produced because racism is largely understood as labelling or namecalling, whilst 'race' (as produced in their everyday lives) and the meanings ascribed to it are not seen as connected. These aspects also overshadowed the complexities of lived multiculture and the convivial qualities of many of their relationships. Indeed, the potential to challenge racist discourses through conviviality was inhibited by the set of restrictions that emerge because of the way integrationist logics dominate. These logics imagine lived multiculture as limited and exclusionary in scope. This meant that these more complex relationships had to struggle for recognition.

For many people, there remains a sense of unease and anxiety about negotiating race and race talk. For this very reason, there remains a sense of ambivalence about how to deal with race and racism. This ambivalence was shared among people who experience race in different ways, though for different reasons. Unease and anxiety about how to navigate the city and encounter difference thus lingered in the background, even when diversity is celebrated within the city in which they live. One of the most pernicious outcomes of this was the difficulty the black and Asian young people had in explaining their own experiences of racism. There was a worrying deeply held anxiety that voicing these experiences would allow them to be

Conclusion   151

read as the problem and as the racist. A number of opportunities emerged in the young people's stories that illustrate ways in which racism can be undermined, principally in relation to how they can disrupt and manipulate how they are identified, and how they can deal with institutional forms of racism operating within their own neighbourhoods. The stories presented here therefore tell us a lot about how racism can be resisted and challenged. They also demonstrate the inadequacy of integrationist paradigms to understand lived multiculture. However, they also alert us to the coercive appeal of the post-racial and non-racism over anti-racism and the complex and troubling situation this creates within which the young people have to navigate and often contest their own identities and relationships.

References

Ahmed, S. (2014). *The cultural politics of emotion* (2nd Edition). Edinburgh: Edinburgh University Press.

Alexander, C. (2002). Beyond black: Rethinking the colour/culture divide. *Ethnic and Racial Studies*, 25(4), 552–571.

Amin, A. (2010). The remainders of race. *Theory, Culture and Society*, 27(1), 1–23.

Back, L. (1996). *New ethnicities and urban multiculture: Racisms and multiculture in young lives*. London: UCL Press.

Bonilla-Silva, E. (2014). *Racism without racists: Color-blind racism and the persistence of racial inequality in America* (4th Edition). Plymouth: Rowman & Leftfield.

Brown, W. (2006). *Regulating aversion: Tolerance in the age of identity and empire*. Princeton: Princeton University Press.

Casey, L. (2016). *The Casey review: A review into opportunity and integration*. London: Department for Communities and Local Government.

Gilroy, P. (2004). *After empire: Melancholia or convivial culture?* Abingdon: Routledge.

Goldberg, D. T. (2009). *The threat of race: Reflections on racial neoliberalism*. Malden, MA: Wiley-Blackwell.

Hall, S. (2000). The multicultural question. *In:* Hesse, B. (ed.) *Un/settled multiculturalisms*. London: Zed Books.

Kaufmann, E. (2017). *'Racial self-interest' is not racism: Ethno-demographic interests and the immigration debate*. London: Policy Exchange.

Lentin, A. & Titley, G. (2011). *The crises of multiculturalism: Racism in a neoliberal age*. London: Zed Books.

Sassen, S. (1996). Analytic borderlands: Race, gender and representation in the new city in King. *In:* King, A. D. (ed.) *Re-presenting the city: Ethnicity, capital and culture in the 21st Century metropolis*. London: MacMillan Press.

Young, R. (1995). *Colonial desire: Hybridity in theory, culture and race*. London: Routledge.

Index

advertisements, Manchester City Council 20–23
Agenda 2010 programme 19
Alexander, Claire 99
'All lives matter' group 68
'the amalgamated other' 23
Amin, Ash 51
anticipation of race 63–65, 146–147; comfortable conceptions of difference 74–78; culturalist discourses 70–71; discomfort in talking about difference 68–71; expectations of difference 65–68; learned encounters 80–84; living with diversity 63–65; proximities to difference 78–80; representation of white working class 71–74
anti-race anti-racism 42
Asian stereotypes: self-segregation discourses 122–123; tropes about 92–94
assimilation: cohesion through 50; demand for 44–45; push for 3–4; *see also* integration

Banton, Michael 100
Big Society initiative 123
Black Lives Matter 68
'BNP Wives' 133
'bodies out of place' 66
Bradford 34n13, 49–50
British identity 99–100; as antidote to 'other' 51; integration and 100–101
British National Party 19, 41
Burnley 33, 34n13, 49

Cameron, David 137
Casey, Louise 50
Casey Review 123
categorisation: mixed versus binary identities 100–102; rejection of 102–107; weight of 127–130
'celebratory' narratives 20–23

'chav' label 25, 71, 94–98, 147
Chicago School 15
cities 15–16; 'celebratory' narratives of 20–23; conflicting narratives of 10–11, 144–145; expectations of difference in 65–68; learned encounters in 80–84; mapping of race onto 4; multi-layered nature of 16–17; 'no-go' areas 66–67; 'other' face of 23–34, 145; racial historicism of 47–50, 123; reinvented identities of 17–20; relationship to broader context 30–33; as 'spaces of difference' 16, 23–24; as state of mind 67; *see also* place, race and
class: class differences 53; white working class 68–71, 94–98
collective identity 50, 105–106
colonialism, repressed references to 6
colour-blindness 43–47
comfortable conceptions of difference 74–78
commodification of diversity 75–76
common ground, identification of 53–54
community: assumed membership of 91–94; conceptions of 71–74; *see also* identity
'contagions' 27
'contamination' 27
continuous process, identity as 89–90
'cosmopolitan' spaces 79, 84
crime in inner cities 26–27
Cultural Ambition report 19
culturalist discourses 70–71, 76–77
culturalist stereotypes 56–57
culture of racial equivalence 125–126

de-categorisation of identities 102–107
deprivation in inner cities 25–26
de-racialised discourses 123–127
devolution 31–32

154 *Index*

diaries: fieldwork diary 8; photographic diaries 9
difference 11–12, 24–30; cities as spaces of 23–24; class differences 53; comfortable conceptions of 74–78; commodification of 75–76; culturalist discourses 70–71; discomfort in talking about 68–71; expectations of 65–68; fetishisation of 18, 23, 77; gender 53, 58n5; indifference to 6, 58; learned encounters 80–84; living with 63–65, 146–147; marketisation of 17–23; mixing 50–57, 66–67, 130–134, 146–149; myth of sameness 43–47; other times and 'othered' places 47–50; politics of 63–64, 146–147; proximities to 78–80; sexuality 53, 58n5; undermining identities of 98–102; *see also* identity
differentiation 4
diversity *see* difference
double consciousness 81, 147
dress codes, racialisation of 45–46

EDL 1
employment, discrimination in 128–130
English Defence League (EDL) 1. 41
equality monitoring form 105, 128–130
ethnic communities *see* difference
ethnographic research methods 6–10
exclusion, processes of 3
expectations of difference 65–68

fantasy of non-racism 43–47
far-right, rise in popularity of 149–150
fear 67
Ferdinand, Rio 103
fetishisation of difference 18, 23, 77
fieldwork diary 8
fixed subjectivities 89–90
forward thinking 11
Front National 1

gangs 26–27
gay spaces, commodification of 18
gender differences 53, 58n5
Gorton: association with crime 26–28; media portrayals of 28–30; racial historicism and 47–50; reputation of 24–25; white working class identities in 71–74, 94–98
Grayling, Chris 29
Greater Manchester Against Crime (GMAC) 26
group orientation 89–90

'hunger' for diversity 63
hybridity 115–116

identifications, resistance to 89–90, 147–148; de-categorisation of identities 102–107; multi-faceted identity 107–110; 'play' with identities 110–116; point of misrecognition 91–94; undermining identities of difference 98–102; white working class identities 71–74, 94–98; *see also* identity
identity 12; bi-cultural 100–102; British 51, 99–101; categories of 100–102; collective 50, 105–106; as continuous process 89–90; de-categorisation of 102–107; 'integrated' 100–101; mixed 100–102; multi-faceted 12, 107–110, 148; 'play' with 110–116, 148; undermining identities of difference 98–102; white working class 94–98; *see also* identifications, resistance to; 'post-racial'
image-making of cities 15–16; 'celebratory' narratives 20–23; conflicting narratives 10–11; multi-layered nature of 16–17; 'other' face of cities 23–34; reinvented identities 17–20; relations to broader context 30–33
indifference to difference 6, 58
inner cities: Gorton, Longsight and Moss side 24–30; media portrayals of 28–30; multiculturalism policies and 92; racial historicism and 47–50, 123; racialisation of 23–34, 145–146; *see also* cities
institutional racism in police 137–138
'integrated' identities 100–101
integration 3–4; British identity and 100–101; cohesion through 50; collective identity 50, 105–106; demand for 44–45; fantasy of non-racism 43–47; 'integrated' identities 100–101; mixing 50–57, 66–67, 130–134, 146–149; myth of sameness 43–47; other times and 'othered' places 47–50; policy approaches to 123–124; push for 3–4; as responsibility of marginalised groups 130–134
inter-cultural contact 50–57
'inter-human' framing 51–52
interviews 9–10

labels *see* categorisation
Lawrence, Stephen 1
learned encounters 80–84

Index 155

LGBT community, marketisation of 18
lifespace, expanded 40, 46, 53–54
Longsight 24–30; association with crime
26–28; media portrayals of 28–30;
positioning of residents of 103–105;
reputation of 24–25

'Madchester' scene 34n4
Manchester 15–16; City Council
advertisements 20–23; discomfort
describing difference in 68–71; Gorton
24–30, 71–74, 94–98; identity as
'radical' city 17–20, 144; Longsight
24–30, 103–105; Moss Side 24–30,
76–78; multi-layered nature of 16–17;
'other' side of 23–34; policing practices
in 137–138; population of 34n2; racial
historicism and 47–50; relationship to
broader context 30–33
marginalisation, lack of recognition of
44–45
marketisation of diversity: Manchester
City Council advertisements 20–23;
'radical' identity 17–20
media portrayals of inner cities 28–30
metatheoretical reification 5, 108
methods of research 6–10
misrecognition, point of 91–94
'mixed' housing projects 66–67
mixed identities 100–102
mixing 50–57, 146; as counter to racism
130–134, 148–149; 'mixed' housing
projects 66–67
Moss Side 24–30; association with crime
26–28; discomfort describing difference
in 68–71; media portrayals of 28–30;
policing practices in 137–138; racial
historicism and 47–50; reluctance to be
associated with 76–78; reputation of
24–25
multiculturalism: marketisation of
17–23; mixing versus 50–57; *see also*
'post-racial'
multi-ethnic networks 50–57
multi-faceted identity 12, 107–110, 148
multi-layered nature of cities 16–17
multiple subjectivities 89–90;
de-categorisation of identities 102–107;
multi-faceted identity 107–110; 'play'
with identities 110–116; point of
misrecognition 91–94; undermining
identities of difference 98–102; white
working class identities 94–98
myth of sameness 43–47, 68–71, 143–144,
146

naming racism 134–139, 149
'no-go' areas 66–67
non-racism, fantasy of 43–47
Northern Monitoring Project 137

Oldham 17, 33, 34n13, 49, 53
open-mindedness, narratives of 50–57
'othered' places 23–34, 47–50, 145

'perpetual outsider' 90
photographic diaries 9
place, race and 3–4; comfortable
conceptions of difference 74–78;
'cosmopolitan' spaces 79, 84;
discomfort in talking about difference
68–71; expectations of difference
65–68; limits of place-based research
15; manipulation of identities and
113–114; 'mixed' housing projects
66–67; 'othered' places 23–34, 47–50,
145; proximities to difference 78–80;
white working class neighborhoods
71–74; *see also* cities
'play' with identities 110–116, 148
point of misrecognition 91–94
policing practices 137–138
Policy Exchange 125
'post-racial' 57–58, 145–146; allure for
young adults 42; appeal of 41–42;
collective identity and 105–106;
comfortable conceptions of difference
74–78; culturalist discourses 70–71;
discomfort in talking about difference
68–71; expectations of difference
65–68; fantasy of non-racism 43–47;
as itself a racist expression 2, 124;
learned encounters 80–84; living with
diversity 63–65, 146–147; mixing
versus multiculture 50–57; myth of
sameness 43–47, 68–71, 143–144, 146;
other times and 'othered' places 23–34,
47–50, 145; proximities to difference
78–80; traction in popular imagination
39–41; 'we-feeling' and 46–47; white
working class identities 68–71, 94–98;
see also identity
Powell, Enoch 126
process, identity as 89–90
proximities to difference 78–80

racial equivalence, culture of 125–126, 131
racial historicism 47–50, 123
racialisation: of inner city neighborhoods
24–30; process of 145–146; racialised
dress codes 45–46; racialised signifiers

156 *Index*

56–57; versus racism 130; significance in everyday lives 130–134
racial profiling 137–138
'racial self-interest' 125–126, 149–150
racism 131; definitions of 12, 125–126, 148–149; denial of responsibility for 143–144; de-racialised discourses 123–127; fear of naming 121–122, 134–139, 149; policy approaches to 121–127; problem of 121–127; racial equivalence 125–126, 131; versus racialisation 130; 'racial self-interest' 125–126, 149–150; recognition of 1–2, 12; 'reverse racism' 125, 149; shifting nature of 149–151; social mixing as counter to 130–134, 148–149; understandings of 1–6; weight of categorisation and 127–130; *see also* 'post-racial'
'radical' city, Manchester's identity as 17–23, 144
rationalisations about racialised groups 125–127
recognition of difference 68–71; comfortable conceptions of difference 74–78; culturalist discourses 70–71; learned encounters 80–84; proximities to difference 78–80; representation of white working class 68–71
recognition of racism 1–2, 12
'refugees welcome' campaign 18–19
reinterpellation of 'radical city' idea 17–23
rejection of ethnic categories *see* resistance to identifications
research methodology 6–10
resistance to identifications 89–90, 147–148; de-categorisation of identities 102–107; multi-faceted identity 12, 107–110, 148; 'play' with identities 110–116; point of misrecognition 91–94; undermining identities of difference 98–102; white working class identities 94–98
'reverse racism' 125, 149
Rivers of Blood speech 126
Rushdie, Salman 34n13
Rusholme 75–77, 92, 121

sameness, myth of 43–47, 68–71, 143–146
'saris, samosas and steelband' approach 58n4
Satanic Verses (Rushdie) 34n13
'scally' image of Gorton 71–74, 94–98
self-segregation, discourses of 122–123

sexuality differences 53, 58n5
Shameless 73
social mixing *see* mixing
Song, Miri 125
spaces: 'the amalgamated other' 23; cities as 'spaces of difference' 16, 23–24; commodification of 18; conflicting narratives of 10–11; *see also* place, race and
Starkey, David 34n12
state of mind, city as 67
stereotyping 56–57; Asian stereotypes 92–94; 'chav' label 25, 71, 94–98, 147; of inner city neighborhoods 28–30; white working class 68–71, 94–98; 'young mum' label 97–98
subjectivities *see* fixed subjectivities; multiple subjectivities

Tebbit, Norman 99
third space 115
togetherness, slogans of 124
tolerance, narratives of 11, 50–57
Trump, Donald 1

UKIP 1, 41
'underclass' white culture 95–96
undermining identities of difference 98–102
United Colors of Benetton advertisement campaign 54, 56–57
'unspoken code' 80–84
urbanism, youthful texture of 5

Walsh, Peter 29
'we-feeling' 46–47
weight of categorisation 127–130
West, Kanye 45
#We Stand Together 124
white privilege: equality monitoring form and 129–130; myth of sameness 43–47, 68–71, 143–146; 'post-racial' as protection of 124; silence around 146
white superiority, sense of 55–56
'white trash' label 72
white working class: identities 94–98; representation of 68–72
'The Wire' 29
WOMEX 20
working class, representation of 71–74

young adults as 'post-racial' generation 57–58
'young mum' label 97–98